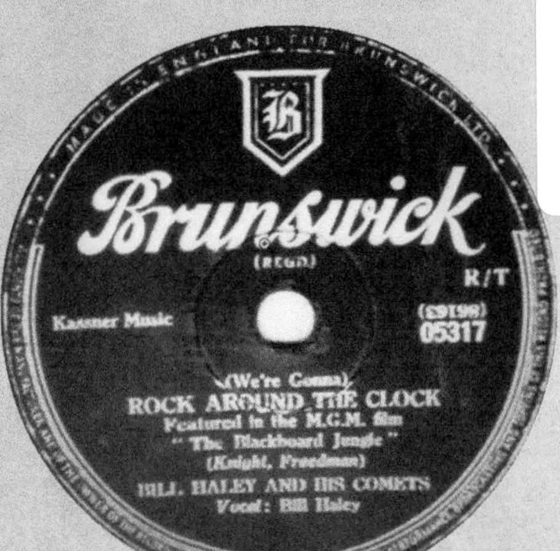
Brunswick
R/T
Kassner Music
05317
(We're Gonna)
ROCK AROUND THE CLOCK
Featured in the M.G.M. film
"The Blackboard Jungle"
(Knight, Freedman)
BILL HALEY AND HIS COMETS
Vocal: Bill Haley

MW00579522

THE DECCA RECORD COMPANY LIMITED
MADE IN ENGLAND
DECCA
78 RPM
JAZZ JAZZ
(DR/X.19299)
F.10647
ROCK ISLAND LINE
(Traditional)
THE LONNIE DONEGAN
SKIFFLE GROUP
(Lonnie Donegan—guitar and vocal;
Chris Barber—bass;
Beryl Bryden—washboard)
Exempt
UNAUTHORISED PUBLIC PERFORMANCE BROADCASTING AND COPYING OF THIS RECORD PROHIBITED

"HIS MASTER'S VOICE"
MADE IN GT BRITAIN
G2WB-209 78
POP. 182
HEARTBREAK HOTEL
(Axton—Durden—Presley)
Sung by
ELVIS PRESLEY
with Rhythm Accompaniment
B. F. Wood. NCB. Frank Music
B·I·E·M

LONDON
AMERICAN
RECORDINGS
78 R.P.M
MADE IN ENGLAND
Recorded by
DOT,
Hollywood
R/T
HLD.8405
COME GO WITH ME
(Quick)
DELL-VIKINGS -Vocal
and Instrumental

The story of one man, his drums, John LENNON, Paul McCARTNEY and George HARRISON

PRE:FAB!

Colin Hanton

with Colin Hall

The Book Guild Ltd

First published in Great Britain in 2018 by
The Book Guild Ltd
9 Priory Business Park
Wistow Road, Kibworth
Leicestershire, LE8 0RX
Freephone: 0800 999 2982
www.bookguild.co.uk
Email: info@bookguild.co.uk
Twitter: @bookguild

Typeset in Garamond

Printed and bound in Great Britain by CPI Group (UK) Ltd, Croydon, CR0 4YY

ISBN 978 1912362 578

British Library Cataloguing in Publication Data.
A catalogue record for this book is available from the British Library.

Colin Hanton dedicates Pre:Fab! to his wife Joan, daughters Allison and Christine, grand daughter Emily and his sons-in-law Gary and Craig.

Colin Hall dedicates Pre:Fab! to his wife Sylvia, sons Alex and James, daughter Hannah, their respective spouses Vanessa, Pavlina and Toby, and grandchildren Riber, Charlotte and Sebbie.

'O youth! The strength of it, the faith of it, the imagination of it!'

Joseph Conrad ('Youth', 1902)

CONTENTS

FOREWORD

By Bob Harris

Colin Hall and I first met at the Cambridge Folk Festival in 2005 and it wasn't long before we began to talk about the Beatles and their impact on our lives. He told me he was the custodian of John Lennon's childhood home in Liverpool and invited me to visit. What an amazing experience it turned out to be. Crossing the threshold at Mendips was like entering a time capsule, the look and atmosphere of the house transporting me straight back to the culture of my own childhood in the 1950s and life before rock 'n' roll.

I felt immediately immersed in the many stories Colin recounted of those distant days and soon we were driving to visit St. Peter's Church in Woolton, the scene of John's first meeting with Paul McCartney at a summer fete in 1957 where John was playing with his skiffle group The Quarry Men. It was a visit that became the inspiration for an award-winning radio documentary Colin and I made together called 'The Day John Met Paul', which was broadcast on BBC Radio 2 on 6th July 2007 to celebrate the 50th anniversary of that historic occasion. Paul gave us a wonderful interview and we talked with Mike McCartney and spent quality time with Cynthia Lennon, which was an absolute joy. And I got to meet The Quarry Men and hear their own stories and reactions to the way Beatlemania grew from the foundation they had created.

I enjoyed making that programme as much as anything I have ever done and underpinning the whole experience was the incredible depth of knowledge and huge enthusiasm that Colin brought to the project. This book has been similarly blessed with his extraordinary attention to detail.

As the drummer with The Quarry Men, Colin Hanton had a close-up view of the Liverpool music scene and 'Pre:Fab!' is his story as told to Colin Hall – a wonderfully warm, humorous and fascinating tale of how the Beatles evolved, providing an incredible insight into the relationships and chemistry that made them what they were. More than that, it is also a vivid and important snapshot of social history – life as a child in the Second World War playing among the Liverpool bombsites, post-war austerity, the rebuilding of the city and the arrival of the Teddy Boys, teenagers and screaming girls.

'Pre:Fab!' is a truly unique and deeply detailed account of life in post-war Liverpool – a culture that gave birth to the biggest band the world has ever known.

INTRODUCTION

It's a story often told. How sixteen-year-old John Lennon picks up a guitar, forms a skiffle group he will call The Quarry Men and just months later on 6th July 1957 meets Paul McCartney. Paul has a pal called George and, as they say, the rest is history.

Just how The Quarry Men morphed into the world-conquering popular musical phenomenon known as The Beatles is a story that continues to captivate and fire imaginations of people around the world. Every year their music continues to win new fans and sell by the truckload. Age has neither withered nor tarnished their reputation or the love the world has for The Beatles.

Sixty years on from that fortuitous first encounter, Beatles fans in their tens of thousands flock annually to Liverpool to discover as much as they can about the Fab Four. They are eager to visit the places where the Beatles lived, grew up, met and played music.

The stories of those who were there with them in those far off Pre-Fab days are highly valued.

As a member of John Lennon's original Quarry Men, drummer Colin Hanton's memories are particularly sought after. He is not only an eye-witness to amazing, life-changing – some would say world-changing – historic events but he was also a participant. It was he who stood side by side with John, Paul and George when their fantastic journey began. At that point in their lives, their story was also Colin's.

He was on the inside, one of the boys: one of the group.

It was Colin who sat rehearsing with the other Quarry Men in the living rooms of Mendips and 20 Forthlin Road (the homes of John and Paul); at John's mother Julia's home; at George's home and in his own home. It was Colin who, as a fellow Quarry Man, shared the thrill and nervousness of stepping on stage with John for the very first time. It was Colin who drummed behind John, Paul and George when they played their first public shows, who sat on the 'bus with the band on their way to and from gigs, who engaged in conversation, shared jokes, drinks and ciggies, ran from the Teddy Boys and competed for the attention of girl fans.

It was Colin who, with fellow Quarry Men, Eric, Len, Pete and Rod, performed with John on the very first occasion he played Liverpool's Empire Theatre and the Cavern Club. It was Colin and John who in 1958 – as the only surviving members of the original Quarry Men – stepped inside Percy F. Phillips's recording studio in Liverpool with 'new boys' Paul, George and keyboard player John 'Duff' Lowe to cut the very first record featuring three future Beatles.

And it is this remarkable story he tells here in great detail, exactly as he remembers it.

And what a story it is, a story not just of friends and family but also of the great city of Liverpool: Liverpool at war and at peace, of bombs and the Blitz, of heroes and villains because Colin has lived through turbulent times as well as good.

Thankfully for all those who love The Beatles, Colin Hanton is possessed of an excellent, insightful memory. Essentially a modest chap he is nevertheless acutely aware of his heritage, proud of his city and of the part it plays in his story and he in it.

He is proud of what he has achieved and both grateful and

amazed by the enduring popularity of 'the band of bands' which has kept himself and his fellow Quarry Men in the limelight for over sixty years since it all kicked off on a hot and humid summer's day at a suburban garden fete.

But Colin is also aware of time passing.

In large part he has recorded his incredible story for the fans: to take them as close as any fan will ever get to how it was in those very early days. And, once told, it will be here for posterity.

But most especially it is told for Colin's family.

This story is first and foremost for them, with love always.

So welcome to 'Pre:Fab!' the story of one man, his drums and John Lennon's Quarry Men.

Colin Hall
Woolton, 2017

THE 'OTHER' COLIN AND THE WRITING OF 'PRE:FAB!'

To be asked by Colin Hanton to write his memoir of his time as a Quarry Man was a huge honour and one I was very happy to accept. Getting to know Colin and his lovely wife, Joan, has been a wonderful experience. They are marvellous people: very modest, caring, unassuming folk but also very lively, great fun to be with and very generous with their time and kindness. Great dancers too.

I have known Colin for over fourteen years. Our paths first crossed one night in 2004 when he and The Quarry Men were playing a gig somewhere in south Liverpool. I had just begun my tenure with the National Trust as live-in custodian of John Lennon's former childhood home, 'Mendips', 251 Menlove Avenue, Liverpool. I remember cramming into a small school hall to hear the group sing, play and reminisce to a very appreciative audience. That night the group comprised Colin, Rod Davis, Len Garry and Eric Griffths.

From that point on our paths regularly crossed at various Beatles-related functions, anniversaries and extravaganzas in and around the city. One event was particularly important in forging our friendship. In early 2007 my friend Bob Harris invited me to help create a radio documentary for BBC Radio 2, 'The Day John Met Paul'. What an experience it proved to be: not only did Bob and I get to interview Sir Paul but we spent a whole, very special fun-packed day with The Quarry Men recording their memories in Bob's home studio in Oxfordshire.

Colin and I discovered we shared an interest in the history of Liverpool, especially the war years, in part because our parents all experienced, and survived, the Blitz, as did Colin himself.

Colin knew I wrote a bit: articles, interviews and reviews for music magazines such as 'What's On In London', 'Get Rhythm' and, latterly, 'R2' music magazine (one of the last surviving independent glossy music publications). Over the years as either a writer or working with Bob on various projects I have been fortunate to spend time in the company of/interviewing Sir Paul McCartney, Bill Wyman, Dr. John the Night Tripper, Steve Earle, Astrid Kircherr, Sir George Martin, Patti Smith, Ray Davies, Bryan Ferry, Boy George, Tammy Wynette and many, many more. Among the many memorable highlights of my work at 'Mendips' has been meeting Yoko Ono Lennon on several occasions and hosting Bob Dylan when he paid a surprise visit to the house. Other guests have included Jackson Browne, James Taylor, Bonnie Raitt, Paul Brady, Alan White, Melvyn Bragg, Clem Burke and Debbie Harry. When I was still living at 'Mendips' I once cooked a curry for Klaus Voormann.

This, however, is the first book I have written: what a way to start!

Co-writing a book focusing on Colin's early life transported us back to the turbulent and traumatic years of the war, then into the Fifties and the advent of rock 'n' roll. In my role as custodian of 'Mendips' I am forever in search of people's memories of those years and of any time they spent with John, Paul and George as youngsters because their recollections help me interpret John's early life at the house with greater accuracy and insight.

From the outset Colin and I were both acutely aware that

the number of books that already exist about The Beatles would fill a wing of the British Library. Consequently any additions to this huge accumulated reservoir of knowledge was going to have to satisfy the vast number of Beatles 'expert texperts' out there who comb any new publication in search of inaccuracies and/or deviations from the 'truth, the whole truth and nothing but the truth, so help me Elvis'.

Of all Beatles biographies Mark Lewisohn's incredibly researched volume, 'Tune In', is the absolute benchmark to which all Beatles biographers should aspire if they wish to be taken seriously. Quite simply, it's the Bible. Mark's veracity has been our benchmark. Colin is also well aware that The Beatles' only 'official' biographer, Hunter Davies, chronicled The Quarry Men's story, and fellow band member, Len Garry, has written his memoir.

Colin's aim has not been to toe any particular party line or add anything controversial or different but simply to tell his story from his own perspective and in the process maybe set some records straight. Of all the original early 1957 Quarry Men – John Lennon, Pete Shotton, Eric Griffiths, Rod Davis, Len Garry and Colin – other than John, Colin was the one who survived the longest, the one who journeyed well beyond the day John met Paul at the church fete on 6th July 1957. Consequently he has much to tell of the group in its formative years. He's been interviewed countless times but his personal story has never been told in such detail. 'Pre:Fab!' is what Colin wanted – his version of the story absolutely as he recalls it and not how others remember it for him.

We have tried our utmost to chronologise Colin's memories and when this has not been possible we have (hopefully) made this clear. Thinking back sixty years Colin has very clear memories of events and personalties he encountered along the way. Nevertheless, piecing together an exact chronology of dates and gigs has been challenging. I think every Beatles expert on earth has

Colin Hanton & Colin Hall,
Liverpool, June, 2017.

been confounded to some extent by the lack of available recorded dates for Quarry Men performances and by the fact no one was keeping a diary because they were too busy living it. There are a handful of dates that can be verified and it is around these that Colin has woven his recollections.

We have spent nearly two years talking, revising and revisiting Colin's narrative, allowing him time to tie together sequences of events. Along the way fresh memories have been sparked and he has gained a better understanding of what was actually going on at the time when he was moving too fast to stop and think it all through.

'Pre:Fab!' is for Colin's family, for the legion of Quarry Men fans and anyone with just a passing interest in recent social and popular music history.

He and I hope you enjoy reading his memoirs as much as we enjoyed piecing them together.

Thanks, Mr. Hanton; it's not just been a privilege but real fun.

Colin Hall
Menlove Avenue, May 2017.

1

TALKING IRISH, BALTIC AND WORLD WAR II BLUES

It was unusually mild (but damp) for the time of year when on Monday 12th December 1938 Colin Hanton was born at Walton Hospital in Fazakerley, north Liverpool.

Fascinatingly there is a distinct possibility that this little boy could have been delivered into the world by a certain Mary Mohin. In 1938 Mary was a sister on the maternity ward at Walton Hospital. In 1941 she would marry a chap called James McCartney and on 18th June 1942 their first son, James Paul McCartney, was born in that very same Walton Hospital in a private room – courtesy of mother Mary's status as a sister.

So the odds are good that, on the day Colin was born, Paul's Mum was the duty sister on his ward.

Colin's parents were John and Ethel. Home for Colin was to be in Bootle. In 1938 Bootle was a thriving, busy area of docklands situated just to the north of Liverpool city centre. As a place to live Bootle has been around a good while: at the time of the Domesday Book in 1086 it was known as 'Boltelai', its name coming from the Anglo-Saxon words 'Bold' or Botle', meaning dwelling.

Colin joined John, Ethel and older brother Brian (born three years earlier on 6th November 1935) in the Hanton family home, number 44 Eleanor Road. John was a grocer's assistant working for the nearby Co-Op store Ethel was a housewife. Within a year

John and Ethel Hanton, 1930s

of Colin's birth his father would join the fire brigade: a change of occupation that was to have grim consequences for him.

Colin's mother Ethel 'nee Jones' (born in 1916) and his father John (born in 1909) were of Irish descent. Mum's father was from Dublin and Dad's family originally came from County Wexford. Grandfather Dennis and Grandmother Mary Hanton lived across the road from them at number 27 with their sons and daughters (Colin's uncles and aunties) Thomas, Dennis, Frank, Jimmy, Terry, Molly and Katherine. Grandma and Grandpa Jones also lived closeby.

Irish antecedents are not unusual for a fellow born in Liverpool. Future Quarry Men John, Paul and George could all claim Irish ancestors in fact a third of all 'Scousers' – as folk from Liverpool are known – have Irish relations, distant or otherwise. No wonder then that the city is often called 'the real capital of Ireland', its growth as a port developing initially from its early pre-1700s trade with Ireland.

'Scouser' is the colloquial name given to the inhabitants of Liverpool while 'scouse' is the name given to the way most Liverpudlians speak and to a meal once eaten by almost every Scouser in the city.

Economically, politically, intellectually and culturally the Irish have contributed massively to Liverpool's colourful history. Their spirit and character can be forever heard in the distinctive nasal twang of the 'scouse' accent while their sense of humour, their love of storytelling, music and a good 'craic' which involves plenty of banter, a love of language, a lot of fun, a pint or several of ale, much dancing and a good sing are all qualities that have become traits for which Liverpudlians are also renowned.

Sadly when Colin was growing up a dark side to that Irish presence was prevalent in the city: sectarianism. During the first half of the twentieth century the Conservative Party dominated Liverpool's local politics and allied itself with the city's Anglican establishment, happily fanning the flames of sectarianism by

Granny Hanton

Granddad Hanton

reminding its Protestant supporters that a vote for the Labour Party was a vote for Catholic domination. The result was a society defined and dominated by religion and ethnicity which, for much of the Twentieth Century proved a combustible combination.

Thankfully things changed during Colin's lifetime: Liverpool today is renowned as a symbol of reconciliation, its spirit of unity epitomised by Pope John Paul II's pastoral visit to Britain in 1982 during which he came to the city and visited both the Roman Catholic Metropolitan Cathedral of Christ the King *AND* the Anglican cathedral.

Unfortunately when Colin was a teenager in the 1950s there were still a good few years to pass before any meaningful sort of reconciliation would be achieved. Consequently a good 'dust up' during the annual Orange Order parades held on or around 12th July to celebrate 1690's Battle of the Boyne was almost *de rigueur*.

In 1938 such divisions were eclipsed temporarily as Brits everywhere drew together to confront German dictator Adolf Hitler and his thoroughly amoral, vile and violent Nazi Party. As Colin and his family were soon to find out, German bombs weren't picky about where or upon whom they were dropped.

As the year unfurled the spectre of war in Europe had drawn ever closer. In March Germany had annexed Austria. In July the Evian Conference failed to resolve the plight of the increasing number of German Jewish refugees attempting to escape escalating violent persecution. Instead they were left trapped to face Hitler's venomous wrath. In late September, Germany's annexation of Czechoslovak Sudetenland left little room for any hope for peace.

It was into this seriously sombre world that Colin had arrived: not even the deepest, whitest Christmas on record that descended on the UK within two weeks of his birth (unsurpassed until Christmas Day 1981) could do little to distract the British from the fact that once again war was just a heartbeat away.

As they built snowmen and enjoyed snowballing and sledging, subconsciously everyone must have been desperately clinging to the hope that the 'peace with honour' Prime Minister Neville Chamberlain claimed he'd achieved in Munich in September would hold.

Of course, it didn't: less than a year later on 1st September, 1939, Germany invaded Poland and that was it. Hitler had crossed the line, there was no way back: within two days Britain declared war on Germany.

The unimaginable loss of life caused by the First World War of 1914–18 was still fresh in the memory: nearly every family in Brtain had lost someone to that appalling conflict. The promise given that it had been 'the war to end all wars' was now broken.

For Liverpool the immediate future was very grim. As a port it is one of the closest the UK has to the USA. As war began and trade with Europe closed down so it turned to the USA to supply its needs and Liverpool provided an alternative and crucial lifeline for the country. In turn this made it of massive strategic significance to the Germans. If Hitler wanted to crush and subdue Britain ahead of any invasion he needed to weaken or better still destroy ports like Liverpool: by doing so he could cut supply links to the west and starve the country, seriously deplete its resources and, most importantly, psychologically smash British resolve. And so, as far as Germany was concerned, Liverpool had to be shut down, bombed into the ground. Menacingly it was within reach of the Luftwaffe. A Heinkel loaded with bombs could just about make it from airfields in France to Merseyside where it would have to lose its payload if it was to have sufficient fuel to take it home. Suddenly the city was a target, its people living on the frontline in the very eye of the storm.

ENDNOTES

See Outtakes #1 'Being a Short Discourse on the Origins of Scouse and Scouser' and Outtakes #2 'The Battle of the Boyne 1690' at the end of the book for more details.

2

LIGHTNING STRIKES

Colin's father, John Hanton, was a fireman, a member of the Bootle Fire Brigade. By Act of Parliament passed in January 1939 fire fighting became a 'reserved occupation' which meant fire officers could not enlist (even though John tried). In reality however, as a fireman living in Bootle near to the north Liverpool docks John was clearly going to see action every bit as intense and deadly as if he were standing directly facing the enemy on a battlefield somewhere in Europe.

Civilians knew that, just because it was an island, Britain would not escape the conflict in Europe. While the possibility of invasion was at the back of everyone's mind, at the immedate forefront was the deadly threat posed by the likelihood of aerial bombing raids on the country.

British people would already have seen evidence of the devastating bombing power of the German Luftwaffe at the cinema where Pathe newsreel footage showed images of Germany's strategic bombing of the Basque town of Guernica on 26th April 1937, during the Spanish Civil War. It was one of the very first times the Luftwaffe had carried out such an intense and sustained aerial bombing attack that took in not only military targets but defenceless civilians as well. Three quarters of the city's buildings had been totally destroyed and modern estimates suggest between 153 and 400 civilians had been killed. It proved to the Germans the effectiveness of aerial onslaughts in 'softening up' an enemy's

Colin's father, John, in his fireman's uniform

resolve to resist, thus they became integral to Germany's plans to conquer Europe.

The British knew it was inevitable that similar bombing raids would be used against them. The Germans called this method of warfare 'blitzkrieg' ('lightning war'), which Brits shortened to 'the Blitz'. They also knew such raids would be sustained. Beyond the immediate destruction and death they caused, the German goal was to break supply lines, destroy the country's infrastructure, terrorise the population and undermine morale.

Very soon the sound of the air raid siren would be a familiar call to action for people to stop what they were doing and take immediate precautions to protect themselves and their loved ones.

Towns and cities like Liverpool would be guarded by anti-aircraft guns. Huge grey barrage balloons would also be put up to force the German bombers to fly higher and so be less accurate in their targeting. (The cables to which these were tethered were so strong they would destroy any plane that flew into them.)

For their own personal safety people carried gas masks everywhere they went and would build air raid shelters ('Anderson' shelters) in their back gardens into which they would go when the siren sounded. Pete Shotton, with whom John Lennon founded the Quarry Men in 1956, remembers that the group's first rehearsals took place *"in an old corrugated iron air raid shelter in my back garden". John Lennon In My Life, Shotton and Schaffner, p.52.*

At first, despite all the dire warnings, nothing happened: instead a strange and unnerving calm settled upon the land, life carried on as normal, nothing warlike happened. From October 1939 until March 1940, neither the Germans nor the Allies carried out any land operations and bombs were not dropped on the mainland and so journalists dubbed this period 'the phoney war'. Despite this, for their safety, children were evacuated from coastal towns and cities deemed likely to be targets for the Luftwaffe's bombs. When the predicted bombing raids failed to materialise, many children who had been evacuated were returned home.

Colin & Brian, Oxford Road, Bootle, 1942

John and Ethel sent Brian and twelve-month-old Colin to be evacuated but the boys weren't gone for long: *"We tried it – for a week"*, says Colin (although he agrees it was most likely for quite a while longer than that). Despite being so young he was already walking – and talking.

"During the 'phoney war' we were sent briefly to Rainford, just to the left of St. Helens. I remember it because Mum and Dad came to see us and I was excited to show Dad the peanuts that were being grown in the big back garden of the house where we had been placed. Like a lot of children evacuated during that period when no bombs were dropped we were sent home. Of course, once the bombing did start up many other boys and girls were re-evacuated but for some reason we never were."

By June 1940 the situation in the UK changed dramatically. In June, 1940 Southampton was bombed and on 1st July during a daylight raid on the aerodrome in Wick in Caithness fifteen people were killed. The Luftwaffe suffered serious losses during such daylight raids and so they switched to night attacks, at which point Liverpool – including Colin's family – truly copped it.

The first major night-time raid on Liverpool occurred on 28th August 1940 when one-hundred and sixty bombers attacked Merseyside: the 'Blitz' of Liverpool had begun. (The London 'Blitz' began on 7th September.)

Between August and Christmas 1940 a further forty-nine attacks on Liverpool occurred. (John Lennon was born on 9th October 1940.) Most raids involved only a few bombers but the biggest raids of that year – including those on the 20 and 21st of December – 'the Christmas Blitz' – involved over three hundred Heinkels.

As a result Colin's father John was kept very busy indeed. His work as a 'fire bobby' was perilous and physically gruelling: long, long hours were worked and when the attacks were at their height little or no rest was possible. The daily bravery of people like John Hanton is quite astounding to contemplate. What they had to do was unimaginably dangerous; the tragedies they witnessed and the situations in which they found themselves were traumatising; through it all death was their constant companion.

It was during the 'Christmas Blitz' – the night of 21st December into the morning of 22nd December 1940 – as they were working at the docks John's crew of five took a direct hit. Only John survived. Thrown into the air by the blast, somehow John did not perish although he was severely injured, his legs particularly so.

Rushed to hospital, it would be many months before John recovered sufficiently to be allowed home. Such was the damage to his right leg, it was rendered shorter than the left: he would spend the rest of his life wearing a calliper and a special shoe on his leg and foot.

"My Aunty Cathy, my Dad's sister, used to tell a story about her friend who was a nurse on duty that night in Walton hospital when Dad was brought in. It was her friend's first night on duty and despite his injuries and all the dirt and blood she recognised Dad when he was wheeled in. Aunty Cathy said her friend literally freaked out and left the hospital immediately to run home to Eleanor Road telling everyone she met that, 'Johnny Hanton has been blown up! Johnny Hanton has been blown up!' Such was the shock and terrifying horror of Dad's injuries she never returned to the hospital or worked as a nurse again."

It says a lot for John's fortitude that when Colin was eventually allowed to visit him in hospital, despite his awful injuries, John was still able to amuse his son to divert him from worrying.

"There was a cage over Dad's legs – to keep the blanket off his wounds. I was fascinated by this and when he told me there was a canary living in it; being so young and gullible, I believed him. I was too shy to lift the blanket

74–76 Gonville Road. Bomb damage 1940. By the end of the war Colin's family were living on Gonville Road and it was where he attended the VE street party. Note the cross-hatch tape on the windows which people applied to prevent flying glass in the event of a bomb blast. The infamous Lord Haw Haw callously taunted the residents of Bootle with the words, "The kisses on your windows won't help you."

and peep underneath; instead I'd sit and listen, waiting for the canary to sing: of course, it never did!"

John's sense of humour stood him in good stead, especially in the most extreme of moments – as in this story he told of an earlier raid when he was standing on the flat roof of an outbuilding that was in flames. Hose in hand, John was desperately trying to put out the blaze when from out of the night sky came a German bomber spraying machine gun bullets. It was flying directly towards him.

"Dad said he didn't know what to do – there were loud noises, bangs and bullets, smoke and flames everywhere but he couldn't leave his post because not only would that have been desertion but he was standing on a flat roof from which it was too high to jump to safety – if nothing else the drop would have killed him. Nevertheless he felt very scared and so he said, 'I just pulled my helmet down over my eyes, squeezed them tight shut and carried on hosing. My thinking was if I can't see that 'plane coming my way then let's hope the pilot and gunner can't see me!' Fortunately for Dad on that occasion it was a tactic that worked…"

As John lay in hospital recovering, the bombing of Liverpool was unremitting: by the end of April 1941 Merseyside had been raided over sixty times. Over 2,000 people had been killed, many more, like John, badly injured, many of whom were badly burned.

Worse was to come: the raids of May 1941 were the most devastating. For seven consecutive nights the area was pounded as some 681 Luftwaffe bombers attacked. 2,315 bombs and 119 incendiary devices were dropped and 2,895 casualties were recorded, while 69 out of 144 cargo berths were put out of action. Liverpool's Anglican Cathedral was hit by two bombs.

As ever, Bootle was in the very thick of it. For its size the town endured the heaviest bombing in the country. On one night alone – 3rd May 1941 – it was pulverised by almost fifty bombs that were dropped on it: together with neighbouring Litherland it was ablaze for all of the first eight days of that month, by the end of which a jaw-dropping 80% of its houses had been hit or set on fire. Rows and rows of terraced houses – homes to the dockers – were simply wiped out. Bootle had become a vast bombsite.

For its inhabitants it must have felt that it would not be long before Bootle would be completely razed to the ground. They were right: by the time the last bombs fell on Liverpool 409 people in Colin's home town of Bootle had been killed, 90% of its houses damaged. It was the most heavily bombed borough in the entire UK.

Amazingly despite all this death and destruction Bootle was to remain home for all the Hantons for all of the war.

"I was only a toddler but I have a very powerful early memory of the 'Blitz'. I can remember being outside, standing with my grandfather Leo Jones (Mum's dad). Being so small – just two or nearly three years old – I was looking up at him, fascinated because he appeared to be all lit up! And he was, for just behind Grandpa Leo the city of Liverpool was in flames."

By the time of this memory Colin was no longer living in Eleanor Road.

"Grandfather Leo and I, our entire family of Mum, Dad, Brian and I were now living with Granddad and Grandma Jones because our homes on Eleanor Road had been so badly damaged by the bombing."

His grandparents' home would have appeared to such a young boy to be several notches up the social scale from Colin's home on Eleanor Road. It was – but there was something else about it that has remained etched into his memory.

Gran and Granddad Jones on their wedding day

"I remember Granddad and Grandma Jones's home in Oxford Road, Bootle because it was so impressive. It was a large corner property with a maid's room and bell pushes in every room! But what really stays in my memory are the large sandstone pillars on either side of the front gate and the words that were engraved into one of them: 'The Jew's House'. They were not written or scrawled but carefully engraved. They were clearly meant to be there. They stopped me in my tracks. You see, for me as a little boy living in those awful times, 'Jew' was almost a swear word. I was not reacting to the horrors that were unfolding in Europe – like so many folk at this time, especially me being such a little boy, I was completely ignorant of the Holocaust. As a small child when I heard it used the word 'Jew' was most definitely as an insult, a derogatory term. I didn't understand what it meant. I just knew from how I heard it used that it wasn't a compliment or complimentary. In my head I couldn't work out why someone would live in a house with a such a 'bad' word written on it."

The sense of shock he experienced as a little boy reading these words has remained with Colin.

"Don't forget this is the 1940s and war was raging. It was a different world. Prejudice against Jewish people, anti-Semitism, was not uncommon in Britain at that time despite what was happening in Europe. It was a fact of life and people didn't think to watch what they said. They were undeniably less enlightened days. I was too young and didn't understand all this back then, I just knew to call someone 'a Jew' wasn't being nice. Of course, there was a back story to all this that I learned as times passed. Apparently the people who had owned the house before my grandparents lived in it had been a wealthy Jewish family. The story I heard was that with the threat of a German invasion they had gone into hiding. Before doing so they had put their home in the hands of a sympathetic lawyer who knew Granddad Leo. Leo was a wages clerk at the Bootle gasworks and the lawyer offered him and his wife the opportunity to rent the house while the family were away. Just who or exactly why those words had been engraved remained a mystery. I never did find out but as a little boy it certainly shocked me. Those gate posts remain but are so overgrown thankfully it is impossible to see anything written on them."

Lynn, Gran Jones, Brian, Colin, Granddad Jones,
Aunty Hylda and Uncle Ray at Oxford Road

Co-habiting with Colin's grandparents was unfortunately short-lived.

"Living with Mum's parents did not work out so, from Oxford Street, towards the end of the war we moved to nearby Gonville Road – one of the few streets left standing in Bootle. We moved there because our home in Eleanor Road remained uninhabitable and I'm sorry to say the reason we had to move was me! I was a bit of a nuisance – untidy, noisy – a normal boy but Grandma Jones had had four girls and I think I proved too boisterous for her; she couldn't cope. I wore her down. She and Granddad were getting on in age, don't forget; the house was full, it wasn't easy and I remember arguments between Grandma and Mum about me. Mum became very upset and so we moved out."

It's incredible to think that despite the fact that Bootle had almost been blitzed into oblivion people actually moved to live there during the war, but they did. Around the same time as Colin moved to live with first one set of grandparents and then the other another little boy, almost two years younger than him, called Eric, moved with his Mum and older sister Joan from their home in Denbigh, north Wales, to live with Eric's grandparents in Bootle.

Eric's father had been in the Fleet Air Arm, Coastal Command but had died in action over the North Sea in 1941. Future Quarry Man Eric Griffiths was this little boy and just after he turned ten he and his family moved again, this time to live in Woolton at number 96 Halewood Drive, just around the corner from where Colin and his family had moved in 1945.

Many years later when both boys spoke to each other of their wartime experiences Colin was impressed to learn that, like his Uncle Jimmy, Eric's father had served in the Fleet Air Arm. This realisation sparked another wartime memory in Colin that during the war whenever an aeroplane could be heard over head he would inquire of whoever was around, *"Is that Jerry or is it Uncle Jimmy?"* This is how he knew the good guys from the bad. If it was Uncle

Jimmy, Colin knew he was safe but if it was 'Jerry' then he knew it was time to skedaddle!

By the time the raids on Merseyside ceased, 4,000 people had been killed, many thousands injured, many docks and their surrounding neighbourhoods destroyed; to obstruct and delay the passage of other vessels and the delivery of their precious cargoes, ships had been sunk in the docks and in the river estuary. Much of the city centre was devastated including main shopping and business areas, well-known buildings like the Cotton Exchange, Lewis's department store and the Customs House were destroyed. The Adelphi hotel was damaged; roads, railways and tramlines were left unusable; houses, churches, hospitals and factories were destroyed. The physical damage inflicted on Liverpool was immense. It would take decades to repair; by the time the raids ended in 1942 over 6,500 homes had been demolished and 190,000 left damaged/uninhabitable.

The raids declined when Hitler turned his attention to invading the Soviet Union. The last German air raid on Liverpool occurred on 10th January 1942, taking out houses on Upper Stanhope Street, one of which – ironically – had been the home of Alois Hitler Jnr., Adolf's half brother. It is said that before he rose to power in Germany Adolf had visited Alois in Liverpool. The houses where Alois had lived were never rebuilt.

It is in this city then, this seriously war damaged city, that Colin and his fellow Quarry Men and all the future Beatles grew up. On a daily basis they were surrounded by ugly reminders of the war and its dreadful, deadly power. The devastating impact of the Blitz on their home town was the immediate backdrop to their young lives. The times were tough but so were Scousers: they were down but most definitely not out.

3

YES, WE HAVE NO BANANAS

Colin was six going on seven when World War Two ended in Europe on 8th May 1945 (Japan did not surrender until 15th August). VE ('Victory in Europe') day was the cue for national celebration: street parties were held up and down the land. Colin clearly remembers the party he attended on Gonville Road in Bootle. All over Britain people were out on the streets, red, white and blue street bunting and the Union Jack much in evidence. Down the middle of nearly every street long tables had been placed on which party food would be served. There was serious celebrating to be done!

Colin remembers that the excitement in the air that day was palpable: excitement and a feeling of great relief mixed with grief for those who had been lost. Letting off steam – singing, dancing, drinking, cheering, weeping, remembering, giving thanks and looking to the future were the orders of the day.

For a little boy whose sweets have been rationed for all of his known life (and which would continue to be so until 1953), Colin was eagerly anticipating the bowl of ice cream everyone who attended the party had been promised. Ice cream was the stuff of dreams – a sure sign of better things to come!

'Like all the children sat at those tables I was so looking forward to my ice cream: this was a big treat. As instructed I had brought my own bowl and spoon from home and put it on a long trestle table from where they said

it would be served. I could see the ice cream: it was in a milk churn and two older ladies were doling it out. As I queued up my mouth was watering in anticipation. But when I came to collect my bowl I couldn't believe it – it wasn't there! Everyone else but me was excitedly scoffing away. I looked around and could see my brother Brian giggling with his friends and enjoying his ice cream. Everyone was so excited, there was so much laughter, talking and noise, that no-one noticed me all alone with no bowl and no ice cream. I was dumbstruck and devastated but too shy to say anything so I just hung my head in disappointment and walked away."

For those expecting a happy ending, it may be best to skip the rest of this chapter.

"As I stood alone and feeling that no one cared about me I spotted two younger women – they were in their late teens/early twenties – standing just near me in a doorway. What I saw stopped me in my tracks – for one of them had my bowl and was eating what should have been my portion of ice cream! As she turned towards her friend I heard her giggle and say, 'I don't know whose bowl this is. I just picked it up.' I was crestfallen. How could she have done this to me? Stolen my bowl! Eaten my ice cream! How mean! But I was just too shy to confront her, too small to say anything, I simply turned and walked away again. So that was it: the war was over, I'd survived the Blitz, had my Dad blown up and my home reduced to rubble, and after all that someone had stolen my bowl and eaten my celebratory ice cream. I'd learned a very significant lesson: Life was not fair!"

For Colin not getting a meal or food he had been promised was to be a bit of a theme throughout his younger years: not long after, compounding the 'ice cream incident', came the banana fiasco.

Bananas had not been considered an 'essential' food during the war and so their import ceased after rationing was introduced by the Ministry of Food on 8th January 1940. Five years later on 18th September 1945, sixteen days after hostilities in Europe ended, the first post-war shipment of this 'rare' tropical fruit arrived at the docks in Bristol. It was headline news. No wonder, for while food rationing remained in place at least bananas were back in the shops!

Colin had of course never seen, eaten or heard the word 'banana' and so his interest was immediately roused when around the same time as that first shipload had arrived he remembers a moment of madness on the street outside his home.

"My friend and I were playing in the street (we kids did that all the time in those days, it was considered safe because there were hardly any cars on the roads because no-one owned one because hardly anyone could afford one). All of a sudden a woman came rushing up from the shops, skirts flying, all of a to-do, shouting, 'There are bananas in the shops! There are bananas in the shops!' We both thought wow! Her excitement stopped us in our tracks. Clearly this was big news. I remember several doors opened and many women came out to gather round and hear what all the fuss was about. Up and down the road the news spread like widfire. 'There were bananas in the shops!' It wasn't long before all the women had dashed back inside, grabbed their shopping bags and were on their way to the shop."

Colin and his friend stood speechless as the gaggle of excited women rushed down the street towards the greengrocer's.

"I still had no idea what was getting them so agitated. I remember turning to the lad I was playing with and asking, 'What's a banana?' He didn't know either; he just shook his head, so we just looked blankly at each other, decided it was an adult thing and carried on playing."

But this was not the end of the story for not long after this incident a single banana did make its way into the Hanton household. By now Colin would be in the know: bananas were something special, a real treat. In the Hantons' front living room the rare and precious tropical fruit was first admired by all present before being ceremoniously cut into pieces and shared by whoever was there at the time.

"It was my brother Brian who told me about this. For some reason I wasn't there. No doubt I was out playing again: I was always outside when the weather was good, always playing. Nevertheless Brian made sure I heard about it in graphic detail. What a treat! So delectable! He wanted me to know just what I had missed and how privileged he had been. Just to make me jealous he laid it on as best he could about how flavoursome, sweet and delectable it tasted. He succeeded: off I went into another sulk. Once again I'd missed out, I just got to hear about it not actually experience it: I didn't get any of the precious delicacy that everyone else sampled and enjoyed. Again I was denied. I could be persuaded to think Life had it in for me."

On the subject of war, peace and bananas, future Quarry Man Len Garry, who was almost three and a half by the end of the war, remembers being given his first banana. Not knowing quite what you did with one he tried to eat it without peeling it. Back then kids not only didn't know what certain foods were; they didn't know how they were meant to be eaten – raw, cooked, fried, boiled, baked… or peeled.

4

MOVING ON

Not too long after the street party, and not unsurprisingly given the physical destruction Bootle had endured, Colin's family moved out.

In August 1945 home now became a rented semi-detached house in Woolton, a 'posh' suburb in south Liverpool and right at the other end of the city that had escaped most of the bombing. Number 4 Heyscroft Road to be precise. It didn't have a garage because in those days most people did not own a car so houses were not built with one attached. Nevertheless it was 'posh', a step up.

A relative of the family had been living there after his home in Bootle had been bombed but had decided to move back because he was a docker and needed to be closer to work. John Hanton seized the opportunity to do a swap and so the Hantons left the bombsites of Bootle for the fields, woods, golf courses, parklands and relative gentility of south Liverpool.

Woolton had always been regarded as one of the most sought-after, middle-class areas of Liverpool in which to live: a definite move 'up' as far as Colin's family would have been concerned.

Colin could tell it was a step up simply by the way people spoke. In Woolton traditionally the accent was softer and more lyrical, less obviously 'scouse'. Elsewhere in the city it can be higher, harsher, more nasal.

It just so happens to be that around the same time as Colin located to Woolton, five-year-old John Lennon came to live there.

Number 4 Heyscroft Road, Woolton,
Mum and Dad's home (circa 1960)

It was also home to other future fellow Quarry Men: Rod Davis, Eric Griffiths, Pete Shotton and their good pals Nigel Walley and Ivan Vaughan. None of them, Colin and John included, developed a pronounced 'scouse' accent.

So just what was Woolton like when these boys raced around its streets on their bicycles, climbed its many trees, played in its parks, attended its schools, went to its shops for their mums (and aunts), sang in its choirs, kissed girls in its shadows and jived in its youth club?

Eight miles from the centre of Liverpool, at the end of the war Woolton still felt very much like a village on the edge of town despite the new semi-detached housing that had been built around it in the 1930s. Many of its original houses were built out of distinctive red sandstone that outcropped in the area. In Colin's day there was still an active quarry on Woolton Hill situated just behind St. Peter's Church. The local grammar school, Quarry Bank, that John will attend, had been named after the quarry that used to be at the bottom of its school field. Quarry Bank was situated across Calderstones Park, which was no more than a quarter of a mile from John's home, 'Mendips'.

Look around Liverpool and you will see many buildings built out of this distinctive stone – none more famous or impressive than the city's mighty Anglican cathedral. The stone for that magnificent structure was quarried in Woolton. Indeed it was from Quarry Bank's school song, 'The Song of the Quarry', that John Lennon and his pals chose the name 'Quarry Men' for their skiffle group. Written by the school's first head teacher, Mr. R. F. Bailey, 'The Song of the Quarry' begins with the line 'Quarry men old before our birth, straining each muscle and sinew'.

"That was the joke John and Pete shared within the group – in life generally they had no intention whatsoever of working hard or stretching any sinews. It was a Quarry Men in-joke."

Woolton was surrounded by parks, fields, woods and golf courses – the parks and golf courses are still there to this day. (Although to their shame these days Liverpool City Council is doing its best to allow building to encroach on its old parklands. As I write the beautiful Allerton Priory and Calderstones Park are under threat.) The village itself was a bustling centre full of shops all owned by local people; there were none of the major chains that populate the streets of today's urban areas, making them almost indistinguishable from one another.

By and large people did not have cars; the 1950s was the 'golden age' of public transport in Britain, so there were no supermarkets: walking or catching the local 'bus was what you did to go to the local shops. This meant that in the 1950s Woolton was buzzing. Among its many shops were grocers (Ashe's and Irwin's), greengrocers (Phythian's), a paper shop (Doris Brown's), sweet shops (there were three – Mantles, Alice Gainey's and Ina Lewis's), a cake shop (Clooke's), two butchers (Morphet's and Gamble's), a fish shop (Cooper's), a toy shop (Grace's, which sold Dinky Toys), two bicycle shops (Arnold Jones' and Parker's), two barbers (Ashcroft's and Dickie Jones'), a pet shop (run by a Mr. Byrom and his sister) a chandler's (Molyneux's) and a chemist's (Fairbairn's). The quantity of your purchases was determined by how much you could carry home. As a result several visits to the shops took place every week.

A last vestige of a bygone and fast-fading age was the blacksmith, Mr. Blackmore, on Quarry Street. Woolton had its own library, swimming baths and a cinema, the Woolton Picture House, known to the local children as 'the bug house'. (As this book is being written in 2017 it's still there, functioning and flourishing.) An important element of village life was religion, as it was everywhere in those days, and Woolton was well served with churches: St. Peter's (Church of England), St. James's (Methodists) and St. Mary's (Roman Catholics).

And in the 1950s as a sign of the changing times Woolton apparently sported its own record shop.

Despite its semi-rural aspect there were regular 'bus services from Woolton into Liverpool and back and, until 1949, it was the terminus for tramcars numbers 4 and 5. These ran down the centre of Menlove Avenue, which was and remains a dual carriageway that connects Woolton to Smithdown Road and Penny Lane. The tram tracks have been replaced by a grassy central reservation running its entire length now graced by beautiful trees. For a time just after the war John Lennon's Uncle George worked on the night shift in the Woolton tram depot preparing the trams ready for use the next day.

Life in his new home was exciting but Colin had to get used to a new environment: bushes, fields and trees instead of bricks, rubble, broken glass and broken-down buildings. Now there were open spaces in place of endless streets and bombsites. And, from the get-go, Wooltonians 'spoke different'!

Being the new kids on the block this could have been challenging but Colin and his brother Brian were soon accepted. The ice breaker was camping.

"It all came down to owning a tent. We'd only just moved in, it was the long school holiday (August) when Mum sent us out to play to meet our 'new' friends – the kids who lived near us. Right away we spotted a gang of boys playing in a nearby field. They had a big white sheet and when Brian inquired what they were up to they said they were trying to make a tent. That was it. We were in. We had a tent at home. When Brian told them we had a 'proper' tent they were immediately impressed. So we nipped home to get our old ridged tent with a pole. It was fairly big but just right for us boys. Once we got back we all set about putting it up and from that moment on we were accepted – we had become friends, we'd shared something, had fun together, we all got on."

In the same month Colin and Brian would attend another street party, which offered another bonding exercise with the neighbours – this time to celebrate the end of hostilities with Japan: VJ Day.

"Like the street party in Bootle we had a bonfire but despite it being held to celebrate the end of the war with Japan, the 'guy' that we burnt was dressed as Adolf Hitler."

As for school, that also brought change into Colin's life. Having been enrolled in St. Monica's Roman Catholic Primary School in Bootle, on moving to Woolton Colin's parents decided to send him to Springwood School, which wasn't Catholic.

"I wasn't too happy about this. Going to school I mean – not what faith it was. That didn't really register with me. I remember Mum taking me there on my first day and in the headmaster's office I started crying. Mum had no alternative but to leave me and as I saw her disappearing out of the office door, I made to follow her. As I did so the head grabbed my arm to hold me back. I wasn't having that and so with my free arm I landed him one on the side of his face, which stopped us both in our tracks. But he never held that against me – he was always kind to me."

Springwood would be Colin's school for several years. Two and a half years behind him was a young lad called Rod Davis. Rod lived at 129 King's Drive in Woolton. Around the same time that Colin moved to live in Woolton so did future Quarry Man, Eric Griffiths who lived on Halewood Road which runs into Kings Drive. Heyscroft Road where Colin lived runs into Halewood Drive. So by the turn of the 1950s all three future Quarry Men lived within ten minutes walk of each other.

Meanwhile over on the opposite side of Woolton from where the Hantons lived was 251 Menlove Avenue where that other little boy, John Lennon, was coming to terms with life in a new home.

This comfortable 'semi' was known as 'Mendips'. Comfortable or not it also did not have a garage. In those days few people –

even among the middle classes – could afford to purchase a motor car of their own. During 1943 it had become home to George and Mary Smith who had married in 1939 and did not have children of their own. Within her family Mary was also known as 'Mimi'. On 9th October 1945, Mary's younger sister Julia's little boy John Winston Lennon would turn five. John was already visiting his aunt and uncle's, staying over, making friends and becoming familiar with the village and its surrounding area.

After the war John's Uncle George secured work on the night shift in the Woolton tram depot. Uncle George's income was quite low but they could afford to live at 'Mendips' because John's Aunt Mary was a nurse in the convalescent home in the village. By 1946 as a consequence of the breakdown of his parents' marriage John would move to live permanently with his aunt and uncle.

During the autumn of 1947 his aunt began taking in students as lodgers. This allowed her to end her employment as a nurse yet continue to earn an income to supplement Uncle George's meagre wages, which in turn meant they could keep 'Mendips'. Crucially it also meant she could remain at home to care for John and be there when he arrived home from school. The damage caused by the Blitz meant that after the war within Liverpool there was an acute shortage of student accomodation, so many folk like Mimi with a room to spare 'took in' students to live with them as lodgers. One of the first student lodgers at 'Mendips' in 1947 was Harold Phillips. He was just out of the navy and would give John his first harmonica.

Just behind John at number 24 Vale Road lived the Vaughan family. (The numbering on Vale Road has altered since then.) George and Gertrude had lived in the house from new. George Samuel Vaughan, a police constable, had purchased the property on 3rd October 1935 for the sum of £750.00. It was identical to 'Mendips', having been built by the same builder. Whilst living here George and Gertrude's son, Ivan, had been born on 18th June 1942. Ivan attended Dovedale Primary School with John Lennon.

A future Quarry Man, Ivan was born on the same day as Paul McCartney, with whom he would become close friends when, aged eleven in 1953, they both became pupils at the Liverpool Institute High School for Boys.

Paul remembered that it was sharing the same birthday that clinched their friendship. Turning up to the 'Inny' (as they called it) that first morning in September 1953, they were nervous young boys; it was a new school and they were strangers in a strange land. Alone in that noisy playground waiting for whatever Fate held in store, Paul and Ivan had recognised each other as fellow 'new boys'. Desperately in need of some moral support they had begun to chat, which is when they discovered they were born on the same date. Paul says that was it, an instant bond was formed: friends for life.

Somewhere behind Mendips at number 83 Vale Road, just up from Ivan on the opposite side of the road – almost on the junction with Linkstor Road – a little boy named Pete with his older brother Ernest, older sister Jean and parents George and Bessie had also come to live. Nearer to Ivan, on his side of the road, in another house identical to 'Mendips' called 'Leosdene', lived Nigel, the son of P.C. Walley. Nigel – a friend of John and Ivan almost from the day John moved in – would later become the manager of The Quarry Men. As a little boy, along with Ive and Pete, he was a member of John's 'gang', the 'Outlaws'. Their name came from the novels of Richmal Crompton, whose fictional schoolboy hero, William Brown, leads a gang of the same name. Mighty fans of 'William', John, Ivan, Nigel and Pete did their best to emulate his and his gang's reckless adventures.

The principal players – the erstwhile pieces of an extraordinary story had begun to settle into place… time and consequence pulling them closer together.

5

THINGS AIN'T WHAT THEY USED TO BE

As the war drew to a close, so life changed dramatically for two little boys. While in 1946 John Lennon moved from living with his mother and her partner Bobby to living with his Aunt Mimi in Woolton, Colin's home circumstances would change equally dramatically.

First there was a brand new arrival to celebrate: in November 1946 he and Brian were joined by a baby sister, Jacqueline, forever known within the family as 'Lynn'.

Sadly Lynn would never get to know her Mum for tragedy struck the family in 1948 when Ethel became ill with tuberculosis. TB, or 'consumption' as it was also known, is a bacterial infection contracted by inhaling tiny droplets from the coughs and sneezes from someone who already has it. One of the biggest killers of the era – as feared then as cancer is today – despite the development of streptomycin, the first antibiotic effective against it, TB still claimed many lives in the Forties and Fifties.

At the time Ethel became ill, husband John had left the fire service and was once again working for the Co-Op. When Ethel went into hospital it became impossible for him to care for three children (one of whom was just a toddler) while continuing to hold down a full-time job. And so, while Mum was away and Dad continued to live in Woolton, Colin, Brian and Lynn returned to live with Granny and Granddad Jones in Oxford Road in Bootle.

Colin was hugely upset by Mum's illness and absence from his life. He missed his mum and continually worried about her and so as soon as he moved in with Granny and Granddad Jones they took pity on him and did not push him to go to school. At the time Brian, Colin and Lynn had arrived to live with their grandparents; they were already under considerable pressure because they were also caring for another grandson called Roger, born to their daughter Hylda. Roger was a lively toddler and quite a handful for the elderly couple.

Fortunately, unlike the first time he lived with Granny and Granddad Jones, this time Colin was not to prove so troublesome: instead he turned out to be a godsend.

"I didn't want to go to school and so in order to remain at home for as long as I could I'm afraid I played on their sympathy. Almost as soon as I moved in I realised my grandparents were struggling to occupy Roger and so almost immediately I made myself useful by keeping him entertained during the day. This had the desired affect: I took the burden off them and in turn they didn't push me to go to school!"

Colin's good fortune couldn't last – and it didn't.

The struggle Granny and Granddad Jones were having caring for four young children and Colin's absence from school were duly noted and changes made. Colin was removed to live with Granny Hanton and Aunty Molly in their home in Eleanor Road. In an instant his protracted break from school came to an end. Granny Hanton would not countenance any of Colin's shenanigans. As a strict, God-fearing Catholic she knew what was best for a child and being soft on them wasn't her idea of good parenting. Thus he was immediately enrolled at the St. Robert Bellarmine Catholic School, Bootle, which shared Granny Hanton's stricter views on child care.

While Colin negotiated the network of new and old relationships and the stresses of beginning a new school, his Mum continued to battle TB. The young boy was constantly reassured she would recover and return home, even though the family knew that with every passing day she remained in hospital the likelihood of this happening was growing ever more unlikely. And so, while it was no surprise to them when in early 1950 Ethel passed away, for Colin it was a massive shock. He was just eleven years old. The world as he knew it had changed forever.

While not surprised the family was nevertheless devastated. The loss of Ethel was a shattering experience. Despite the support of his extended family Colin felt adrift in the world. He loved his Mum and for her to no longer be there was difficult to understand or accept. It was hard for such a young boy to imagine life ever returning to normal.

"What upset me was that right up until the end the adults in my family continued to reassure me Mum would come home. I comforted myself with that knowledge. Thus it became almost unbearable when she didn't. I don't think I ever forgave them."

Of course life would never be the same but that did not mean Colin's new life would be as unbearable as he imagined it would be. In fact it turned out to be much, much better than he ever imagined it could be.

A year passed after their mother's death before the children found themselves returning to live with Dad once more at 4 Heyscroft Road in Woolton. (Just ahead of him, Eric Griffiths, future guitar player with The Quarry Men, had moved from Bootle with his Mum to live on Halewood Drive just around the corner from Colin's house.)

It was at this point in Colin's life that he found some much-needed permanence and security. His sense of 'family' was gradually restored with each passing day and 4 Heyscroft became a 'proper' home again where he would live for the next fourteen years. Coming back was not simple however: more dramatic twists and turns would accompany the children's return to living with their dad that were challenging but ultimately positive.

There had been a very special reason why the family had not been reunited after Mum had died: Dad had found a new 'friend'. Sometime after the death of Ethel and before their return to live with him, Dad would regularly spend Saturday or Sunday afternoons with his children at Grandma Hanton's. On these occasions he would be accompanied by his new 'girl friend', Aunty Peggy Shaw.

"We three children immediately took to Peggy: we felt comfortable with her and Dad as a couple, as 'Dad and Peggy' as we called them. She was younger (23) than Dad (41) and fun to be with. She liked being with us and we with her. So when we did return to live in Woolton she was already an accepted part of our life. We had all grown fond of each other. In fact when we moved back in with Dad in April 1951, Peggy became our 'new Mum': she and Dad had married on the 26th March that year. Even more to the point not long after in November 1951 Brian, Lynn and I were joined by a new brother, John Dennis – or 'John D' as he has always been known."

All the moving around, the death of his Mum and the arrival of Peggy and John D into his life inevitably took some getting used to. The shape and nature of Colin's close family had changed irrevocably. It says a lot for how John and Peggy conducted themselves and cared for the children that Colin now always refers to Peggy as 'Mum'.

"That's how I think of Peggy: she's my Mum. When we first all lived together I did call her Aunty Peggy but one day Dad took me aside and said how she'd like it if I called her 'Mum'. I had no problems with that at all and neither did Brian, for by then we had grown very close to her. From the start Lynn, who had no memory whatsoever of our Mum, was already calling Peggy 'Mum', and John D of course naturally called her that. We needed a Mum in our lives so much. So we were happy Dad had found Peggy. We were a family again. As Dad said – Peggy would not replace Mum in our affections – but would become a new mum to us. He was right: we have always got on well."

Lynn, Brian, Colin and John D, Heyscroft Road

Dad John and Mum Peggy (1959)

6

SCHOOL DAZE

'If you don't pass the Eleven Plus you're finished in life. So that was the only exam I ever passed, because I was terrified.'

(The Beatles Anthology, p.8)

So said John Lennon. So powerfully had this dictum been drummed into him and every other middle class youngster in the Fifties and Sixties, failure was simply not an option. As a consequence John became a grammar school boy. Predominantly the province of the middle classes, grammar school carried the educational kudos of the time and its pupils were regarded as the cream of the crop, the educational elite. And so in September 1952, as he entered the portals of Quarry Bank High School For Boys for the very first time, for John Lennon of Woolton, Liverpool, academia, university and the prospect of a golden future beckoned. Known locally as the 'Eton of the Labour Party', it was a prestigious institution (even if, academically, a step or two behind the Liverpool Institute High School for Boys, where future Quarry Men, McCartney and Harrison would be pupils, or Liverpool Collegiate, where Pete Best was a scholar).

The Eleven Plus was a result of the Butler Education Act of 1944, which also raised the school leaving age to 15 (inadvertently creating 'the teenager'). The only problem was failure was built into the Eleven Plus. In Liverpool annually approximatley only 10% of eleven-year-olds passed the exam to go to Grammar School. The remaining 90% were headed for a secondary modern or technical school. To put it bluntly – in the perception of the time – secondary modern equalled second class, i.e. 'thick'.

Colin didn't pass the Eleven Plus. Indeed he even failed the test his primary school set to see if you were actually worth entering for the real thing.

"I failed so miserably they did not even enter me for the big exam."

Oops!

There would be no golden ticket of opportunity for Colin. Instead a place at Horrocks Avenue Senior School in Garston (his local Roman Catholic Secondary Modern) awaited him. Generally considered as clearing houses for the working classes, most secondary modern pupils were destined to become 'factory fodder' or would fill low-level clerical positions. Only the fortunate few gained an apprenticeship to learn a craft.

Sadly Horrocks Avenue was no great shakes as a school. Quickly constructed after the war it comprised just four 'prefabricated' units (or 'prefabs'), which were to be used until something better came along. After the war 'prefabs' were used widely throughout Liverpool to house displaced families

"I was taught in a school made out of four prefabs! There's an irony in there somewhere. The one I was in was divided into three classes: Sister Gertrude's, Mr. Rouss's [Colin is not too sure of how he spelled his surname], and a young attractive female teacher whom we all fancied… but whose name – like most of what I learned at school – I have forgotten."

Despite the class and academic divides the disciplinary regimes at either grammar or secondary modern were equally harsh.

Corporal punishment had yet to be abolished hence a good thrashing with either a strap, cane or slipper or straightforward slap across the face with the front and/or back of the hand was generally regarded as a just reward for any misdemeanour.

Back then such physical punishment was almost considered a rite of passage on the way to becoming a 'well-adjusted' member of society: its proponents would churn out phrases like 'it will make a man of you', 'it's character building', 'it never did me any harm' and other similar guff. All opinions for which Colin gives short shrift. For him schooldays do not qualify as 'the best days of your life'.

While future Quarry Men Lennon, Shotton, Davis and Griffiths at Quarry Bank faced a caning for any misdeeds committed, Colin was not only subjected to the 'stick' but also to a good face slapping. Canes were made from rattan, which has a natural flexibility which meant it could deliver a very painful sting indeed.

Colin has always maintained that his familiarity with the cane was unfairly gained. He was not a particularly errant or naughty pupil but getting out of bed in time for the start of the school day was something he found difficult to master.

"I always felt it was unfair to be punished with a caning for being late because at the time of my so-called wrongdoing I had actually been unconscious, unaware and definitely behaving myself!"

A good caning was always on the cards from the moment Colin began junior school but on entering senior school a harsh face slapping courtesy of Sister Gertrude became a distinct possibility. A nun as well as a teacher she was as strict as a sergeant major: memories of Sister G in action remain irrevocably scarred into Colin's psyche.

"The most violent attack occurred during my last year at Horrocks. It was a Monday morning before lessons had started when Sister G almost casually

asked my whole class, 'Did everyone attend Mass on Sunday?' Usually we all just automatically intoned, 'Yes Sister' but for some reason I've never been able to work out on this occasion a particularly foolhardy lad on the front row put his hand up and said, 'No, I didn't.'"

Like all his classmates Colin was stunned and immediately turned to get a better look at this boy whom he feared had suddenly lost his mind. Such an admission was tantamount to saying you'd turned to worshipping the Devil! Always good news to deliver to a nun.

"Sister Gertrude had gone very quiet. We all had. I can see her now: she had the boy fixed firmly in her gaze. Unblinking and in a very low but steely voice she inquired further: 'And why was that?' Apparently not sensing any danger whatsoever and without any pause for thought or consequence the boy innocently replied, 'I went fishing with my Dad, sister'. That was it – there was no way back for him now: had he said he'd accompanied his father to administer an exorcism there might have been a chance – but 'fishing'? He might as well have asked Gertrude to kiss the Devil's arse. By now the tension in that room was unbearable."

Within the instant Sister Gertrude moved to stand directly in front of this errant child. As she did so, the two became locked eyeball to eyeball within each other's gaze. If he didn't know before he certainly knew now that he was in trouble and there was no way out. Without any warning whatsoever the excruciating tension broke as Sister G began slapping the boy vigorously across the face. Colin remembers every blow.

"Slap, slap, slap, slap – forehand, backhand, forehand, backhand. So sudden and violent was her assault the boy had no time to move out of the way. His face was a blur as it rocked from side to side. We were completely dumbstruck. He was wondering what day it was."

The attack was over almost as soon as it began. Sudden, violent, terrifying to witness.

"I can see Sister Gertrude now, collecting herself before stepping back from her assault, leaving the boy slumped, stunned and speechless in his desk. You could have heard a pin drop. Knowing she had our attention now she once again turned her attention to the rest of us, staring us all down before addressing us very clearly and precisely, 'Boys – let me ask you again – did you all go to Mass on Sunday?' There was barely a moment's hesitation before – in total unison – we replied: 'Yes, Sister!!!' (Even though, in my case, I hadn't.)"

Almost as stunned as the boy with the ballooning face had been all those years ago, when asked Colin struggles to recall other memories of school: he has no thoughts or stories about the institution itself, about his actual education, any books he read, his teachers or his lessons. His mind is blank. But when asked about school meals he smiles and waxes lyrical.

"I did enjoy the dinners there – especially the fish and chips on Friday! I also liked their semolina. In those days, for all us kids, food was thin on the ground. Getting a meal each day at school made it almost worthwhile getting up to go there – even on days when I got the cane for being late. I was never late for school dinners. Don't forget rationing continued until 1954. What was on offer at home and at school was very basic fare by today's standards – treats like chocolate bars were almost unheard of – to find an orange inside your Christmas stocking was considered a real treat. Consequently being fed at school was very important to us, especially the indulgence of school puddings. All sweet, sugary, treacly and covered in custard they made school bearable: true schoolboy heaven!"

Hand in hand with the pleasure of school meals and school puddings came pain. Not the tooth decay the puddings caused, but the stigma. Colin's was a big family – four children – and Mum and Dad's incomes were stretched to the limit.

"I can still feel the piercing discomfort I felt for being deemed eligible for 'free school meals' and 'free school milk'. This was a source of real embarrassment, one of those things that singled lads like me out from the others. It made me a bit different, uncomfortably so because it marked me as 'poor': in other words a potential target for those nasty 'gets' every school has who like to make the lives of other kids a misery. It was a stigma, a stick for the bullies with which to beat me. And so, as best I could, I kept quiet about it – or tried to, it wasn't easy."

Colin's eligibility for free meals led directly to him and his sister Lynn experiencing another unpleasant aspect of life in post-war Liverpool: the antipathy between certain members of the city's Orange (Protestant) and Green (Catholic) communities.

"My sister and I received free school dinners and one time when I was at secondary school I remember one Catholic School holiday (that Protestants didn't celebrate) when my parents inquired of the Education Committee exactly where on that particular day my sister, Lynn and I would receive our free school meal. We were told to attend St.James – a non-Catholic school in Woolton – where we would be fed. I didn't want to go but had no option: I had to take Lynn so she could have her school dinner, she was too small to go on her own. On arriving at the door we were met by a sympathetic young woman but before I could relax, almost immediately from behind her there appeared this big battleaxe of a woman all hustle and hatred who told us in the harshest of terms, 'No, we are not feeding Catholics – we only have enough food for our own kids!'. I didn't stop to argue, I just grabbed Lynn's hand and took her away."

The woman watched them go. Colin says he could feel her eyes boring into the back of his neck as they pushed the door open and exited.

"Although I hadn't wanted to go to that place all the way there I'd been comforting myself with the prospect of sampling St. James's semolina.

However I wasn't going to argue our corner given the woman's size and aggressive demeanour: she could have had us for dinner and still come back for seconds. Nevertheless as we trudged away I was certainly upset and humiliated by her attitude. And very angry. When we got home Mum listened closely to what I had to say before making us some bread and butter: meagre fare but all she had.

My parents must have complained to Mr. Cunningham, the head master of my school, because two weeks later he asked to speak to 'the Free School Meal pupils' to inquire if any of us had had any problems with any of our meals recently. He asked this in a roundabout way rather than directly. I'm not sure why, possibly to save Lynn and I from any embarrassment.

Unfortunately I was too distracted by his black and white border collie that he brought with him to school to realise he was referring to the incident at St. James's. My attention was so focused on making friends with the dog I didn't stop to think and simply said, 'No, no problems, Sir'. And so I suppose nothing ever happened. Mr. Cunningham must have wondered just what my parents were on about, making a fuss when I was seemingly quite happy and oblivious to any problem. Clearly he had not encountered the battleaxe of St. James's. If he had, he would not have had to ask."

Colin's general disillusionment with school went back to Junior School, where he witnessed a particularly outrageous incidence of corporal punishment being meted out.

"I was at St. Mary's, my Junior School in Woolton when two young boys, almost infants, broke into the school and stole some dinner tickets. I don't know how they'd managed it, they were so small. Mr. Cunningham assembled the whole school to witness their punishment. (Mr. Cunningham was head of both *St. Mary's and Horrocks Avenue, even though they were situated on different sites, the junior school in Woolton, Horrocks Avenue in Garston.) Quaking and crying the two tiny criminals were brought into the assembly hall where the entire school population stood watching and waiting."*

The two little boys were made to stand in front of the assembled throng where Mr. Cunningham – in infinite detail – described their misdemeanours and the exact nature of their punishment.

"Utterly humiliated the boys stood heads bowed in front of the rest of us. The time it took Mr. Cunningham to describe their crime and their punishment only served to intensify the impending catastrophe the little boys believed was about to hit them. Despite their size and clear remorse they were going to receive a caning. A beating. A thrashing. Cranking the tension within that room to almost beyond bursting point was the knowledge that it was to be administered in full view of us all. The two little boys looked utterly shamefaced and terrified. This was horrible but we onlookers were a mixture of emotions. Horrified but equally thrilled and excited. To us this was as close as we'd get to witness a public hanging! It was pure theatre, a public flogging: perversely fascinating but horrific at the same time because on any given day it could have happened to any one us. We were gripped by the all-consuming tension of the situation, inwardly thanking God it was they and not us who would be on the receiving end of the merciless length of stick Mr. Cunningham held in his hand.

The older brother of one of these boys, a lad named Joey, was standing next to me in the assembled throng. I will never forget how – as he stood waiting to be hit – his young brother turned towards him crying, 'Joey, Joey, please help me, Joey!' And of course there was nothing that poor Joey could do for his little brother except stand speechless like the rest of us to witness Mr. Cunningham strike him six times across each hand with the cane. Six times on both hands. Twelve swipes in total! The same then meted out to the other boy. It's incredible to comprehend that such outrageous cruelty was acceptable back then – and publicly demonstrated. I felt terrible for Joey and the two little lads who were so terrified. Sixty-five years on it still makes me wince, a moment seared irrevocably into my memory.

No wonder school days were not the happiest days of my life. How could they have been when stuff like this was going on? The fear of violence – from teachers and bullies alike – was the daily backdrop to all our school days."

One positive Colin does take from his school days occurred during his last ever school summer holiday in 1953.

"That's when I met Rod Davis for the very first time. He lived on Kings Drive, just around the corner from my home on Heyscroft. There were a group of youngsters who lived in this vicinity and we'd get together to play cricket or football on our road. Rod was one of that cricketing and football gang. Heyscroft, being a T-shaped cul-de-sac, was not very bothered by traffic at all and so that's where we'd congregate to kick the ball around or play cricket. We could quickly and easily move out of the way if a car came along, which in those days they rarely did because not many people owned one anyway, consequently we were as safe there as anywhere. Our biggest hazard was putting a ball through someone's window!"

Inevitably school ended in anti-climax when, in late December 1953, amidst no fanfare whatsoever, Colin left. Nothing marked the occasion: no exams, no school certificate, no qualifications; there was no band playing or farewell party, just a simple report and commendation from his headmaster, Mr. Cunningham. Ten words were all it took to say goodbye: 'Works well, tries hard, will tackle willingly the labour set.'

Like his father's generation before him despite the new fangled Eleven Plus exam Colin left empty handed. He did so on a Friday afternoon and two weeks later on Friday 1st January 1954 (New Year's Day, which, in those days, was not a public holiday) he was suited, booted and walking out as an adult: his working life had begun. He was just fifteen.

7

THE WORK, THE WORKING LIFE

As effortlessly as his schooldays ended so Colin's working life began. Old school friends quickly faded as new friends from work took their place.

If 'life' had taught Colin anything up to this point it was to embrace change. Finding a job, going to work did not faze him. These were the necessary next steps you took in life – and anything was better than Horrocks Avenue Senior School!

Colin's destination that first day of work was Guy Rogers, a furniture manufacturer situated in Speke just a mile or so down the road from his home in Woolton.

"Just before I left school in December I'd been to the Job Centre in Garston to see the Youth Employment officer. He'd read my report from school, which, let's face it, didn't say an awful lot. Based on Mr. Cunningham's words of wisdom there wasn't much he could ask me. So when – after much pursing of the lips and furrowing of the eyebrows on his part – he asked what I was good at. I'd had plenty of time to prepare myself and so immediately I replied 'working with my hands': I was good at carpentry."

As Colin sat wondering what else he could say to help, this small nugget of information he had imparted acted like switching on a light inside the poor chap's head.

"He immediately told me there was a furniture factory out in Speke, at the

same time he quickly scribbled an address on a piece of paper, which he thrust triumphantly into my hand with the advice: 'That's probably the place to go for you.' I looked at him and he at me. Without speaking another word I took my leave."

How right that Youth Employment Officer was.

"I wasted no time. I went directly to 'Guy Rogers furniture factory' and saw the senior man, Mr. Beniworth. He also looked at my school report, which of course did not take him long. He looked me up and down, also had a few words with me and told me I could start on January 1st. That was all it took for me to get a job. A brief interview and I was sorted for life."

Ten words on a school report, one for every year of his education, and in less time than it took him to remove his school tie Colin had found himself a job for life.

As this had all been done and dusted before Christmas 1953 it was on New Year's Day 1954 Colin began his first job. (New Year's Day did not become a public holiday until 1974.)

"Monday to Thursday I began at eight each morning and finished at six each evening but on Friday we finished at four pm. The firm had not long moved from their original city centre premises into a purpose built factory out at Speke. The move had been originally scheduled to happen in the mid-1930s but when the war broke out the factory had been commandeered by the RAF who used it to manufacture aeroplane parts. Even by the time I started in 1954 there will still a few RAF bits and pieces like desks lying around. In those days everywhere you went in Liverpool there were bombsites around every corner, gaps where buildings had once been, physical evidence of the war."

Although he had a job Colin had no idea just what it actually entailed. No one had thought to explain it to him. It was just assumed he'd do what ever it took. Any thoughts Colin may have had before he started work of being given an apron, saw, chisel and bench and making a chair or desk from scratch were immediately dispelled.

"I thought I'd be starting as a carpenter but I wasn't. I was allocated work as a general labourer. I was sent through to what's known as the 'French polishing shop': that was my base. I was given a manual 'truck' that I would push up to the mill where they produced the wooden furniture. There I would load three settees or a dozen chairs, take them down to the first polishing shop where I would push them in. There they would be given the first coat or spray of polish which would bring out the grain of the wood. I'd then hand sandpaper them down and push them back in for another coat. After that I'd load them up again and take them to the top polishing shop to be finished off. As you can imagine I was kept fairly busy!"

Colin didn't argue. This wasn't strictly carpentry but it was work: hard, physical work. But he had a job and that is what mattered. He also knew his Dad was watching. John Hanton had led by example: work hard, don't shirk, support your family, take the opportunities life handed out.

"I'm not sure quite what I expected to happen next. I was just going with the flow but I knew my Dad felt I was capable of more, that I needed to learn a skill, a trade: something that had more of a future, something that would offer greater security, better prospects and pay better. Consequently he'd left me in no doubt just how important it was to learn a trade, to get an apprenticeship. In fact he'd given me an ultimatum of twelve months: 'If you don't have an apprenticeship after twelve months I'll find you one!' So there was pressure on me from home to find something better but I was also being given a period of grace – time to find my feet, make my own decisions."

As so often in Colin's life, the answer to a problem came to him before he'd had time to properly ask the question.

"After about six months Mr. Beniworth approached me to say the firm were starting an apprentice upholstery scheme. He said they'd noticed how hard I worked on my own and thought I deserved a chance on an apprenticeship, would I be interested? I didn't need asking twice. This was something that had been drummed into me by Dad for as long as I could remember: 'an apprenticeship, an apprenticeship, an apprenticeship!' So obviously this was a 'eureka!' moment for me – this *was exactly what my parents had been on and on about. More to the point – the offer had beaten my Dad's deadline by six months."*

Colin's enthusiasm and sense of relief were so overwhelming he accepted on the spot.

"Mr. Beniworth said if I was interested I should go and see Mr. Baird, who would be taking charge of the apprentices."

That was exactly what Colin did – but before doing so he had to sort out one niggling problem that was worrying him about the whole plan.

"Before I actually saw Mr. Baird to 'sign on' as it were I went into the French polishing shop to seek out my mates to ask them the very simple but crucial question, 'What's an upholsterer?'"

Up to that point no-one had actually thought to impart this vital piece of information to Colin. Mr. Beniworth had clearly assumed that from the moment Colin arrived he knew what an upholsterer was.

"My mates looked at me quite thoughtfully but didn't make fun of me when it would have been very easy to do so; instead they nodded towards the chaps in the middle of the factory floor banging away with bunches of tacks in their mouths. As I looked at them they said, 'They are upholsterers, what they are doing is upholstery'. All my co-workers that I spoke to encouraged me, 'to go for it!' so, I did. I sought out Mr. Baird and put my name down."

Not long after he signed up for the scheme, one Monday morning when he arrived for work there were six work benches laid out; two had settees on, the other four chairs. That was it: Colin's five-year apprenticeship had begun. He was shown how to put the padding on the arms and how to put an arm in and then how to put a back and seat in. This and all the other skills of upholstery were learned exceptionally well by Colin; so much so, he has been in demand and never out of work since.

For a measure of how much the world has changed since 1955, Colin's memories of how much he earned as an apprentice and what it would buy are quite startling.

"My starting wage was about two pounds ten shillings (worth approximately £48.00 in today's money) a week rising gradually. That's ten pounds a month: I don't ever remember being particularly well off. The majority of my wage went to my parents for my board and keep, which left me about ten shillings (50 pence in modern currency, which would buy the equivalent of £9.50's worth of goods in today's money) a week to spend on myself. Don't forget that back in the Fifties ten shillings would buy a lot, a lot more than it would today. There were twelve pennies in one shilling, twenty shillings in one pound i.e., 240 pennies in a pound. You could go to the pictures (cinema) for nine pennies or 9d as we wrote it then, I think a pint of milk cost two pennies or '2d', it wasn't a lot but somehow I managed, we all managed. Everybody was in the same boat: i.e. struggling!"

Colin's right. In 1954 a pint of milk cost only two old pennies or '2d', a loaf the same, six eggs 3d, a bag of sugar 5d and a pint of beer 9d. After fourteen years food rationing would finally end that year on 4th July. What could be bought for pound in 1954 would cost approximately £19.00 in today's money. The average weekly wage for a man was £9, nine shillings and two pennies (£9/9s/2d). For a woman it was £5. (In 2017 that's approximately £180.90 and £95.71 respectively.)

And so the pattern of Colin's life after school had begun:

working hard, learning his trade, paying his money to mum and Dad. As for that excess ten shillings, Colin doesn't remember saving any of it. He says he spent quite a bit of it on frequent trips to the cinema – a major passion in his life. As far as entertainment went, there wasn't really a lot more to do back then except go out to the pub, the pictures or a dance (all of which he liked to do – but, of course, he had to wait until he was 18 to start going to the pub).

8

SITTING ON THE BACK ROW

As a regular cinema-goer, Colin was typical: out of a population of about 47 million in 1948, it was estimated that one third of Britons went to the cinema at least once a week. Cinema attendances peaked in Britain in that year. As for home entertainment, by the end of the Forties there were only 14,500 television sets in the whole country: radio remained far and away the main entertainment centre at home.

All this would begin to change as the Fifties progressed and more television sets found their way into British homes. Until they did, it cannot be understated how moving pictures, especially those from Hollywood-influenced that immediate post war generation. Fictions though they may have been, they helped shape and inform both preceding and post-war generations' view of the world and life beyond their hometown, especially that in the USA.

"As I grew up I didn't really have any hobbies. Basically my pastime was the cinema. There was the Woolton Cinema (which is still there to this day). There was another on Allerton Road, in fact there were picture houses all over the place. These were the days 'before television' and a night out at the cinema was hugely popular. The picture houses all showed different films. I mean you could go to the Woolton twice or even three times a week because there would be a new film on from Monday through Tuesday and Wednesday which changed for Thursday, Friday and Saturday and then there'd be another film shown on Sundays."

A night at the cinema or 'flicks' or 'pictures' was real value for money.

"You got a lot for your ninepence. Trailers for forthcoming attractions, Pearl & Dean advertisements, a Pathe news bulletin, usually a low-budget 'B-film' as well as the main feature, maybe even a cartoon short and you could purchase refreshments. Many cinemas were very luxurious – no wonder they were called 'Picture Palaces'. Stepping inside a really good cinema removed you from drab reality; there'd be lots of deep pile carpet, velvet and ornate decorations, portraits of famous stars adorned the walls. Once inside you were in a different and glamorous world, you felt privileged. On the other hand those that had seen better days were often referred to as 'flea pits' because that's exactly what they were."

More often than not the cinema would be be packed and smoke-filled. For a couple of hours folk could disappear into the darkness to fire their imaginations. It was a public place but felt almost private, a place to treat yourself: somewhere to be entertained while you consumed tubs of ice cream or bars of chocolate or bags of sweets or popcorn and drink Kia Ora Orange Squash through a straw. The back row was usually the province of courting couples, where, in the depths of darkness, they could enjoy hot moments of passion: a sloppy kiss and a furtive grope.

The cinema helped shaped young people's vision of the world and their place in it. War was glamourous, men were heroes or villains, women beautiful, alluring and largely ornamental. Films with Marlon Brando and James Dean especially appealed to the younger generations. Being a film fan, Colin went to see all James Dean's films when they came out. Dean made only a handful of films before dying in a car crash aged just 24 in 1955 but the way he looked and the films he made had a profound affect on the new and emergent teenagers in both the USA and the UK.

"James Dean was a rebel. I remember going to see 'Rebel Without A Cause' (1955) even though it was an 'X'. He looked cool. I saw him in 'Giant' (1956) as well. You were meant to be 18 to get into an 'X' but some cinemas were well known for being less vigilant than others. 'Blackboard Jungle' (1955) was another 'X' I distinctly remember going to see at the Odeon on London Road – the same cinema where John Lennon went to see it. I'd read all the newspaper stories about Teddy Boys down south smashing up the cinemas where it was first shown. As an apprentice upholsterer I resisted the temptation to rip up the cinema seats when I went to see it – even if it might have given me some work. Rock 'n' roll was happening by the time this film came out. I'd heard and enjoyed Bill Haley's 'Rock Around The Clock', which played over the titles to the film but the raucous response to 'Blackboard Jungle' never really happened up here. I know John Lennon experienced the same audience reaction as I did when he went to see it: nothing."

It's hard to be a juvenile delinquent when everybody else remains seated, too busy eating their choc ice.

9

FLUORESCENT SOCKS 'N' SMOG

As a fashion statement the Fifties were something else. War was over; it was time to step out and enjoy life. The era of 'make do and mend' was slowly coming to an end. The 'teenager' had emerged thanks to the raising of the school leaving age and when conscription ended at the end of the decade young people could enjoy an even longer extended period of adolescence.

As ever, commerce stepped up to the plate to cater for this emerging class of moneyspenders. Teenagers would soon be offered styles especially designed for them.

Movie stars and mass media would be the biggest influence on fashion although teens were soon tuning in to what those new and exciting rock 'n' rollers were wearing.

For boys, the roll call of cool included blue suede shoes and winklepickers, drape jackets with velvet collars, leather jackets and blue jeans, drainpipes and pegs, slicked-back hair, quiffs and ducktail or crew cut.

For girls, the choice almost expanded by the day: wasp waists with full skirts, pencil skirts and blouses, pumps and flatties, stilettos and mules, sandals and kitten heels, Italian cut and bubble cut, pony tail and poodle cut, bouffant and brushed under bob.

Tuned in to all of this crazy stuff as it happened, Colin is philosophical when asked if being a new-fangled 'teenager' really resonated with him. Did the themes of teenage restlessness and disaffection as portrayed in such films as 'Rebel Without A Cause' strike a chord?

"I didn't feel restless or disaffected but I felt very much that it was 'our own time' if you like – 'ours' meaning us as young people, or 'teenagers' as we were beginning to be called. It still wasn't that long after the war and Liverpool was still in a mess physically and economically. It didn't look great because of the destruction. Don't forget how much of the city had been bombed. That takes time and money to rebuild. It wasn't just the place it was the people who were in recovery. I would describe what was happening back then as living in black and white when suddenly life became 'Technicolor'.

It could be dangerous to be a teenager. Teddy Boys were the teenagers to be avoided – even by their fellow teens: youths dressed up like Edwardian dandies with drape jackets and crepe-soled shoes ('brothel creepers' we called them), a bootlace tie and often armed with flick knives and chains. They usually hung about in gangs and were most definitely out for trouble: just looking at them could get you beaten up. New music aimed directly at young people was being heard; clothes were in the shops for the 'younger man' – not a suit like your dad would wear but something more stylish. Most young blokes like me still wore a suit to go out in but something sharper than older blokes: there was more choice – I could buy something else, something stylistically different.

I remember going into town and – big spender that I was – buying some fluorescent socks! One pair was fluorescent pink, the other fluorescent green. So when I went into town that Friday night with my pink socks on I really thought I was the bee's knees: the epitome of cool. In my mind this splash of colour set me apart from a lot of other people. My socks were a statement: they made me feel different, good about myself."

Colin doesn't remember if his wild socks drew the attention of the girls that particular night but he says it was being able to wear something made in such a vivid colour that was the breakthrough – a big attraction for him and his fellow teens.

'Everything was so grey in those days; the buildings in Liverpool were black from the soot, the mixture of dirt and the dust present in the air. I remember trying to get home in the 'smog' – we don't have smog in Britain today but we did back then. It was a toxic atmospheric mixture of smoke and fog that was a regular feature of lives in big towns and cities in the Fifties. 'Pea soupers' they were called. Not only were factories burning coal, churning out black soot and smoke into the atmosphere, but so was everyone at home; there was no central heating back then. We sat huddled in front of coal fires during winter, smoke pouring out of our chimneys.

People could die in the smog. They'd suffocate: anyone with a lung infection was in real peril. People died. It was so bad everything would stop: the buses would stop because the drivers could not see the road in front of them; we'd have to get off and walk home. Not just occasionally but frequently. You had to pay attention, it was so gloopy, like swimming in muddy water – you could easily miss a turn, get lost. It completely disorientated you. You couldn't see your feet in smog, even if you were wearing fluorescent socks!"

Smog, gloom, grey, damp, old and worn down is how Britain felt as a place to live at that time. And of course most of those Hollywood films that Colin loved so much were shot in California, USA, and the world they depicted was a million times brighter, sunnier, lighter, warmer and cleaner.

"It did seem better in America. Again it was all about colour and brightness. We seemed mired in gloom compared to Americans. They seemed to have sunshine from day to day. They hadn't had bombings, black outs or experienced the 'Blitz'; there was lots of food – no rationing. No smog! No bombed-out buildings! Everyone had a car. To us it looked to be a bigger and better place to be. Not that I particularly wanted to go there or be there but it certainly looked better.

Although I got the socks, looking back I'd describe myself as just this dizzy kid floating through life, taking things as they came, working hard but I was not too socially conscious or politically aware of what was going on around me. I wasn't motivated to change the world. That was going on around me all the time, instead I was just dipping into what was there that I liked, what attracted me – like dancing, I definitely liked rhythm: I'd found my niche."

ENDNOTES

Teddy Boys

Teddy Boys or 'Teds' and Teddy Girls were a uniquely British phenomenon who rose to notoriety during the 1950s. They were the first youth group in the UK to identify themselves as 'teenagers'. Now associated with the emergence of rock 'n' roll in the mid-Fifties their emergence actually pre-dated the genre. The subculture began life as 'cosh boys' and comprised working-class youths who adopted the sartorial style of the Edwardian era and listened to jazz. (Jazz musician Bill Eckstine often wore an open high-necked white shirt, which was adopted as part of the Teddy Boy apparel and was known as a 'Mr. B' after him.) Along with the 'Mr. B' shirt Teds wore long drape jackets with velvet collars, slim ties, rubber-soled suede creeper shoes ('brothel creepers') and sported 'greaser' hairstyles featuring a quiff at the front and at the back the hair would be combed into a D.A. 'duck's arse'). A 'Boston' was an alternative hairstyle for which the hair was greased, combed straight back and cut square on the neck.

After the war ended, Savile Row tailors attempted to re-introduce the style of clothing favoured by Edwardian 'dandies' amongst their wealthy young clients but the style became increasingly popular with working-class youths who could afford second-hand Edwardian suits or clothing which could be found on sale in markets. Soon the suits Savile Row tailors had made for their posh clients also became available second-hand because of their increasing assocation with the working class.

It is usually claimed that the style began in London in the early Fifties (1951) and from there spread around the country but some commentators suggest it emerged in other areas of the country around the same time as it did in London. It was in 1953 that a headline in the Daily Express coined the term 'Teddy Boy' when it shortened 'Edwardian' to 'Teddy'. When rock 'n' roll became popular in the UK in 1955/56 so it became the Teds' favoured style of music. They would sometime form gangs who fought with each other (often in ballrooms where they would assemble – ostensibly to listen to the music), which brought them notoriety and media attention. And although the violent male Teds claimed the headlines, there were also Teddy Girls and Teddy Girl gangs who wore drape jackets, rolled up jeans, and flat shoes and favoured straw boater hats, espadrilles, brooches and clutch bags. Less violent than the boys, they did join them at dances and concerts and enjoyed rock 'n' roll.

British teens putting on the style, 1955

10

THE JOY OF RIDING

Five other young men were taken on at Guy Rogers at the same as Colin. They became good friends and would socialise together.

"I'm still in touch with three of them – Ronnie Bamton, Brian Doyle and Alan Kinsley. I soon lost touch with my friends from school. That was how it was, you would leave school, you and your pals would disperse all over the town and lose touch as work and your new workmates filled up your days. We didn't have mobile 'phones and computers and all the social media people have access to today to keep us in touch. We also didn't have cars. Even though I only lived around the corner from Rod Davis, who'd I'd met playing footie on the street, he was one of those with whom I lost contact once I started at Guy Rogers because he was still a schoolboy."

Age was more of a 'thing' back then. Just being a year older than someone was a barrier to becoming friends. Whole year groups would snub the pupils in the years below, which is how it was at the Institute. So the older you were, the less likely you were to associate with younger folk. Both Colin and John Lennon would initially find it difficult to treat George Harrison seriously or as an equal simply because he was nearly five years younger in Colin's case and two and a half in John's. In their eyes he was 'just a kid'.

"Ronnie, Brian, Alan and I would go to the cinema together and once we were old enough we'd go to the pub together. I never started drinking until I was

eighteen. The Brook House on Smithdown Road was popular with us, the Pegasus in Speke was another favourite: places where we could get served – we all looked so young. Pubs were serious drinking and smoking places in those days, the particular habitat of men. I mean seriously adult places. No food, no slot machines, no bar snacks. A young lad with fluorescent socks would have stood out like a sore thumb so you had to choose where you drank carefully. The first pub I went into was the Rose of Mossley on Rose Lane. It's still there, still thriving."

Warming to the subject of old friends, Colin recalls a neighbour from both school and those early days at work through whom he was introduced to someone who in turn became a good friend and would one day offer the fledgling Quarry Men a now famous 'booking'.

From this point on links to Colin's future life as a Quarry Men and friendship with John Lennon begin to pile up.

"Michael Handley lived on our road. While I went to Horrocks, Michael went to St. Francis Xavier, or SFX as it was/is known locally. It was a Roman Catholic secondary school situated in Woolton. Of course we nicknamed Michael 'Tommy' after Tommy Handley, a famous comedian from Toxteth Park in Liverpool well known for his appearances on the BBC radio programme ITMA ('It's That Man Again') that was very popular during the war. Michael was part of our cricket and football gang that played on our road and one day he brought a friend around called Kevin Hanson to meet me. Kevin was a pal of his at SFX and his dad was the caretaker of Woolton Manor on Woolton High Street.

In those days Woolton Manor was a huge convalescence hospital. John Lennon's Aunt Mimi had worked there as a nurse. It's just across the road from where John's Uncle George used to own a small dairy farm and some dairy cottages before the war. Although he and his brother sold the farm Uncle George kept the dairy cottages and for a brief time during the wat John and his mother Julia lived there at number 120 while dad Alfred, was away at sea. Alfred notoriously visited them there at least once when he was home.

Kevin Hanson (left) and Charlie Roberts (right), 1959

Anyway I'd stayed friends with Kevin and sometime later at the end of 1956 or beginning of 1957 when I'd turned eighteen and would be frequenting pubs, Kevin and I were out for a pint when we bumped into an old friend of his called Charlie Roberts. The three of us became drinking buddies. Charlie became an early fan and friend of The Quarry Men and got us a crucial early gig… more of which later."

A while before Colin met Charlie, for a brief time he and Brian Doyle discovered a very enjoyable hobby: driving!

"When I was still only sixteen or seventeen I remember Brian and a friend of his turning up to my house in a Ford Popular. Today this would not raise an eyebrow; back then it was a big deal. Half the neighbourhood came out to see. No one I knew owned a car so this was more than exciting. Ford Pops as they were known had only just started to be manufactured in 1953. It was the UK's lowest priced car of its day. Brian's mate worked in Blakes garage in Speke and he had keys to the garage which meant he also had the keys to the cars. So legally it wasn't actually his car – it was one Blakes used for hire – but that didn't matter to me (or Brian) – I didn't even think about it – at first."

The glamour of a brand new car – albeit one as down-to-earth as a Ford Pop – proved irresistible to the three teenage boys with time on their hands.

"I remember the lads arrived and asked me if I wanted to go for a ride – which, of course, I did. I didn't think twice about it. I never inquired whose car it actually was. It was only when we were out and about that they told me that the car was 'borrowed'. No one at Blakes knew a thing about it: in other words we were driving a stolen car. Even so that didn't deter us: the thrill of being in a car was utterly irresistible. To us we weren't really 'stealing' it because we had every intention of returning it."

The thrill of cruising around became irresistible. Once sampled the boys could not get enough.

"Over the next few months it became a regular thing with us. We would drive around Halewood to where there was a big lay-by and there we'd all take a turn at driving. I'd never sat behind a wheel before so it was completely reckless – but oh, so exciting (even though we were all very cautious). Of course by now we knew it was all illegal but that had become part of the thrill: 'joy-riding' I guess you'd call it – although certainly much more benign and careful than what some youngsters get up to today. It was that very element that made it thrilling."

Inevitably Colin's dad found out what they were up to and although he didn't directly try and stop Colin – he wasn't that sort of a dad; he preferred that he would come to his own conclusions – he did warn him off by pointing out that when he and his friends did this they were driving without a safety net: they had no insurance. And being a good dad he pointed out what that actually meant.

"Dad pricked my conscience. I'd known it already but had been burying my head in the sand. He simply woke me up to the reality of our bit of fun: it was against the law all ways round; we'd cop it if we crashed. Other people could suffer. The police would be involved and we'd end up in court, owing lots of money we did not have, maybe having injured ourselves or someone else, ending up in jail seemed a certainty.

From then on it was in my head and so the 'joy' just drained away. Even if we didn't crash or injure anyone if we were caught we'd still be in deep trouble. In those days this was the kind of thing that could lose you your job. That was too much for me to risk. The more I thought about it the more I knew it was wrong. What had I been thinking? So while Dad categorically never said, 'Don't go in that car again', he'd done a good job, he'd set me right: he'd made me think about the possible repercussions of what we were up to. He let me come to my own decision in my own time. The right decision. Dad was good like that."

Not long after the prank came to an end.

"Soon after Dad's 'talk' the car experienced some mechanical trouble and in an instant from enjoying a bit of a lark we began to panic. It became imperative to get it back to the garage immediately before it broke down completely. We were on tenterhooks every inch of the journey back, afraid it might conk out on the road and we would have to leave it to be discovered. Our necks were on the line. We felt sure the police would stop us. Fortunately the car managed to limp back to the garage. Once we'd got it back inside we frantically legged it out of there, desperately hoping no-one had seen us. Luckily no-one had but we lived in dread for the next few days. Needless to say we never 'borrowed' that Ford Pop again."

11

STANDING BY THE FIRE

Colin wasn't just making new male friends. Girls were also very much a part of the scene. As his school days drew to a close he met someone very special, although it took him a while to realise just how special.

"I came home from school one day – sometimes towards the end of my school career in 1953 – and standing by the fire in the living room, warming herself, was this very attractive young girl who my mum introduced me to as Joan, a colleague of hers from work. To this day that's how I remember seeing her for the very first time, standing next to the fire in our front room. At that time my mum, Peggy, worked in the Co-Op on Prescot Road and Joan worked in the same branch as her. In fact that's how Dad had first met Peggy – when he worked for the Co-Op – and that's how their friendship developed."

One of the idiosyncrasies of life in Britain both before and after the war was that most shops only worked half a day on Wednesdays (a law that had been introduced to ensure shop staff had a half-day off work, bringing the average working week down from six to five and a half days). This meant that it was on Wednesday afternoons Joan became a regular visitor to Colin's house. An avid film-goer herself she started to attend the Woolton Picture House on a Wednesday for the afternoon matinee or early evening screenings.

Joan with Colin's brother John D, Heyscroft Road, 1954

Joan was a few years older than Colin so she could get into the cinema on her own.Your age determined what films you could see unaccompanied. It wasn't long before she agreed to take Colin with her.

"That's why I started to accompany her, because she could get me into the pictures. Usually youths like me who weren't sixteen but wanted to see an 'A' certificate could only do so if we were accompanied by someone aged eighteen. This resulted in kids like me standing on the corner near the cinema asking passersbys if they would 'take one in please'. Cheeky but it usually worked."

As Colin remembers the system of film certification, there was a 'U', an 'A' and an 'X'.

"For an 'X' certificate everyone who attended was expected to be 16 and older. 'Rebel Without A Cause' was rated 'X', as was 'Blackboard Jungle', despite cuts being made to both before they were shown here to make them more palatable to sensitive British audiences. Despite looking young I managed to get in to see them because I was seventeen."

The 'X' Certificate replaced the 'H' Certificate that had been introduced in 1932 to indicate a film was a 'horror' film, the 'H' stood for 'Horrific', to which only over-sixteen could be admitted. Only some councils enforced the 'H' certificate but the 'X' was enforced by all councils.

"As I have already mentioned I went see 'Blackboard Jungle' at the Odeon on London Road when it came out in 1955. I didn't go to see it with Joan however, I went with other apprentice upholsterers from Guy Rogers. One day a week we were sent into Liverpool to a day school on Gambier Terrace (attached to the Liverpool Art College which John would attend in 1957) a road that runs along one side of the Anglican Cathedral. We registered in the Art College on Hope Street but the course itself was held in nearby Gambier Terrace in a big terrace house in the cellar of which there were a couple of

rooms where we were taught. Upstairs, above us, the Art College ran a junior art school where Cynthia Powell was still a student.

I remember that it was for the song 'Rock Around The Clock' as much as the film that I went to see 'Blackboard Jungle'. It was played over the opening titles and it was an electrifying moment to hear the song played at such a volume over the cinema's loudspeakers. The film wasn't a musical; it was a very tense and violent teen drama set in an inner-city American High School. Very contemporary and edgy for the times, it portrayed a dark side of life in the USA.

A year or so later in 1956 after college we all went to see 'Rock Around The Clock' at the Odeon. It starred Bill Haley and his Comets and was a cash-in on his success in the USA; it featured lots of his songs and was the first proper rock 'n' roll musical I saw."

Meanwhile back in Woolton: as time progressed so did Colin and Joan's relationship.

"From those early days when to be hospitable Joan would take me to the cinema, as I got older and could get in by myself, we continued to accompany each other until one time the inevitable happened: we held hands during the film. At the time we had boy and girl friends of our own but not long after we became boy friend and girl friend in our own right. I was in love: and that's how I met my wife."

12

RECORDS AND RADIOGRAMS

Music has been an ever-present in Colin's life. Its significance increasing as he grew older.

"The first songs that made an impact on me were what I'd call 'wartime' songs. Two in particular: 'Yes We Have No Bananas' – that was a big hit because no-one had any bananas – especially me! The other was 'Its A Long Way To Tipperary'."

'Yes We Have No Bananas' had originally been a number one hit in the USA in 1923. When the British government introduced food rationing during the Second World War and so effectively banned the import of bananas for the next five years shop keepers put signs up in their windows saying, 'Yes we have no bananas'. Consequently the song became a hit in Britain all over again during the Second World War. 'It's a Long Way to Tipperary' was a tune from the First World War that also proved popular again during the Second World War.

"As young lads however we were never in, we were always out. Out in all weathers as well – too busy playing football or cricket to spend much time actively listening to music – that came later in life. What music I heard was usually in the background, seeping into my subconscious. When we'd come home from school we'd have a bite to eat, go out and play and then it was time to go to bed. Nine o' clock was my curfew: no radio allowed after that."

For Colin's generation and his parents' before him the radio was the all-important means of communication with the outside world.

"There was no television. Radio was our window into the world. More like an ear-piece really! That's where we got our news – there, in the papers and at the cinema via the Pathe News. Hardly anyone had a telephone so the radio was a big part of life although there weren't the music stations or music programmes there are today."

Radios were often housed in wooden cases resplendent with knobs and dials that you turned to 'tune in'. They were pieces of furniture, often ornate, quite big and bulky.

"Anne Shelton had a radio programme during the war ('Calling Malta') and sang especially for the soldiers. (Later, in 1956 she had a top ten hit with 'Lay Down Your Arms' engineered by Joe Meek who later produced 'Telstar' for The Tornados in 1962.) Vera Lynn was also very popular and known as 'The Forces Sweetheart'. She was famous for her hugely patriotic and stirring songs like 'The White Cliffs of Dover', 'We'll Meet Again' and 'There'll Always Be an England'. I guess they were just played or sung so often at home they became part of your DNA. You just knew them but couldn't remember how you did or when you first heard them. That's what I mean about seeping into your subconscious.

For me and my pals in those post-war years (and when we were just a bit older) the radio was important to us beyond music: it was a vital source of adventure and comedy. When I was back in Woolton for the second time I couldn't wait for 'Dick Barton Special Agent' to come on the radio at quarter to seven in the evening. It was a thriller serial and at the end of every programme Dick would be in some perilous situation from which escape seemed impossible. We would be glued to the radio and left in suspense wondering just how he would escape. He always did, of course."

Another massively popular and hugely influential radio show for Colin and all of his Woolton chums – and those soon-to-be-pals living in Allerton and Speke – was 'The Goons'.

"That was a really big hit – one you just couldn't miss. It was zany, anarchic comedy that always featured a song or two with performances by Max Geldray, a virtuoso harmonica player, and singer Ray Ellington and his quartet. The Goons began in 1951 and was still being broadcast when we were Quarry Men. (All of us, all of The Beatles loved 'The Goons'.) John would be tuned in at Mendips. Spike Milligan's way with words firing his imagination – I learned later that he was a real inspiration and John would have been really taken by Max Geldray because the harmonica was the first instrument John learned.

Sunday lunchtimes and the 'Billy Cotton Band Show' (1949–68) was really popular – and an early favourite on telly (1956). Everyone knew Billy's catchphrase: he was a Cockney and each show he'd begin by loudly exclaiming 'Wakey, wakeeeee!' After which his band went into 'Somebody Stole My Gal', the show's signature tune. It was all very lively."

As Colin crossed the line into teenagehood the sounds of jazz became an integral part of life in Heyscroft Road courtesy of older brother Brian's brand new radiogram. Not bebop, more Trad, jazz you could move to like 'Swing'. Big dance band stuff.

Radiograms were state of the art hi-fi: a piece of furniture for the home that combined a radio and a record player or 'gramophone'. Housed in stylish wooden cabinets, they were equipped with a loud speaker that was larger than the usual domestic radio speaker. Look inside and there was space to store records and the auto-changer could hold six records and played them one after another without you having to rise from your seat. As the Fifties grew into the Sixties so the record player inside could spin discs at different speeds: 16rpm, 33rpm, 45rpm and 78rpm. As the size and speed of records changed this feature meant you could continue to play older records as well as new. Record sales were increasing and in the early to mid-Fifties '78s' was the favoured format. Twelve inches in diameter, made from shellac and very brittle, they broke easily so needed careful handling. Despite this hazard record sales soared and, as they did, so did sales of Radiograms. As the Fifties progressed so the 78 gave way to the smaller, more durable 45rpm single.

"Brian got his radiogram in early 1956 just before he was conscripted into the army. I could/would listen to his records (tunes like 'Whistlin' Rufus', 'When the Saints Come Marchin' In', that kind of jazz) while enjoying films like 'The Benny Goodman Story' (1956) at the cinema."

A popular jazz record released in 1956 that Colin remembers that influenced The Beatles was 'Bad Penny Blues'.

"Of course, 'Bad Penny Blues' by Humphrey Lyttelton and His Band – a British jazz band – and they made the top twenty which was unheard of!"

Colin's right. Not only was it a great tune produced by the aforementioned legendary Joe Meek but it was indeed the first British jazz record to make the New Musical Express top twenty. Released on the Parlophone label (where George Martin was already in charge), it was a jaunty instrumental that enjoyed a six-week run on the charts, peaking at number 19 in mid-July. A large part of the record's appeal was its catchy boogie-style piano riff as played by Johnny Parker. Meek had recognised this riff as a major hook and bumped it up to the front of the mix. It did not fall on deaf ears: in 1968 Paul McCartney adapted Parker's hi-stepping riff for his own piano part on 'Lady Madonna'.

Trad jazz enthusiast Colin recalls these early pre-rock 'n' roll days with great affection. He wasn't just an armchair listener; he was spending his hard-earned cash to go out and enjoy 'live' music.

"It was not long after that I started going down to The Cavern – for the jazz. Alan Sytner who opened the club on January 16, 1957, was an aficionado and opened it specifically as a jazz venue."

Cave-dweller Colin was a regular and saw many great acts down The Cavern.

"I saw Liverpool's legendary Merseysippi Jazz Band down there many, many times; they were always really entertaining. I also saw the great Acker Bilk and his Paramount Jazz Band make their debut at The Cavern in 1958. He played clarinet and sang and was a very popular figure on the Trad jazz circuit. He sold a lot of records. The night of his debut was a Friday night, Valentine's Night in fact, and he played an all-nighter.

I sat right at the front by the stage. Acker Bilk came on with his band in the early hours but when they left the stage – and the club – Acker stayed behind: in fact he sat right in front of me. When the next band came on he asked them if he could sit in with them. They agreed and he remained on stage until eight 'o' clock in the morning. As they were finishing and about to take their leave Acker asked what time it was and when they said it was five to eight he persuaded them to stay on and do one more number. What a performer! It was clear he just loved to play – I think he would have stayed around even longer if it had been up to him."

Warming to his subject, Colin recalls another Liverpool jazz and dance hot spot.

"The Temple was a bar just off Dale Street and another venue where I would go to hear jazz. (As did young Frieda Kelly, who later become The Beatles' Fan Club Secretary.)

As keen dancers, later in our relationship on Saturday nights Joan and I would trip the light fantastic at the Grafton Ballroom on West Derby Road. To prevent groups of lads going in on their own and causing trouble The Grafton had a 'couples only' policy on Saturdays: everyone who was in there had to be already paired up with a girlfriend/boyfriend or their wife/husband.

No fisticuffs – it was all very civilised: waltzes and quick steps. Joan not only taught me these dances but – crucially – she taught me to jive. To this day music, jazz and dancing remain very much an important part of our life."

The arrival of brother Brian's radiogram could not have been timed better: it coincided exactly with Colin's rapidly developing interest in music.

"It was jazz, which was so popular in those early years of the Fifties (and continued to be so through into the early Sixties), that grabbed my undivided attention. It was the rhythm that did it for me. Once a record came on it was the sound of the drums, the percussion on which I focused.

Sometime during 1955 or early 1956 I became fascinated by drums, with rhythm. Whenever the opportunity arose and I found myself listening to music it would be the drums that held me transfixed. I'd load the radiogram and tap along with each record. Somehow – and I can't recall how – I had obtained a pair of drumsticks. Even now I can see myself sitting in our front room, one of my brother's jazz records blaring out and me drumming for all I was worth on the back of an armchair!"

From then on there was no turning back. Colin was entranced.

"I just loved the sound of drums. I liked the way they looked. I loved the way they sounded. Whoever the star might have been fronting a band it would be the drummer on whom I would be focused. It remains that way to this very day. Whenever I went to the cinema in those early years to see a film about music I was excited to watch famous drummers in action like Gene Krupa or Buddy Rich. There is something about the beat, the rhythm that fascinates me: it fires my imagination until I become absorbed in it. To this day I can't hear Glen Miller's 'In the Mood' or Bill Haley's 'Rock Around the Clock' without either getting up to jive or to tap out the beat on my thigh or chair."

Surprisingly it was not a jazz record but a Bill Haley rock 'n' roll record on which Colin first shelled out his hard-earned cash to buy. For Colin it's all down to the rhythm and as he says: those Bill Haley records are just great to dance to.

"It was 'Rip It Up', released in November 1956: I bought Bill Haley's version of the Little Richard song. Such was Haley's popularity at the time it had climbed to number 4 in the UK chart and it hung around for weeks and weeks (eighteen to be exact)."

Little Richard's version was released in December 1956 in the UK – after Haley's version had already charted – which meant Richard's original version only spent one week in the singles chart at #30. When it had been released in the USA earlier in the year in June, Little Richard had taken it to #1 in the R&B Best Sellers chart and up to # 17 on the Billboard pop chart, whereas Haley's version only reached #25 in the USA. Haley was massive in Britain: he dominated the UK charts.

"Haley and his Comets performed their version of 'Rip It Up' in their second film, entitled 'Don't Knock the Rock', which also featured Little Richard singing 'Long Tall Sally' and 'Tutti Frutti'. Released in December 1956, the film was a huge hit, which, of course, I went to see."

The very first purchase of a record is a red letter day in any young rock 'n' roller's life – and so it was for Colin. It was the A-side 'Rip It Up' that made the charts but Colin always refers to the record's B-side as the 'first' record he bought. It is that song that has remained uppermost in his memory.

"That was the one, 'Rip It Up' may have made the Hit Parade and why I initially bought it but it was the B-side, 'Teenager's Mother (Are You Right?)' – written by Curtis R. Lewis and J. Leslie McFarland – that I ended-up liking the best."

Colin clearly played this song a lot and paid attention to the lyric because sixty years later whilst recording his memories for this book

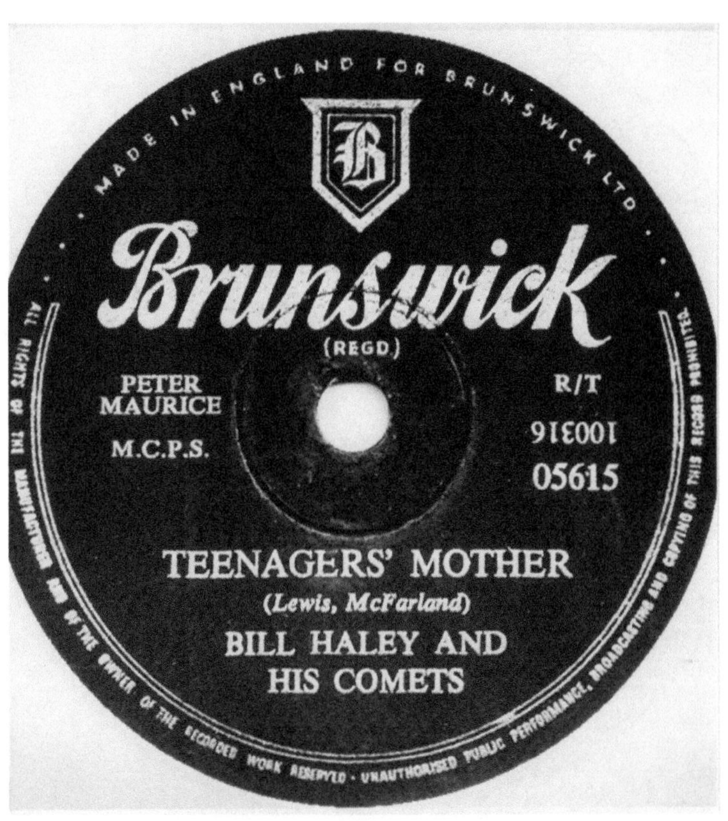

'Teenagers' Mother', Bill Haley

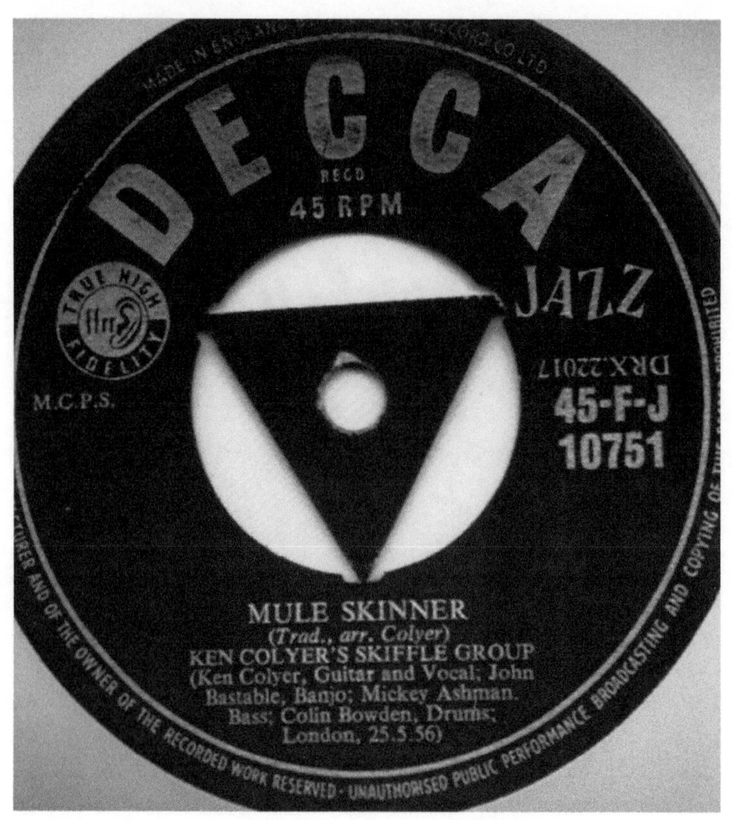

'Mule Skinner', Ken Colyer's Skiffle Group

he could still quote and sing every one of them. As he points out, with hindsight the song's lyric can be seen as prophetic. The singer gently castigates a mother for disapproving of her son 'Johnny' liking rock 'n' roll, going out dancing and staying out late on a date.

"In the song the singer reminds the mother to whom the song is addressed that she used to be young herself and enjoyed dancing to the Charleston and had herself stayed out late on a date: 'That rocking music you called bad, Was just about all Johnny had, But with a shout, you threw it out, And so you made your Johnny sad'. To my mind, it could almost be Aunt Mimi talking to her nephew."

Another record Colin remembers buying or 'acquiring' was 'Mule Skinner Blues'. This is a record that has endured and has a long and varied history of being covered and recorded since originally being written and recorded by Jimmie Rodgers in 1930. (George Harrison was a big Jimmie Rodgers fan.)

In the UK it was the B-side of a Ken Colyer's Skiffle Band single release in June 1956, the A-side of which was 'Down Bound Train'. This is interesting because 'Down Bound Train' was a song written by Chuck Berry. Berry had released his version of 'Down Bound Train' on the Chess label in December 1955 as the B-side to 'No Money Down'. Colin bought the Ken Colyer single and again he preferred the B-side.

"Later, when I'd joined the group I remember one time asking The Quarry Men to come up to my house to listen to it, I thought they might like 'Mule Skinner Blues' enough to do as part of our set. I put it on my brother's radiogram thinking John might be impressed with it but he didn't like it, so that was that, it wasn't mentioned again. John was the arbiter, the leader: if he didn't like a song we didn't do it. So there was no debate, we didn't return to it – and I didn't suggest any more!"

With hindsight it's interesting to speculate what might have John's reaction been had instead Colin played that Chuck Berry-penned

A-side to him. Like most Sixties rock and rollers John Lennon was a massive fan of Chuck Berry.

As Colin's memories run ahead to his days as a Quarry Man he catches himself, pulls back and recalls the impulse that lead him to pursue his interest in drums and rhythms even further.

"It was sitting in our front room in Heyscroft drumming on the back of an armchair to one of Brian's records that it all started in a practical sense for me. It wasn't long before that just wasn't enough: I wanted a set of drums all of my own. I wanted to be the man in the band sat on the stage pounding the skins, even if that stage was just our front room at home."

And so it was, for the teenage Colin Hanton of Woolton, Liverpool, the call to arms rang loud and clear: 'Let there be drums!'

13

INTERLUDE: 1956, PART 1 ELVIS

1956 was pivotal. It was the year that Colin Hanton laid down the deposit for his first set of drums and John Lennon acquired his first acoustic guitar.

It was the year the all-important (for British youth) 'skiffle' craze swept the nation. Spearheaded by the one and only Lonnie Donegan, skiffle is the door through which British teens will pour to form thousands of bands…

Above all else, transcending all else it was also the year the world would tilt that extra degree on its axis to send us weak at the knees, loose at the hips and gone in the head, for that was the year God gave us Elvis.

(And for good measure he'd add Gene, Carl and Little Richard…)

In 1955 Bill Haley had turned us all on. With the advent of Bill Haley and his Comets rock 'n' roll had landed in the UK. Teenagers stepped up to the plate, juvenile delinquency and Teddy Boys threatened to destroy the entire world and the generation gap split wide open.

This was seismic: no two ways about it.

But compared to Bill or anyone else you care to mention, Elvis was somethin' else. He was that brand new book of rock 'n' roll ripped up. He was the book rewritten. He was a whole new

Album cover, 'Elvis Presley'

vocabulary. Elvis took us so totally out there we didn't know if we could ever come back. And what's more – we didn't care.

Check the music charts. Bill Haley and his Comets were the messengers: 'Shake Rattle and Roll' hit in December '54; 'Rock Around The Clock' charted big-time in 1955 and 1956 respectively. In 1956 he and his band had taken up residence in the UK singles chart but the arrival of Elvis in May of that year with 'Heartbreak Hotel' for twenty-one weeks blew everything that had come before completely out of the water.

So while throughout 1956 we British continued to be enamoured with Bill Haley and his Comets, his days as rock 'n' roll's leading light were numbered. His song 'Rock Around the Clock' featured in the soundtrack to the film 'Blackboard Jungle' and this and other Haley records were all over the UK charts during that year. (Eight singles and an LP spent a combined and dizzying total of ninety-nine weeks in the Top Thirty.) But the truth was Bill was already passé in the USA and when he finally got to tour the UK in 1957 he was mobbed but it was more for what rock 'n' roll promised than what he actually delivered as as a teen idol. For kids pumped up and ready to to rock, seeing Haley was not believing. He was not the stuff of heartache or heartbreak. He didn't look right. He wasn't one of them; seeing Haley was like watching your dad perform. However good a musician he was (and he and his band were very, very good) he looked too old, dressed 'too square' and his act was too 'show biz'. He was as unhip as unhip gets. He was already sounding outdated. His rotund shape and signature kiss curl could not compete on any level with the animal magnetism of the boy from Tupelo, Mississippi. By March 1957 Haley wouldn't be seen in the UK charts again until 1968 when a re-issue of 'Rock Around the Clock' made the UK Top Twenty.

But this is not to knock or dismiss Haley, he is a massively important figure in rock's history: crucial. His music opened doors and broke down barriers. With 'Rock Around the Clock' there was no going back: the genie had been released from the bottle.

11 May 1956 is the date Elvis and 'Heartbreak Hotel' hit the UK singles chart. Later that month Carl Perkins hits the UK top twenty with his own song, 'Blue Suede Shoes'. Elvis's version of Carl's tune will also chart, climb higher and stay around longer. Gene Vincent followed on 13 July with 'Be Bop a Lula' while on 14 December Little Richard closed out the year with the prophetic 'Rip It Up'.

John Lennon knew immediately: *"Nothing really affected me until Elvis."* (The Beatles, The Authorised Biography, Davies, p.19.) The exact moment John's life changed forever was clearly etched into his memory: *"When I heard 'Heartbreak Hotel' I thought 'this is it'."* (John Lennon in His Own Words, Miles, p.17.)

Paul was equally attuned: *"I remember being in the assembly hall at school one day – it was a free period… somebody pulled out a music paper, and there was an advert for 'Heartbreak Hotel'. Elvis looked so great: 'That's him, that's him – the Messiah has arrived!' Then when we heard the song, there was the proof."* (The Beatles, The Authorised Biography, p.21.)

14

INTERLUDE: 1956, PART 2 LONNIE DONEGAN

1956 was massive because of Elvis but equally crucial in Britain was Lonnie Donegan.

Elvis blew your mind.

Lonnie made it real.

Elvis was the leap of the imagination that inspired a musical revolution: his voice, his records, his looks, his very being took teenagers to another level.

It was Glasgow-born, London-based Lonnie Donegan however, who, as a member of Chris Barber's Jazz Band, provided British youth with the tools to fashion a musical revolution of their own that took them to within spitting distance of real rock 'n' roll.

Hailed as the 'King of Skiffle', Lonnie opened the door for British youth to follow when his version of 'Rock Island Line' entered the UK charts in January '56 (peaking at number 8). This was some five months before 'Heartbreak Hotel' hit the UK charts. 'Rock Island Line' was also American music but it was not rock 'n' roll. It was something called 'skiffle'.

With this record and the instruments on which it was performed, Lonnie enabled cash-strapped British youth to play a form of music that was as close as they could get to rock 'n' roll without having the need for those beautiful expensive electric

Album cover, 'Lonnie Donegan Showcase'

guitars which were rock's crucial instrument. They also didn't have to fork out for expensive music lessons.

'Skiffle' did not rely on electric guitars. It was played on a mixture of acoustic and home-made instruments. For cashstrapped British teens this was a godsend. Skiffle was cheap, cheerful and accessible. Anyone could be in a skiffle group.

An existing wartime trade embargo with the USA and a resulting trade deficit made it virtually impossible to import American goods into the UK. For a nation that didn't make or sell electric guitars of its own in great or affordable quantities (Grimshaw guitars were the most famous) the UK's teenagers were immediately thwarted in their ambitions to play rock 'n' roll'. Although restrictions on American imports were lifted right at the end of 1955, as late as 1959/60 imported luxury items from the USA such as electric guitars remained prohibitively expensive. Consequently the difficulties British youths faced just plugging in, made playing rock 'n' roll a real challenge.

The first known Fender Stratocaster to be imported into the UK from the USA was in 1959. It was Hank Marvin's iconic 'Flamingo Pink' Strat – as he called it – but which was actually a 'Fiesta Red'. Bought for him by Cliff Richard, Hank played this on 'Apache' a guitar instrumental that took The Shadows to the top of the UK charts in July, 1960.

In Germany, Hofner began manufacturing guitars from their new factory in Bubenreuth in 1949 but the instruments were not officially imported into the UK until Selmer of London took on their distributorship sometime in 1958. The instruments Selmer sold were built specifically for the UK market by Hofner and therefore different from those available in Germany.They were to prove very popular with the UK's emerging rock and rollers.

Back in 1956 however, Lonnie's simple rambunctious 'skiffle' was as close as British kids could get to rock 'n' roll without electricity. Up-tempo, acoustic, immediate, word-propelled, highly rhythmic, blue collar, anti-establishment, American in origin and played on homemade instruments, it was the kissing cousin of rock.

'Homemade' is the crucial word here. Suddenly comb and paper kazoos, old tea chests, broom handles, string, pots, pans, washboards and thimbles took on a currency of their own as they could be converted into simple instruments with which to equip a skiffle group. A hybrid of folk, blues and jazz, it was the creation of poor black workers in the USA in the early 20th century. 'Skiffle' was one of many names given to rent parties where folk held a party and charged a small fee to help pay their rent. In 1925 the word was used by Jimmy O'Bryant to name his band the 'Chicago Skifflers'. 'Hometown Skiffle' and 'Skiffle Blues' were two records cut by Dan Burley and his Skiffle Boys. The latter tune was the B-side of a record he released in 1949. (Burley was a journalist and musician whose barrelhouse style of playing is believed to have influenced Humphrey Lyttelton's 'Bad Penny Blues'.) Skiffle itself is thought to have developed in 'jug bands' who played blues and jazz in the southern states of the USA in the early part of the 20th century. During the 1920s, very few black workers in the USA could afford to buy any kind of musical instrument at all – but nevertheless they wanted to make music and dance – so they improvised and made instruments out of what was to hand.

Pots and pans – over which animal skins could be stretched became instruments of percussion, wash tubs or tea chests became sound boxes which, with the addition of broom sticks and a single strand of string, turned them into simple upright basses. Other ingenious applications included washboards, saws, comb and paper kazoos and cigar box fiddles, while wire could be stretched along a length of wood to form a rudimentary guitar. So long as it made a decent sound, anything could be fashioned into an instrument.

For a brief while this style of music was called 'skiffle'

and it arrived in Chicago during the 1920s along with African-Americans from the South who were moving to work in northern industrial towns. Earlier Ma Rainey (1886–1939) – billed as 'The Mother of the Blues' – used the word to describe her music to rural audiences.

Sometimes called 'Spasm' music but refined as 'Skiffle', it was the product of imagination and ingenuity. And so under this label songs by acoustic American guitar troubadours – in particular Woody Guthrie and Huddie 'Lead Belly' Ledbetter – along with blues musicians like Robert Johnson – all from the very core of American 'roots' music – entered the British charts and British teen consciousness via British adherents performing their tunes. Lonnie's 'Rock Island Line' was a tune written in 1930 by Clarence Wilson but later made popular by Lead Belly who also wrote additional lyrics for it.

Lonnie opened the door for a whole generation of post-war British teens who seized upon his example. No musical expertise or expense was necessary for skiffle was easy to play, it encouraged audience participation and – damn it – was a lot of fun! It provided that immediate post-war generation – those so-called baby boomers – a means to an end: the ability to stand up and make a big noise all their own.

> **George Harrison**: *"Lonnie Donegan had a much bigger influence on British rock bands than he was ever given credit for… He had a great voice, a lot of energy and sang great songs – catchy versions of Lead Belly tunes and things. I loved him."*
>
> *(The Beatles Anthology, p.28).*

As George noted, Lonnie's example encouraged thousands of teenagers to get guitars and form skiffle groups. Coming out of the blues and because of the way it was performed it was eagerly embraced by a legion of cash-strapped white Liverpudlians.

> **George**: *"It was dead cheap – just a washboard, a tea chest, a bit of string, a broom handle and a £3 10s guitar… it was a simple way into music because a lot of the songs had just two chords and the maximum was three…"*
>
> *(The Beatles Anthology, p.28).*

And through the door that Lonnie opened came not only John, Paul, George and Ringo but Gerry Marsden, Keith Richards, Van Morrison, Eric Clapton, Mark Knopfler, Jimmy Page, Robert Plant and countless others.

And so it was into this cauldron of challenge and change, of jazz and dance bands, of Elvis, emergent rock 'n' roll and the down home sounds of skiffle, that, seventeen-year-old drum fanatic Colin Hanton – accompanied by his mum – on a sunny day in 1956 tumbled into Hessy's Music Store on Stanley Street.

15

FRANK HESSY'S

Hessy's was situated in Liverpool city centre on Stanley Street, just around the corner from Whitechapel, where Harry Epstein had opened NEMS and where his son Brian worked. Hessy's was literally also just a stone's throw away from 10 Mathew Street where on 16th January 1957 a jazz club called The Cavern had opened its doors for the very first time. By then a keen jazz fan himself, Colin would be a drummer in his own right playing in a skiffle group fronted by a sixteen year old tearaway from Woolton by the name of John.

Hessy's was Liverpool's most wondrous music emporium. If you were in a group Hessy's was where you went. Although Rushworth's was truly awesome and renowned as the 'largest music house in Europe', if you were an aspiring rock 'n' roller or jazzer in those halcyon days of the late Fifties, throughout the Sixties and beyond, Hessy's was always your first stop: this is where it was all happening. It was far, far smaller, less palatial than Rushworth's but packed with guitars and drums. It sparkled and shone full of beautiful instruments and by the Sixties resplendent on a silver papered wall were photographs of all the 'beat' groups who bought their equipment there.

Fronted by Frank Hessy himself, the undoubted 'star' of the shop was his assistant Jim Gretty. Everyone's friend and a fine musician himself, it is to Jim that everyone gravitated – and with every guitar bought he donated a free lesson to help them on their way. It is at Hessy's that The Beatles will buy most of their equipment. On Friday, 28th August 1959 John Lennon's Aunt Mimi accompanied her nephew to the shop to lay down the deposit on his first ever electric guitar. A Hofner Club 40. Mimi and John handed over £17 and his Aunt acted as guarantor for John's purchase. Its total cost including hire purchase payments was £30, nine shillings, which would be approximately £500 today: a major commitment for any youngster in the Fifties to say the least.

By the time Colin and his mum entered Hessy's on that fateful Saturday afternoon in the summer or autumn of 1956 he'd already visited on several other occasions. While other boys may have gone inside to fantasise about guitars, for Colin it was always the drums that irresistibly drew him within to gaze in wonder.

"It's true; I bought my kit from the famous Frank Hessy's in Stanley Street, just around the corner from Mathew Street. The Cavern hadn't even been opened at that time. I went down with Mum one Saturday and I told Frank I wanted to buy a drum kit so he showed me this 'Broadway' kit made by John Grey. The name 'Broadway' was printed on the drums and on the drum sticks it just said 'John Grey'. It cost £34.19s.6d. [Approximately £600+ today, an even mightier financial commitment than John Lennon would undertake nearly three years later for his Hofner].

Initially I was drawn to a better, more elaborate set up on the top shelf – all blue and gold sparkly. It looked like the Rolls Royce of drum kits. When I inquired about their price Frank asked me if I'd like to sit down before he informed me. I knew then that particular kit was out of my range and, it was. At £65 (£1100+ at today's prices) *it was almost twice the price: an absolute fortune in those days. The more my jaw dropped the more my enthusiasm waned and so I settled on the cheaper version. Truth was to me the Broadway looked fabulous and professional: very much the real thing. And at half the price that sealed the deal."*

What Colin had bought was a budget-priced John Grey 'Broadway' set made by British manufacturer and distributor Rose-Morris.

"It comprised a small bass drum, a snare, a high tom tom and a cymbal. There was no hi-hat. The drumheads were made of calfskin and it was finished in a white, lacquer paint. As drum kits go it was very basic but it suited me fine. I was really proud of it: they didn't sparkle but to me they still shone. They looked absolutely great!"

It's no wonder Colin needed Mum there to act as guarantor. £34. 19s. 6d. was a mighty financial undertaking for a young man, even if he was in work. That day in Hessy's he was putting down a deposit on the kit that would bind him into a hire purchase deal for twenty-four months. Peggy signed as his guarantor, agreeing to undertake responsibility for the payments should Colin fail to do so. She clearly had faith in him to keep his side of the deal. He wasn't going to let her down.

Deposit paid, 'hp' agreement signed, Colin left the shop the proud owner of his first set of drums.

"They were only a small set but that was to my advantage. Don't forget in those days not many people had a car so their small size came in useful especially when as a Quarry Man we travelled by 'bus to all our appearances. In fact the day I bought them I took the full kit home on the 'bus. It fitted into a small suitcase except for the bass drum, which I carried separately in my other hand. Once on the 'bus I stored the kit in the luggage compartment under the stairs that lead up to the top deck which is exactly what I would do when I was a Quarry Man and we were playing away from home."

It says a lot for John and Peggy and their tolerant natures that they obviously raised no objections to Colin's purchase. He'd not touched a set of drums before this momentous day. He'd never had a lesson but here he was piling into the living room with a brand new kit and a debt as big as Europe. Life at home was about to become a lot noisier and relationships with the neighbours potentially somewhat strained.

16

HAVE DRUMS WILL TRAVEL

Amazingly, despite now being the proud owner of a dazzlingly new drum kit Colin had never really thought about taking lessons or playing in a band and performing in public. He had not bought them with that aim in mind. Initially they were purely for his own pleasure at home, so he could play along to his beloved jazz records. No more, no less. Fate however was about to deal him a hand that would change all that and mark the rest of his life.

"That is how I learned to play: tapping along to records in the living room at home. Like all the other boys in The Quarry Men I was self-taught."

Colin's new acquisition proved to be of especial interest to one old friend in particular whom he still occasionally bumped into on the 'bus on the way home from work, Eric Griffiths.

"How I actually came to meet John Lennon and be invited to join The Quarry Men was through Eric Griffiths. Eric was at Quarry Bank with John, Pete and Rod. He lived near me around the corner on Halewood Drive at number 96. Eric was a very friendly guy who was easy to get on with. I'd known him for a year or two. We first met on the number 66 coming home from Garston; we were still both at school at that point – although I was just about to leave – we used to get the same 'bus home and had begun chatting to each other. We'd also bump into each other at the local shops on Kings Drive.

I saw less of him once I started work and would be going out drinking with Brian Doyle, Alan Kinsley, Charlie Roberts and Kevin Hanson. This meant I was not around as much in the neighbourhood as I was when I had been at school. Even so when I went to work in Speke, I'd occasionally see Eric on the 'bus home to Woolton. I guess it was during one of those 'bus rides I must have mentioned that I'd recently acquired a set of drums."

Colin's casual comment registered more with Eric than he realised.

"Once Eric knew that I had bought a small drum kit it wasn't long before he came knocking on my door to check them out. It must have been a Saturday because I wasn't at work and he wasn't at school. It must have been about a month or so after I'd got my drums, maybe early September or thereabouts, I can't remember exactly when. Naturally I was proud to show them off and took him into the living room, where the kit was now permanently set up.

Eric was immediately impressed and took no time in asking if I could play something for him. I was only too happy to oblige: I put one of my brother's jazz records onto the record player and played along, which impressed Eric even more. As soon as I'd finished he asked if I'd like to go round to his house and 'meet the rest of the group.' His request took me completely by surprise. I had not thought about joining a group up until this very moment. There'd been no prior mention that Eric was even in a group or that they were all round at his house at that very moment. He told me there were five of them in the group and that he and another lad played guitars. Once he told me all this it put his fervent interest in my drums into perspective: he'd been auditioning me! In all honesty I was flattered and pleased to have been asked: lucky for him I was at home."

With no more ado Colin packed his kit into its small suitcase, grabbed the bass drum in his other hand and they were on their way to Eric's. Colin had passed Eric's audition; the question now was would the group agree with his assessment?

"Within minutes we were at his house, where he took me straight into his living room. Sitting around in front of me were a group of lads clutching a variety of instruments. Eric introduced me first to a lad called Pete Shotton, who was holding a washboard – which immediately told me they were a skiffle group – and then to someone called 'Nige' Walley, who wasn't holding an instrument. John Lennon was sitting in an armchair, a guitar in his hands, one leg over the arm, sorting of lounging back, almost distracted, not getting too involved, just watching me, weighing things up.

As I was to learn – this was John's way: on meeting new people he held back – it was almost like he was weighing up the opposition. I don't recall meeting Len Garry (tea-chest bass) or Rod Davis (banjo) on that occasion. I met them a week or so later at another rehearsal at Eric's. Ivan Vaughan – 'Ive' for short – a close friend of John's, was also not there that day, I met him later. Anyway, here I was, a new lad for John to contend with, potentially a new presence in the group who was older, already working. He must have been wondering was I going to be a threat, a challenge to his authority because right from the start it was clear to me that 'The Quarry Men' were John's band. He was the leader: he was the one who made all the decisions."

John's nonchalance was his shield. Make no mistake: he would have been fully focused. It certainly had the effect of focusing Colin's mind. Within an instant from not having even given thought to playing in a group suddenly it really mattered. Something was at stake here and Colin didn't want to lose out.

"Keenly aware that all eyes were on me I carefully set up. The other lads seemed impressed – however cheap they may have been those Broadway drums must have looked impressive – don't forget they didn't know anyone with a drum kit, they hadn't been this close to a proper kit before – and it was absolutely brand new, sparkling white, they did stand out. Most skiffle bands did not have a drummer because drums were expensive, like electric guitars. The expense meant drums were way beyond the pocket of most young people, especially schoolboys, which they all were. I'd also noticed that the instruments

they had with them weren't up to much at all. My drums were the Rolls Royce in that room.

Once I was set up I played a little for them, just enough to impress. Short, sharp and just long enough for my nerve to hold. Of course, the moment I finished they all wanted to have a little tap as well, the way people do. I think everyone finds a drum kit irresistible; they just want to touch it to hear how it sounds. Basically that was it – that was the audition: nothing was said, no comment on my ability, no formal offer was made – from the get-go I was a Quarry Man. In all honesty I don't think it would have mattered how good I was on the drums, the fact I was an amateur, self-taught didn't matter. What mattered was that I had a kit, it looked good, professional, and that was enough. I was in."

For John Lennon this was a key moment: he'd formed the group at school with Pete and another lad called Bill Smith (Bill was no longer in the group by then). The Quarry Men were skiffle. Skiffle was one thing but for John rock 'n' roll was the ultimate. That's where his heart lay. With Colin, a drummer, in the group they now had the potential to move on up and play some rock 'n' roll.

ENDNOTES

Who played what?

The Quarry Men took a step up instrumentally the day Colin joined their ranks. His brand new drum kit was in a different league to their cheap guitars and home made instruments.

John: Throughout Colin's time with the group John always played a relatively inexpensive Gallotone Champion flat-top hollow-bodied acoustic guitar. No scratch plate. It was three-quarter size compared to a regular instrument. Famously inside the soundhole it bore a label on which the words 'GUARANTEED NOT TO SPLIT' were written.

John always said it was advertised in 'Reveille' magazine and he had it sent to his mother's house (John's sister, Julia Baird, says their mother bought it for him) to avoid any problems with his Aunt Mimi, who wanted him to focus on his forthcoming O-Level exams. The Gallotone was made by a South African company and sold over here to meet the demand for cheap guitars generated by the skiffle boom. (Prior to this John had borrowed a guitar from his friend Geoff Lee at Quarry Bank school. Geoff had a guitar but did not play and generously loaned it to John until he got his own. Geoff cannot recall the make of his guitar but it was he who suggested to John that he start a skiffle group of his own. John clearly thought Geoff's idea was worth a try.)

Eric: Eric's guitar was most probably an Egmond (the name of the Dutch company who manufactured them). Also inexpensive it was an archtop, non cutaway, hollow-bodied with a scratch plate and more distinctive than John's Gallotone because it had cat's eye-shape f-holes.

Eric and John attended two guitar lessons in Hunt's Cross (next village on from Woolton) but gave up because their tutor wanted to teach them 'properly'. Instead they turned to John's mother, Julia, who, being a banjo player, taught them banjo chords. Consequently John and Eric only tuned four of their guitar strings. The fifth and sixth were left un-tuned and "flapping about" as John described it.

Rod: He played a second hand banjo. A Windsor Whirle Victor Supremus, most probably from the 1920s. Within days of telling Eric at school he'd bought his banjo, he was in the group. Not because he could play it but because he owned one!

John, Eric and Rod played Cathedral strings.

Len: Tea-chest bass, homemade, various designs.

Pete: Washboard and thimbles.

Colin: John Grey Broadway (white). Bass drum, a high tom tom, a snare drum, a cymbal.

(**Sources**: Beatles Gear, Babiuk, p 7–12; The Quarrymen, Davies, p.40; The Fab One Hundred And Four, Bedford, p.50, 51 and, of course, Colin Hanton.)

17

A QUARRY MAN!

"I was excited to be joining a group. I hadn't expected or planned to be doing so but now the opportunity had arisen I found myself really excited at the prospect. This would make playing more enjoyable. I was no longer a closet drummer but was suddenly surrounded by friends who could play guitars and banjos and we would soon be performing in public. I was in a group! This would significantly expand my social life and increase my prospects of meeting young ladies, which was very cool to my way of thinking."

Colin's pride in being asked to join a group manifested itself in his immediate desire to personalise his kit and tell the world just who he was and for which band he drummed. Without realising it, this simple gesture of putting his name on his drums that didn't bother any member of the group at the time has many, many years later become a source of debate among Beatles fans: how exactly should the group name be written, Quarry Men or Quarrymen? One word or two? (The school from which they took the name was 'Quarry Bank High School For Boys'.)

"A weekend or so after I joined the group I actually made a logo to go onto the drum kit. I put my name 'Colin Hanton' at the very top of the bass drum slightly to the left, and below that in large capital letters the 'QUARRY MEN', just the two words – the word 'Quarry' curving above 'Men' because the way I'd made the logo I couldn't fit Quarry Men on in one word, it had to go on as two. That has caused a great deal of controversy in

later years as to whether the group name was one word or two. If you look at the programme and posters for the St. Peter's Parish Church Garden Fete and the business cards Nigel Walley had printed they all print the name as two words, 'Quarry Men'. So initially it was definitely two."

Colin was simply following a tradition among drummers that he liked.

"Just why I put my name on the drum kit I don't know; looking back it may seem a bit big-headed to do so but at that time I was heavily influenced by all the American big bands, Glenn Miller in particular. (I'd seen 'The Glenn Miller Story' (1954) at the cinema.) Eric Delaney was a British-born drummer of whom I was a big fan. He'd formed his own up-tempo dance band in 1954 and had his name 'Eric' written on his bass drum. Then there was Gene Krupa, who'd drummed with Benny Goodman and formed his own orchestra before rejoining Goodman. (A film was made about Krupa's life in 1959.) He had his initials on his drums. 'The Benny Goodman Story' – another biopic – had been released in 1956 and featured Krupa. Krupa was my favourite. I used to watch all those films.

Eric Delaney used to do 'Oranges And Lemons' on kettle drums. [Eric signed to Pye Records in 1956 and in July released it as the 'A' side of his second single – backed by 'Delaney's Delight'.] I saw him at the Liverpool Empire with his big band; he had luminous drumsticks and so all the lights would go down, and every time he hit a skin it lit up, all we could see were illuminous sticks waving all over the place and individual drums lighting up as he hit them. It was very effective, very impressive – and very exciting.

Later in 1959 I went with Joan (my wife, girlfriend at the time) to Manchester to see Louis Armstrong and his All Stars, out at Belle Vue. I also saw Glenn Miller at the Empire; well I should say the Glenn Miller Band – obviously by then without the big man himself.

All of the drummers that influenced and inspired me did have their name and, if not their name, certainly their initials, on the top left hand corner or on the left hand side of the bass drum and that's probably what inspired me to put my name on the top left hand corner.

The first name I made for my drums was in the style of how I saw my favourite drummers individualised their kits. It was simply a series of letters cut from cardboard that spelt out my name and 'Quarry Men'. Joan and I made these at my house on Heyscroft Road one afternoon, we coloured them black to stand out and stuck them on the bass drum skin with sellotape. They were on my bass drum for quite a while (you can see them on Charlie Roberts's photos of us playing Rosebery Street). Later Charlie, who was my drinking buddy and a screen printer at Littlewoods at the time, made me two professional personalised circular covers for the bass drum. They were printed on paper and were attached under the rim of the drum over over the skin. They were both very professionally done. The first one I used and particularly liked was excellent. The background colour was a sort of orange fluorescent colour with black writing on top and my name was up there again. I had a really good photograph of that, but like lots of things you lend people something and they never come back, that's what I did with that photograph and I never saw it again. That cover lasted quite a while and then I used the other one he'd made, which was black lettering on white paper. However the point I really want to address is about my name being on the drums and especially The Quarry Men being written as two words."

Like many stories surrounding the early days of The Quarry Men, Colin is not always sure where some of them come from. It was all a long time ago but these stories take hold and pass from being conjecture or hearsay into cold hard fact that people believe. One such 'story' is the existence of 'The Black Jacks'. The story is that the band we know as The Quarry Men originally were called The Black Jacks and actually played a gig under that name. Colin has no memory of this ever happening.

"I have no knowledge at all about the Black Jacks. I saw an article somewhere where we were supposed to have played at the Pavilion in Lodge Lane as the Black Jacks but I have to ask the question why on earth would we call ourselves the 'Black Jacks' if I had gone to the trouble to have the 'Quarry

Men' written all across my drum kit? I'm sure there's others who might take issue and claim to know better than me."

Well the suggestion has certainly been mooted that, when they first formed a skiffle group at school, John and Pete did call themselves the 'Black Jacks'. Another original member and banjo player Rod Davis has a vague memory of the name but of no gigs being played under it. No one else associated with the group has substantiated this and if it was their name it would only have been for a matter of weeks. So brief in fact it is highly unlikely they ever appeared in public under that name. Certainly Colin is correct in his memory that by the time he joined the group the name was most definitely the Quarry Men: as he says – why else would he have had this name put on his precious drum skin?

One thing is for certain with Colin on drums the Quarry Men were something approaching a proper band, to play in public was now their goal and so group practices or rehearsals were essential. What they needed now was a set.

18

REHEARSALS

The Quarry Men desperately wanted to play in public but before they could do this they needed some songs to perform. Colin has clear memories of the boys gathering to rehearse.

"In those very early days we would rehearse on Saturday afternoons. We practised at my house quite regularly because both my parents were out at work so it was ideal. We certainly spent time in Eric's house, indeed that was where we did our first so-called 'rehearsal'. Later we would also rehearse at John's Mum Julia's. Julia was very encouraging and would even join in on banjo. We'd also occasionally rehearsed at John's Aunt Mimi's and later at Paul's. I also remember on at least two occasions rehearsing at Rod's."

Rehearsing or 'practising' became a regular Saturday afternoon affair for the Quarry Men but they were not particularly disciplined sessions and were also excuses to simply get together and mess about.

"It was during one of those Saturday afternoon practises that I met the other boys in the group: banjo player Rod Davis – which was more a case of a reacquaintance because Rod was an old friend from our football in the street days. He was the same age as John, Eric, Pete and Nige. There was also tea-chest bass player Len Garry who didn't come from Woolton and was a pupil at the Liverpool Institute. Len was a year or so younger than the other lads, the same age as Ivan Vaughan whom I also met. Ive was John's back

garden neighbour who'd known John since they were both little. He didn't go to Quarry Bank; he attended the Liverpool Institute, where he was pals with Len. It was Ive who, thinking John would like Len, had introduced the two. The success of that introduction will inspire Ive to introduce John to another good friend of his from the 'Inny' just a few months later… more of which later!

One early rehearsal at my house I recall included my friend Kevin Hanson. He could play harmonica and he asked me if he could have a go for the group. I asked John if Kevin could and one time in my front room Kevin was there and he did play along to a song. When we split at the end of the rehearsal Kevin asked me how he'd got on because no one had said anything. I knew anyone joining the group would be entirely John's decision so I caught up with John on the front path as he was about to leave and asked him. He just looked at me and simply said, 'No, I can play harmonica if we need one in The Quarry Men'. So that was Kevin's 'audition' – if we can call it that – John did not want to expand the group. It was also the moment when I found out John could play harmonica but he didn't use it with The Quarry Men.

Whenever and wherever we got together there was certainly an amount of time spent in rehearsal, but there was also a lot of playing around. As I recall there were always young ladies there. I clearly remember one in particular who certainly fancied John: whenever it was time for her to go home, she always asked him if she could 'borrow his comb?' One time that she did sticks in my memory because I remember John obliged but on removing it from the inside pocket of his jacket he immediately stuck it down the front of his pants for her to retrieve. To my surprise she wasn't fazed one iota; she just dived in there, grabbed his comb, combed her hair, handed it back and went off home.

That particular incident came to mind several years later in 1963 when The Beatles were breaking big here in Britain and they had a radio show called 'Pop Go The Beatles' on which I heard them playing 'Lend Me Your Comb'. [It had been the B-side to Carl Perkins' 'Glad All Over' in 1956.] When I heard the opening line, which goes, 'Lend me your comb, it's time to go home' I instantly remembered that girl and her request and wondered if that memory also went through John's mind when he sang those words."

Colin's memories of rehearsing at Eric's reminds him of another boy, a key member of the Quarry Men's 'inner circle', Nigel Walley, John's long-time friend from when they were both briefly together at Moss Pitts Primary School ('briefly' because John left to attend Dovedale).

"There were lots of rehearsals in Eric's house. I had met Nige Walley by this time and not really being a musician but being part of the group circle and wanting to do something useful he decided he would act as our manager, which suited us down to the ground. We needed someone to organise us. It would be the ever-enterprising Nige who would have business cards printed to hand to people – especially folk who might book us for a gig.

Nige wasn't a Quarry Bank High School boy; he was a pupil at the Liverpool Blue Coat School where John's father had been educated. He lived on Vale Road in Woolton in 'Leosdene' a few doors up from Ivan Vaughan, who lived in 'Vega'. Pete Shotton also lived on Vale, on the opposite side to Nige and Ive, just a few doors away from the junction with Linkstor Road. Pete's house was not identical to Mendips as were Leosdene and Vega, but it was also a semi and similar in design. As junior school boys the three lads were John's partners in his first gang, 'The Outlaws'. They took their name from the 'Just William' books. William was a middle-class boy who together with his three friends also had a gang called 'The Outlaws' and were the authors of outrageous pranks, forever in trouble with figures of authority. I sometimes think that whatever John Lennon became in his adult life, it's all there in his childhood years."

These early skiffle and rock 'n' roll years were undoubtedly unchartered waters into which The Quarry Men were sailing, albeit they were doing so alongside thousands of others like themselves who had embraced the vibe and formed groups. There was no real blueprint for what was happening, no existing platform or network for young groups to access. They were making it up for themselves.

The Quarry Men were so eager to perform and become part

of 'the scene' but breaking into this new youth music 'scene' was not easy. Finding places to play became a process of hit and miss. The boys needed someone like Nigel to find 'a way in'. Although he was a complete novice he had the confidence to succeed.

"One time we all left Eric's house to walk up to the village when Nige decided to stop at the 'phone box: he said he had a plan. Eager to hear what he was up to we pulled the door open and gathered around to listen in as he telephoned the Liverpool Empire. Now, remember we were a group with just half a dozen songs under our belt but who nevertheless believed we were ready for the big time. First however, we needed somewhere to play. Even so the Liverpool Empire was not what we had had in mind. Talk about thinking big and starting at the top, Nige clearly had faith in our ability to make it!

The Empire was the prime variety theatre in Liverpool. In fact it still is. Straining to listen we could hear that they hadn't just hung up on him but were listening to what he had to say. Those of us close to the earpiece could hear that they were being very polite and taking pains to point out that they didn't actually book people in this manner: a 'phone call out of the blue from someone unknown was not the usual protocol. They told Nige there was a correct procedure, everything had to be done through an agent, blah, blah, blah. So that was no good: equally politely Nigel listened, thanked them and hung up."

Colin and the boys were impressed by Nige's style and his confidence in them. Another of Nige's great qualities was he was dogged, not easily deterred.

"He wasn't daunted one iota by this rebuff but proceeded to try the other theatres around Liverpool – all of whom, of course, gave the same response. Basically, the Empire had told it as it was – theatres just didn't book people they didn't know via a cold call; you had to be 'represented'. There was a protocol to follow. It was a lesson learned so we gave up on that approach, wandered up to the village, hung around, speculating just what we would have to do to get some gigs. Before we split Nigel promised to give the matter

even greater thought. But he was on the case, determined to get us out there performing."

The answer, of course, would be to go local, to start at the bottom and work their way up. A good start would be to play the local youth club, of which some of them were members, and to engage the help of friends and family to spread the word that The Quarry Men were open for business.

"Nigel was to prove particularly adept at this. One of his best ideas was to have some business cards printed up: for a sixteen-year-old boy that really was enterprising. It certainly impressed us and made us feel we were going somewhere."

19

JULIA'S BANJO

Of all Colin's memories of The Quarry Men none are more poignant than those of the time he and the boys spent in the company of John's amazing mother, Julia.

"I remember the first time I ever met Julia. It was within a couple of weeks of joining the group – by which time I'd already been round to John's home with the other boys to rehearse and had met his formidable Aunt Mimi. On this other occasion I was walking up to see him at Mendips – just as a mate, to call in, as we all did – but when I reached the house John was at the gate on his way out. He said he was going to see his mum and asked did I want to go with him. I was a bit surprised by this because up to this point no one within The Quarry Men had mentioned John's mum and I'd never thought to ask if he even had one. I just accepted he was living with his aunt for whatever reason. It wasn't unusual at the time – post-war – for a parent to be missing. Think about it: Eric's dad was missing and Ivan's was too, both casualties of the war. In those days many families were missing people. Not just dads but mums too, because of the Blitz. It was something you almost took for granted, so you didn't talk about it. It was private. Anyway I went along with John to visit his mother."

Colin and John took the 'short cut' John often took to his mum's: over the Allerton municipal golf course to 1 Blomfield Road just off Mather Avenue where his mother, Julia, lived with her partner Bobby Dykins and their two little girls, Julia and Jacqueline (who respectively turned nine and seven in 1956).

"John knocked and Julia enthusiastically invited us in. John introduced me but she knew who I was, he'd obviously already told her my name, that I was in the group and played the drums."

Julia was not your average 1950s mum. Indeed Colin had never met a 'mum' quite like her.

"I was immediately taken with Julia: she was vivacious, full of fun and friendly, not like most mums I knew who could be a bit guarded when you first met them. For a start Julia looked young, her whole demeanour was young, the way she dressed was stylish: she seemed more like an older sister or a younger aunty than a mum. She showed us into the living room, where I sat on a chair while John and she sat next to each other on the settee. On this occasion I don't recall Julia's partner Bobby nor her daughters being with us or being introduced to them. It was just Julia, John and I in the living room. We hadn't been there very long before she produced a banjo and began singing a song. I was fascinated: a mum playing a banjo and singing. In my experience this was a bit different. And she was really good."

Different from a lot of mums but, as Colin will quickly learn, this was very much the norm for Julia who loved to sing and play her banjo whenever she could. She and her partner Bobby Dykins even owned a gramophone: their love of music meant that for the times they already had a large collection of records. Julia would buy Elvis records for herself. Buddy Holly too. For mid-Fifties Britain this was astonishing. Most parents were very wary of rock 'n' roll, viewing it as subversive, a bad influence, at best 'a five minute fad', not to be encouraged. It's certainly how it was perceived at Mendips by Mimi. Initially Aunt Mimi, as may be expected, had resisited buying a gramophone – most probably in the vain hope of focusing John on his schoolwork and impending O-Level exams and well away from his obsession with Elvis and Lonnie. In the battle of wills currently waging at Mendips, Mimi's opposition to the presence of a record player in the house would eventually be broken just as her opposition to John owning a guitar would. To get his hands on his Gallotone Champion, a 'Spanish-style' acoustic, he had appealed to his mum, who had been more than happy to help him acquire the instrument via mail order. By the time Paul McCartney arrived on the scene just a few months later a record player was ensconced in John's bedroom at 251 and John had a small collection of records. Paul remembers sitting on the bed in John's room listening to records – often with a view to performing them with The Quarry Men. They would work out the chords and keep playing the record over and over until they had transcribed all the words.

What happened next at Blomfield Road held Colin spellbound.

"As Julia sang so she talked the chords of the tune to John, at the same time showing him their shapes. His attention was rapt. This was very impressive to me but as a drummer the technical stuff – chords, shapes. etc., went over my head, even so as an observer Julia had my absolute attention. She was charismatic. She was a very good singer, would sing some words, show John the chord she'd played and then hand the instrument to him to strum the chord for himself at the same time singing the words back to her. As memory serves she was teaching him 'Maggie May', which became a mainstay of The Quarry Men's repertoire. Once they had finished working through the song Julia sang it all the way through before leaving us to make us a cup of tea."

'Maggie May' was a traditional Liverpool folk song (circa 1830s) very popular with skiffle groups up and down the land. In March 1957 The Vipers (produced by George Martin) reached the UK singles chart with their version of 'The Cumberland Gap', on the B-side of which was their expurgated/sanitised version of 'Maggie May', a song about a notorious 'lady of the night' who frequented Lime Street in Liverpool. The version Julia was teaching John, as Colin recalls, was the rather more full-blooded original. The date of its release by The Vipers helps to suggest it was during the Spring of '57 that Colin accompanied John to Julia's.

One of the student lodgers at Mendips, Michael Fishwick, can recall Julia turning up to see Mimi one afternoon when he and John were also there. He says Julia was always good fun. On this particular occasion she noticed John's guitar (which, according to his story, appears to have been in the Morning Room), picked it up, began strumming and started to regale the two young men with her 'unexpurgated' rendition of 'Maggie May'. When Julia had finished, Mimi quickly joined her sister in explaining the meaning of the lyrics for the benefit of both Michael and John. Words such as 'the cast iron shore' were explained and details of the pawn shop on Canning Place shared for it was familiar to them from being girls living around the corner from it.

John of course would return to 'Maggie May'. He led The Beatles in a spontaneous version that found its way onto 'Abbey Road', and was still making home recordings of it shortly before his death in 1980, suggesting the personal connection he possibly felt towards the tune.

Colin was really very impressed. He cannot recall their conversation over tea but remembers Julia being very entertaining.

"When we left, John and I walked back over to Woolton before splitting towards our respective homes. We didn't talk about his mum or why he didn't live with her. Back then that was just another day in the life of John and The Quarry Men. Many years later I realise just how privileged I was to witness John and Julia together playing music, to see first-hand how important she was in his life and musical development. It was an intimate moment that showed me how close they were and how easy they were in each other's company. Privately I couldn't help but wonder why he was not living with her when he clearly loved her so much and there was such a bond between them. It must have been tough for both of them.

As a group we always looked forward to rehearsals at Julia's because they were always fun and she was very entertaining. Sometimes she would pick up a banjo – her own or Rod's – and join in."

People often ask Colin where The Quarry Men would rehearse at Julia's house to confirm the stories of them practising in the bathroom and toilet because of the reverb in those rooms, which John always liked on his vocals.

"In my memory at Julia's The Quarry Men would always rehearse in the living room not the bathroom. The bathroom and toilet are separate and way too small for six lads to squeeze into with drums and all their other instruments. Logistically it would have been impossible. However, maybe before the group expanded to include me and my drum kit, some of the boys may have gone up there once or twice to take advantage of the echo. I think Rod has a memory of that. John's sister Julia certainly does."

At this stage in John's life no-one was more important, emotionally, than his mother. After years of being cared for by his Aunt Mimi (and her husband George until he passed away in June 1955), he was now reunited with Julia and spending time with her, her partner John 'Bobby' Dykins and his sisters, Jacqueline and Julia. This was so important to him: it enriched his soul in so many ways. In his mum John had discovered a kindred spirit: Julia loved music and she could sing and dance really well. She was an accomplished player of the banjo, piano, piano accordion and ukulele and was teaching and encouraging her son on banjo. She had a great sense of humour. All the boys in The Quarry Men – including Paul – speak with great affection and admiration for her. She sparkled and shone and embraced what they were doing. She made them feel good about their music and about themselves. She took them seriously and was their first real adult fan.

When she could Julia liked to hear them play. However, as a mum with two young daughters getting to bookings was not easy, especially as Bobby worked at nights.

"Apart from the church fete, where she was with her girls, the only time I remember seeing Julia in the audience after the church fete in July 1957

was when we played a club on Penny Lane, which is now the Penny Lane Community Centre. It was at a party organised by members of the Liverpool Vespa Club. [Vespas were scooters, so beloved in years to come by Mods.] We were the only 'live' band on that night – when we weren't performing the organisers had set up a record player at the front of the stage for dancing: it was a sort of prototype 'disco'. Paul, who was in the group by then, and I were sitting on the front of the stage where a young man and woman were spinning the discs. They turned to me and asked if each time they did so, would I play a drum roll? I shrunk back in horror; this was my worst nightmare. I didn't play solo. On stage I didn't like to be the focus of attention. Paul put his arm around me and told them 'He's very shy'. This did the trick: they simply smiled and turned away.

We could all see that John was really pleased when his mum turned up that night. The rest of us were too – for one thing her presence almost doubled the size of the audience. As I looked out from my drums she was sitting almost at the front on the right hand side of the stage quite close to where we were while other members of the audience were dancing. John acknowledged her from the stage and played up to her quite a lot – as if he was performing just for her. Every time we finished a song Julia clapped very loudly and enthusiastically which was great because not many others were. She was clearly pleased and proud to see and hear John performing with his group.

After we had finished Julia came over and told us how much she had enjoyed our set. As ever she was great to be around: one of the few parents who appreciated what we were doing. Jim McCartney was another. However, there was something special and engaging about Julia. All these years later I still feel privileged to have known her and to have witnessed the musical bond between she and John: it was very loving and very strong."

20

NIGEL, THE GOLF CLUB AND THE CAVERN!

Meanwhile back on the bookings scene Nigel Walley was having some success.

"The first gig that I particularly remember was at Lee Park Golf Club in Gateacre. Nige Walley had left school at fifteen to work at Rushworth & Dreapers – the premier music shop in the city. He has told me that John used to come in to the shop quite frequently when he was there to look at the harmonicas because Nigel would let him play them. These were top-of-the range instruments and Nigel knew John could not afford one but he was happy to let him try them. Not long after Nigel become a golf professional at Lee Park and that's how we got the gig: Nigel used his influence. I told you he was enterprising."

Apparently Nige had been playing golf at the club with a Dr. John Sytner, whose son Alan had opened The Cavern only a few months earlier. Sensing an opportunity, Nigel had asked the good doctor to put in a word with his son about the chances of The Quarry Men playing the club. Although principally a 'jazz' venue, The Cavern also ran mid-week 'open mic' nights to give emergent talent a chance to strut their stuff. For these evenings it would bend its rules to accommodate skifflers, having deemed skiffle's musical roots more authentic than rock 'n' roll's, which the management considered completely unworthy.

John and Nigel and their amazing lapels, Lime Street, Liverpool, May 5th,1958

Dr. Sytner suggested to Nigel that The Quarry Men should play the golf club first to allow his son to hear the band before committing to a spot on 'open mic night'. And so that is exactly what Nigel arranged.

"We arrived late afternoon, were shown into a room where we could hang around and where they eventually provided us with some food. It wasn't particularly fantastic, basically just some sandwiches. I remember I was in the golf shop talking to one of the other guys when it arrived. Rod came running up to me saying, 'Come on, the food's out'. I started walking back behind him but he broke into a jog, saying, 'Oh no, you'll have to run, they'll (meaning the other boys in the group) eat it all, it will all be gone.' I can't remember if the sandwiches had all gone or not – but I can remember the urgency in Rod's voice. He seemed really concerned. Looking back now I wonder whether they were feeding him enough at home."

Colin cannot recall any first-gig nerves or incidents of stage fright but being their first public performance it remains etched into his memory.

"Once the time came for us to perform we were escorted into the big ballroom where people were sitting on two sides of the space. On another side was a professional band – a proper dance band – they had set up towards one corner, while we were invited to set up along the side of the stage that ran along the back wall. I wasn't positioned behind John and the rest of the lads, which would become the norm; instead we were spread out in a bit of a line and I was at the end."

The Quarry Men were at floor level and being level with the audience proved to be an immediate disadvantage.

"Just as were starting to play a young lady dragged a chair over and sat down right next to me on my left hand side and immediately grabbed hold of my left arm. I was taken by surprise but she seemed very keen. I had no idea

who she was but there was no doubt, unless she let go, she would make my bad drumming (as I perceived it) even worse. John announced the first song, turned to us and asked, 'Are you all ready lads?' He kept his eyes on me because he could see what was happening. I returned his gaze and shrugged my shoulders. Bemused John just remarked, 'Uh-oh Colin seems to be having a bit of trouble but we'll carry on anyway.' And that's exactly what we did; we started playing even though the young lady persisted in holding onto my left arm – I just couldn't get her to let go. We sort of got away with it but I don't think it was a particularly good session. I know afterwards the hat was passed round and we got something out of it, but I can't imagine it was an awful lot."

Any thoughts that the evening was over, it definitely was not: there was still time for some rock 'n' roll high jinks. Rod Davis's dad arrived in the family car, an Austin A70 Hereford, to take Rod and Eric home, while Len, who didn't live in Woolton, caught the 'bus back to Wavertree. That left John, Pete and Colin to make their way home together.

"We dropped lucky. When we came to go another young lady (not the one who'd held my arm) approached us and said she had a car. A girl with a car! Offering us a lift! I think it was her dad's – but so what, she could drive and that was a start. This was the stuff of a teenage boy's dreams. It wasn't just any old car by the way: it was a limousine – quite spacious, definitely impressive. She offered to take us back up to Woolton Village.

I put my drums in the boot, Pete's washboard went in there too. John had his guitar with him inside the vehicle. There were no seat belts in those days. I was made up, we all were – maybe a bit too much because as we put the equipment into the boot I heard John say to Pete something like, 'I'll make a move on this girl'. From what I could gather John was going to get in the front seat with her.

For some reason this brought out the chivalrous side of me and I thought, No, I can't let this happen: she had been good enough to give us a lift, and she doesn't want one of us to make a pass at her. I wasn't being entirely noble however; I was also being practical: I wanted to get all the way home, not stranded, kicked out half way there with my drums on the side of the street just because John had messed things up by making a move. So, as soon as the passenger door opened, I jumped into the front seat right alongside her.

Pete and John saw what I'd done and began complaining, 'Get out! John's going to sit there!' I was determined not to let him do so and held my ground by simply taking no notice of them until the girl herself intervened to end the dispute by shouting at us to 'stop fighting and shut up!' Embarrassed we did just that and good to her word she kindly took us to Woolton Village, where she dropped us off at the Milk Bar. Not another word passed among us about the evening's escapades."

Despite that clinging girl The Quarry Men's performance passed muster: they did secure themselves a debut booking (of sorts) at The Cavern. Alan Sytner recommended to Nigel that they came along to the club on a Wednesday night when it held its 'open mic' session. On these occasions aspiring groups could play the venue in the hope of impressing the management and securing a paid booking at a later date. So this is what they did. Later, as the skiffle boom erupted, The Cavern's 'open mic' nights became dominated by skiffle groups for a while, consequently The Quarry Men played the club on several occasions.

The journey had begun.

21

JOHN BREAKS A STRING

The exact venues and when they played them around the time of Spring 1957 are not easy to trace because no-one was keeping a diary. Somewhere between Lee Park and their first appearance at The Cavern, however, there was a gig both Colin and Rod Davis recall which was to have a consequence in 1999 long after John's death.

"Even before our first night at The Cavern another early gig I remember was at St. Luke's Church out in Bootle. We played there just after the golf club. It was a youth club gig run by younger members of the church. There was another group on with us at the time, and they actually had a double bass but it only had one string. It was literally one step up from the tea-chest bass and they certainly couldn't play it properly, they just plucked away on that one string. In fact they weren't very together at all and asked if they could borrow my drum kit. Well musicians are always protective of their equipment and I'm no different. I could see them ending up giving my kit a real hammering and there was no way I was having any of that, so my answer was a resounding no.

I recall most clearly that it was that night at St. Luke's when John broke a string as we were performing. Immediately he turned, swapped his guitar for Rod's banjo and carried on regardless. There was a chair at the back of the stage where Rod sat and one song later he had restrung John's guitar. In my mind's eye I can clearly see Rod sitting out a song, fixing John's string."

Colin's memory sits well with Rod's own recollection of tuning John's acoustic Gallotone Champion guitar that he played in those early skiffle days.

Rod: *"John had broken a string and in the process had also skinned the edge of his index finger, probably as a result of playing too hard – don't forget we had no amplifiers. He handed me the guitar to replace the string and took my banjo to play the next number. I noticed that a fine spray of blood droplets from John's cut finger had gone through the sound hole of the guitar and had landed partly on the label on which were printed the words 'Guaranteed not to split' and partly on the wood above the label."* (The Quarrymen, Davies, p.260.)

This vivid memory of Colin's (the location of which Rod is less sure of, pondering that it might have been St. Peter's Church Hall) equipped Rod in 1999 to positively identify a guitar that was up for auction at Sotheby's described as John Lennon's 'original' Gallotone. By simply looking inside the sound hole for the evidence of the blood stains he was able to confirm the instrument's provenance.

Two eye witnesses remembering the same story also reminds us that those were indeed simpler days: no amplifiers, no monitors, no PA stacks – no turning up the volume, no group vans – it was acoustic, the volume dependent entirely on the collective on-stage noise the group could muster. And, of course, they travelled to all their gigs on the 'bus.

"On stage it was a case of simply having to thrash the guitars in order to be heard above the noise of the audience. This was skiffle and it was unplugged. When we first started playing there was no room for finesse like intricate guitar solos, only for stomping, strumming and drumming as loud and hard as we could to my bass drum, all thrashing away just to keep the beat. The beat is what mattered: keep the beat, keep the audience on their feet."

As John, Paul and George would say when Colin had quit the band and they turned up to gigs *sans* a drummer: *"The rhythm's in the guitars!"*

22

THE CARROLL LEVIS DISCOVERIES AT THE EMPIRE

In the adrenalin rush of youth that can convince angels to rush in where the more considered may hesitate to tread, The Quarry Men were game to appear on talent shows almost before they had learned to tune their guitars.

As now, so then, talent shows – both local and national – were very popular. Cheap and cheerful they were a fun night out and in some instances did promise at least one lucky contestant the chance of overnight fame. As skiffle was so hugely popular and relatively easy to perform, such extravaganzas became magnets for local groups who found themselves competing against each other on a regular basis at such events. Indeed they became a bit of a theme running through The Quarry Men's entire existence.

And so on 27th May 1957 the boys found themselves on Lodge Lane at the 'Pivvy' – otherwise known as the Liverpool Pavilion Theatre – where they appeared on a 'Spot The Stars Variety Show'. It was compered by singer-impressionist Don Arden but needless to say The Quarry Men's star remained unspotted.

Despite this set back, they remained undeterred.

Almost before they could retune their guitars opportunity came knocking a second time for Woolton's fledgling skifflers when on Sunday 9th June 1957 auditions for the hugely popular TV talent show 'TV Star Search' rocked up in Liverpool at the

Empire. Fronted by ITV's 'Mr. Star-Maker' himself – the one and only Carroll Levis – it was the 'Britain's Got Talent' show of its day. A place on this TV show was the ultimate goal for all budding artists the length and breadth of the nation, be they ventriloquists, comedians, acrobats, jugglers, singers, magicians, instrumentalists, bands or skiffle groups.

It's hard to imagine just how coveted, how important an appearance on television was for entertainers back then. It was instant stardom – fortune and fame there for the taking. It was a dream. Most never made it beyond an initial audition. But that didn't stop people: it guaranteed you overnight celebrity – or, even better, stardom, your face on the front page of every paper – the importance of entering was utterly compelling.

Such an unmissable opportunity provided a real buzz for The Quarry Men.

"Carroll Levis was the Simon Cowell of his day and when we heard that he was coming all the way from London to Liverpool, for us kids in a group it was a big, big deal. It wasn't every day a real big shot in the entertainment industry – a star maker no less – deigned to set foot out of London. A little bit of glamour was coming our way. Uppermost in our minds however, was, first and foremost, it gave us an opportunity to tread the boards of Liverpool's biggest and best theatre, The Empire. We would be standing on a stage graced by likes of Laurel and Hardy, Mae West, Frank Sinatra, Roy Rogers AND besides all this came the possibility that we just might end up appearing on television ourselves. It was a chance we weren't about to miss. Television was new and so exciting – it was changing the British way of life. There were no second thoughts: we were ready, willing and totally up for it!"

Hosting his own TV show was the portal of celebrity for Levis and earned him big money. Equally important for this early starmaker were the extremely lucrative supporting national theatre audition tours and regional winners shows that he hosted. These drew sell-out audiences and were relatively cheap to stage: costs were kept low because the artists who were auditioning were amateurs and so performed for free.

The Quarry Men were typical of the acts up and down the land who turned up in their thousands to audition: youngsters with stars in their eyes looking for a short cut to stardom. As for all such acts however, it was a case of first things first: for the dream of appearing on television to stand any chance of coming true, it was imperative The Quarry Men made it beyond the preliminary round.

"First round auditions were held on the Sunday and then those who were successful would perform at one of a series of second auditions held on the forthcoming week-nights (which I think for us was the following Tuesday the 11th). These second auditions would be in front of an audience. The winners of each week-night audition would then perform on the Saturday in a grand final event. During that final show a past winner from the TV series itself would also appear – having now become a 'star' in their own right. Stretching these audition shows throughout a week kept the theatres packed and the cash rolling in."

What the parents of Rod, Pete and Eric must have been thinking as their sons announced their intention of entering a talent show is interesting to contemplate. Aunt Mimi was no doubt shaking her head in barely suppressed frustration and disbelief, pointing out in no uncertain terms to her nephew the error of his ways. She had good reason to be concerned.

The reason why she and those parents in particular might have been anxious was that this was June 1957 and so all these boys were in the midst of their O-Level examinations: fail these and any hopes they may have had of staying on at Quarry Bank Grammar School for A-Levels and a shot at university would be dashed. There was no safety net back then; their chance would be blown and it would mean having to leave school and get a job – a job without qualifications: low pay, future uncertain, a dead end. Grammar school boys were meant to pass exams not flunk them!

Colin was his own boss, however: no exams to sit, his future already determined, he was a working man already on the road to learning a trade and ensuring a good living for himself.

Whatever debates, arguments, warnings, pleading and persuasion had gone on or deals been struck in the privacy of John, Eric, Rod and Pete's homes only four of the Woolton-based Quarry Men – all fired up and ready to sock it to Mr. Levis – were waiting at the 'bus stop on Sunday: Colin, Eric, John and Pete. (Len, who did not live in Woolton, was making his own way there to meet up with the lads.)

"When Sunday 9th arrived there was a genuine sense of anticipation among us when we met up to catch the 'bus down town to the Empire. All of us I should say except Rod. His parents had other plans for him: Sunday was the Lord's day and so he wasn't allowed to attend, although he desperately wanted to be with us."

Having been joined by Len along the way, when the five boys did arrive at the Empire it was immediately clear The Quarry Men weren't the only ones with stars in their eyes.

"As we walked along Lime Street we were confronted by a huge queue three or four people deep that stretched all the way round the corner of the Empire. Half the city's youth seemed to be there. Despite the inevitable wait, spirits were high. The atmosphere crackled with the banter there always is in Liverpool when something exciting is happening. The Quarry Men joined in – letting our imaginations run wild – laughing and joking, talking about what we wanted to do and what we hoped would happen – dreaming out loud that we would become big stars.

Eventually the door opened and gradually we shuffled towards the entrance, where a guy was handing out forms to be completed by everyone entering the audition. He explained that there was one form for an individual act and one for a group but that one member of the group could fill in the form for everyone – which in our case was John. I think there was an age limit; everyone competing was supposed to be a certain age, I don't know whether it was sixteen or seventeen, but it was irrelevant because irrespective of our actual ages on the day – on paper we were all whatever age it took!"

This was it – The Empire: Liverpool's great and famous variety theatre. Colin had been there before as a patron but now here he was about to step up on that famous stage as a performer. That took some taking in, the very thought was mind blowing.

"It felt strange to be inside the Empire as a performer – it was a huge space and it made me stop and think, a kind of hush descended upon us all as we absorbed just where we were and what was happening. The banter stopped and we spoke in lowered voices as we were shown into the auditorium, where we took seats in the stalls to watch what was going on. Every now and then a number of people would be called up from the stalls to go back stage before going out to perform. The great Carroll Levis was sitting on the left hand side of the stage as we looked at it facing across the stage and so the right hand side his body was visible to us. He was sitting at a very small table surrounded by all his paperwork while in front of him people were coming on stage to perform. They weren't there long: Mr. Levis didn't mess around – you very quickly got his verdict – a simple 'yes' or 'no'. No debate, no second chance whatsoever. He didn't waste any time – there were a lot of hopefuls to get through."

The number of acts, the brevity of the allotted time on stage, no allowance for error, it all cranked up the tension amongst the boys.

"Finally we were called backstage, where we waited in the wings with another group of people until it was our turn to go on. We were nervous, no doubt about it. I remember mentioning to John just how nervous I felt, to which he replied – 'You're nervous, how do you think I feel – I've got to go out there and introduce the group as well as sing!' Knowing John – who always seemed so sure of himself – was also nervous had a strangely calming effect on me."

During their wait one of the groups that The Quarry Men watched with interest was fronted by a lad called Nicky Cuff, who worked with Colin at Guy Rogers Furniture Factory. He was a dwarf and a singer in a skiffle group, The Connaughts. (They weren't the only skiffle group to emanate from Guy Rogers, which was clearly a veritable hotbed of emerging talent. Another contemporary of Colin's was Phil Robinson, who used the amazing skills he'd learned as an apprentice at Rogers to build high-quality guitars for his group, The Crossrocks, a successful skiffle group based in Hunts Cross just next to Woolton. They played many of the same venues as The Quarry Men including St. Peter's Church Hall.)

"When it was their turn Nicky's band came on without him and started to play, only for Nicky to follow a moment later. The band stopped playing as he appeared on stage and one of them asked where he'd been because he was all dressed up in top hat and tails and carrying his tea-chest bass. Nicky joked that he'd been to the Adelphi Hotel. Immediately Caroll Levis stood up and stopped him from saying any more, instructing the group: 'No, no, you all get one song, you've only got three minutes, you can't do a joke routine as well, you either sing a song or you tell some jokes. One or the other, not both.' Having witnessed that little episode we knew exactly what we had to do: strictly one song, no more, no less. Three minutes and your future was sealed. No wonder John said he was nervous.

Once on stage we set up very quickly indeed – we didn't want to lose any of our precious three minutes. John introduced us as 'The Quarry Men' and proceeded to sing. I remember the song was 'Railroad Bill', but he'd only got a line or two out before Carroll Levis stopped us and said, 'Yes'. That was it, our big moment over in a flash. We were through to the next round. We didn't even get to finish our song – but we had passed the audition. We were booked to return on the Tuesday night: that was it, almost before we knew it we were out of the theatre, on the 'bus and headed home."

Nicky Cuff and the Connaughts

Phil Robinson and The Crossrocks

The adrenalin surge of going on stage at the much-vaunted Liverpool Empire to play in front of the mighty Carroll Levis now ebbed away, leaving The Quarry Men almost speechless on the way home. Not a condition that often afflicted John Lennon.

"When I got home Mum, Dad and Granny Hanton were having tea but they were so excited to know what had happened they immediately put down their knives and forks, fell silent and looked directly at me, their faces full of anticipation. And so, as nonchalantly as I could – pausing for dramatic effect – before I inquired of them, 'What are you doing Tuesday night?' For a moment everyone was agog as the penny slowly dropped that we'd actually got through to the next heat. They were really quite surprised, taken aback – but then clearly very relieved and pleased for us. Proud too. If truth be told, so was I."

Two days later, Tuesday, the big night arrived. All The Quarry Men had to do was pass the second heat and they would be perfoming on the Saturday night grand final. On this occasion a posse of supporters turned up to help cheer them to victory.

"Remembering just who was there in the audience is not easy. My mum, dad, younger sister Lynn and a neighbour most definitely were, I think Pete's mother was there. Rod's mum and dad were there along with Rod's brother and sister. I can't recall if Len's parents or Eric's family were there, I somehow doubt Eric's mum would have been there. She was a single parent and by Eric's own admission as a teenager he proved quite difficult for his mum. I cannot remember whether Aunt Mimi or John's mum, Julia, attended. I somehow doubt Mimi would have been in attendance. It might have been difficult for Julia to be there because of Bobby working evening/nights even though I'm certain she would loved to have gone. Nigel would have been there but I'm not sure about Ivan, I'd be surprised if he hadn't gone along – after all it was a bit of a big deal for us to be playing the Empire and he was one of the 'inner circle'.

I do remember we were buzzing – a mixture of high spirits and nervous energy as we headed off down to the Empire carrying our instruments, sitting one to a seat on the 'bus. John and Eric who never carried their guitars in cases were strumming all the way there. John would occasionally sing and we were all telling jokes. Spirits were truly high.

When we arrived we took all our gear inside via the stage door, which made us feel like we were proper stars. Once inside we were shown up several flights of stairs into a huge dressing room. The window looked out over the side of the Empire facing the side of Lime Street Station. We were almost over the stage door, and of course we were looking, shouting and waving at the girls below. I don't know who they thought we might be but they were waving back very enthusiastically. It all added to the excitement of occasion.

We were mightily impressed by our big dressing room, which had showers. That particularly impressed me because I didn't know anyone who had a shower in their home – don't forget this was the era when showers weren't particularly common in houses in Liverpool or anywhere in the country; we all had a bath and many of us still had outside toilets. So for us this was the big star treatment – we lapped it up. Of course, for John, little did he or any of us realise, the girls standing outside the theatre waving and shouting at him was a taste of things to come."

They also tasted the other side of life as an entertainer: time spent just waiting around before going on stage to perform.

"The theatre had a PA system so we could hear what was going on stage down below. We were ensconced in that dressing room for the best part of two hours. I set my drums up ready to carry downstairs and on to the stage but we didn't rehearse. John would normally have played his guitar – any opportunity to do so – but we became becalmed and just sat around chatting, smoking, telling jokes – and waving to the girls. Eventually a call came over the small tannoy inside the dressing room: the Quarry Men were due on stage.

Suddenly this was it – no more sitting around, this was our opportunity – and so once more the adrenalin began to pump and the nerves kicked in. Grabbing our equipment we went gingerly down the narrow staircase onto the back of the stage. Before we knew it we were lined up in the wings ready to go on. Pete was carrying my snare drum for me as well as his washboard and as I stood there holding my bass drum replete with small tom-tom, small cymbal and a foot pedal, I can remember telling myself, 'Don't mess up, don't mess up!'"

From then on time speeded up, the wait was only brief: before they knew it Carroll Levis had introduced them and to loud applause The Quarry Men were walking on stage.

"The lights were so bright I couldn't see the audience but I could hear them. They weren't screaming but there was some cheering and a real buzz of anticipation. I set up at the back of the stage while Carroll Levis interviewed John asking him where we were all from (there was an act from north Wales about to follow us on so not everyone was from Liverpool). And then we were off – our time had arrived. We performed our song – and then in the blink of an eye it was over, we were off stage. We were definitely pleased with our performance. I remember there was lots of applause as we trooped off and among us as a group a sense of relief mingled with pride."

Buzzing with excitement the boys returned to the dressing room to pack their stuff away. But the night was not yet over. Decisions had to be made: a winner had to be decided.

"We didn't have long to wait after our performance. We soon had to go back down to the stage to assemble with all the other acts for the grand finale. When we got there we were amazed that the final group – that group from north Wales – was still on stage. We were really miffed because they had been allowed to perform two songs when we had been told it was strictly one song per group. Among ourselves we began to grumble because we felt this was unfair and gave them an advantage over everybody else – especially us. It was deeply frustrating because there wasn't anything we could do about it."

Sitting in the audience cheering for all her worth for her brother's group, Rod's sister Rosemary remembers her family also being very put out that the last group had been allowed to perform two songs. They thought it was unfair and that The Quarry Men had been stitched up. The Quarry Men's displeasure was short-lived and replaced with a keen sense of anticipation as the act on stage finished and they found themselves standing on stage with all the other acts for the grand finale. This was the climax of the evening when that night's finalist who would go forward to appear on the all-important Saturday night show would be chosen – not by Mr. Levis – by the audience!

"Carroll Levis marshalled us onstage. As he pulled me forward to stand in front of the other members of the Quarry Men (me being the shortest) he said to us all, 'I'm sorry I may have been a bit unfair there lads' – a reference we assumed to the group from north Wales being allowed to perform an extra song."

To decide the evening's winning act the audience had to cheer for the artist or artists that they thought were the best. The volume of noise each act received was to be the deciding factor. So the clapping began as Levis reintroduced each act one by one to the audience. By the end of the clapping it turned out that The Quarry Men and this other group from north Wales were tied. Levis simply could not distinguish who were the outright winners. Of course a tie also cranked up the level of excitement and tension within the auditorium, just like a penalty shoot-out. And so turning once more to the audience he informed them that – having eliminated all the other acts – all he could do to decide the winner was to have a clap-off. The next rounds of applause were to be between The Quarry Men and the group from Wales.

"And so it was decided: the clapping began again and when it all subsided it was judged that the applause for the group from Wales had been louder and so they were announced as the evening's chosen winners. We felt really deflated.

For us them being allowed to perform two songs had swayed the outcome in their favour. It really rankled with us and our friends and family in the audience but that's the way it was, the choice had been made."

Colin believes that Levis himself who, given his line of work had no doubt developed a bit of a tough skin regarding people's hopes being dashed, also felt some sort of pang of conscience for allowing the final group two bites of the cherry.

"As he was bringing proceedings to a close Carroll Levis did take time to seek us out and say, 'I am awful sorry boys, but don't be too downhearted, I thought you were very good'."

Levis's words of encouragement might not have altered the result but it puts into perspective how well The Quarry Men actually did that night.

"Some commentators have said the evening was a disaster for us, but in my mind it wasn't. We'd come within a whisker of winning. To me that was not bad at all for six lads who'd played only a handful of times before that performance. And despite everything it had been a thoroughly entertaining evening shared with our parents and friends who were in the audience. But that was it, we hadn't won, our shot at making it onto the telly had gone: that, for us, was the Carroll Levis Discoveries. Opportunity had not knocked."

23

IT WAS 750 YEARS AGO TODAY

"So I'd joined a group. I could officially call myself a drummer. I attended rehearsals; I was one of the boys. We even had a name that was emblazoned on my bass drum. We were raring to go. Crikey – we'd even played the Empire as part of the Carroll Levis 'TV Star Search' auditions. Talk about running before you could walk."

In between those early performances and audacious shot at 'overnight' stardom The Quarry Men followed the same low-key route as most youngsters who form a band whilst still at school.

"We'd rehearse in different homes, at friends' parties; youth club nights at St. Peter's – John, Ive (short for Ivan), Pete and Rod were all members of St. Peter's Youth Club in Woolton. John sang in the church choir. They were that sort of performance. More like rehearsals really. We were basically just kids entertaining our friends. A bit of a captive audience – but appreciative. To be honest I can't remember just everywhere we did play.

As a group we are agreed that – various youth club appearances and audition try-outs aside – that infamous night at Lee Park Golf Club in Gateacre in early 1957 was our first 'proper' show. Our first 'memorable' public appearance as a group, however, was in the open air on the back of a lorry in Toxteth."

The venue was Rosebery Street, the date Saturday 22 June 1957. Party time! The Quarry Men were truly on their way: they'd been invited to perform – they were a gigging band.

"That was the day we played a street party as part of a city-wide celebration of the 750th Anniversary of King John granting Liverpool its first Royal Charter."

Rosebery Street is in Toxteth, Liverpool 8, just off the magnificent Princes Boulevard. All around the neighbourhood the streets were decorated with bunting but it was on Rosebery where the party was really happening; it was the place where the crowds had gathered in anticipation of hearing 'live' music. Lots of young people – lads in particular – turned up to hear The Quarry Men skiffle group. Skiffle was all the rage among youngsters. This was a chance to hear the real thing and let off a little bit of steam.

Several miles and a gulf in class away from The Quarry Men's more genteel stomping ground of Woolton, it was through Colin that they had got the gig.

"We'd got the booking through Charlie Roberts, my drinking buddy. Charlie lived at number 84 Rosebery Street. He had come with The Quarry Men to that Youth Club dance at St.Luke's Church in Bootle – one of our early bookings, the one where John broke a string. He'd helped me carry my drums. He'd spoken to someone in his neighbourhood who said we could play on the back of a wagon in the road that they'd organised for the street party. We were up for that. It was all very simple: the electric cable came out of someone's house and plugged into some kind of a basic PA system. The Quarry Men were all acoustic, only the mic John would use fed through the PA."

Age and employment had forged Colin's friendship with Charlie. Charlie recalls that it was a chap called Fred Tyler who supplied the wagon and wired up a speaker system for the microphones.

"I can't remember any other acts performing on that day. Just The Quarry Men – Rod Davis, Len Garry, Eric Griffiths, John Lennon, Pete Shotton and myself – the original six. There were people around the truck that I knew

Charlie Roberts outside his house, No. 84 Rosebery Street

like Kevin Hanson, another drinking buddy of mine, and Chas Roberts of course because we'd used his house – number 84 – as a sort of 'Green Room' to store our belongings. I don't remember any of John's family or Woolton friends like Ivan being there. They could well have been but they certainly didn't register with me at the time."

Occasionally people ask Colin if, while he was a member of The Quarry Men, in the very early days the group ever performed under a different name such as 'Johnny and the Rainbows'.

"Personally I have no recollection of playing with John under any other name but the Quarry Men. The photographs taken at Rosebery Street, which was one of our very first gigs together, clearly show the name on the drums is 'Quarry Men', plus there is a photograph taken of Charlie Roberts standing outside his house right next to a poster promoting the event that was displayed in his window on which it clearly says 'Special Attraction 5pm QUARRYMEN Skiffle Group'."

John's mother Julia's influence on the group was clearly apparent in John's stage attire. Photographs taken on the day show the boys performing on the back of the truck with four of them wearing open-necked checked shirts – John, Eric, Len and Pete (under his jacket). These *had* been bought for them by Julia at an open-air market in Garston. Interestingly, Colin is seen in these photos to be sporting a patterned pullover over a white shirt and tie. Rod appears to be wearing a plain shirt. The check shirts are a reminder that, as well as skiffle and rock 'n' roll, Country & Western music and the whole cowboy genre was hugely popular in Liverpool in those days. It was fairly easy to pick up American style 'western' apparel, which, in turn, visually strengthened skiffle's American roots. They were a great choice for The Quarry Men.

As for familiarity with the neighbourhood, only Colin could claim this.

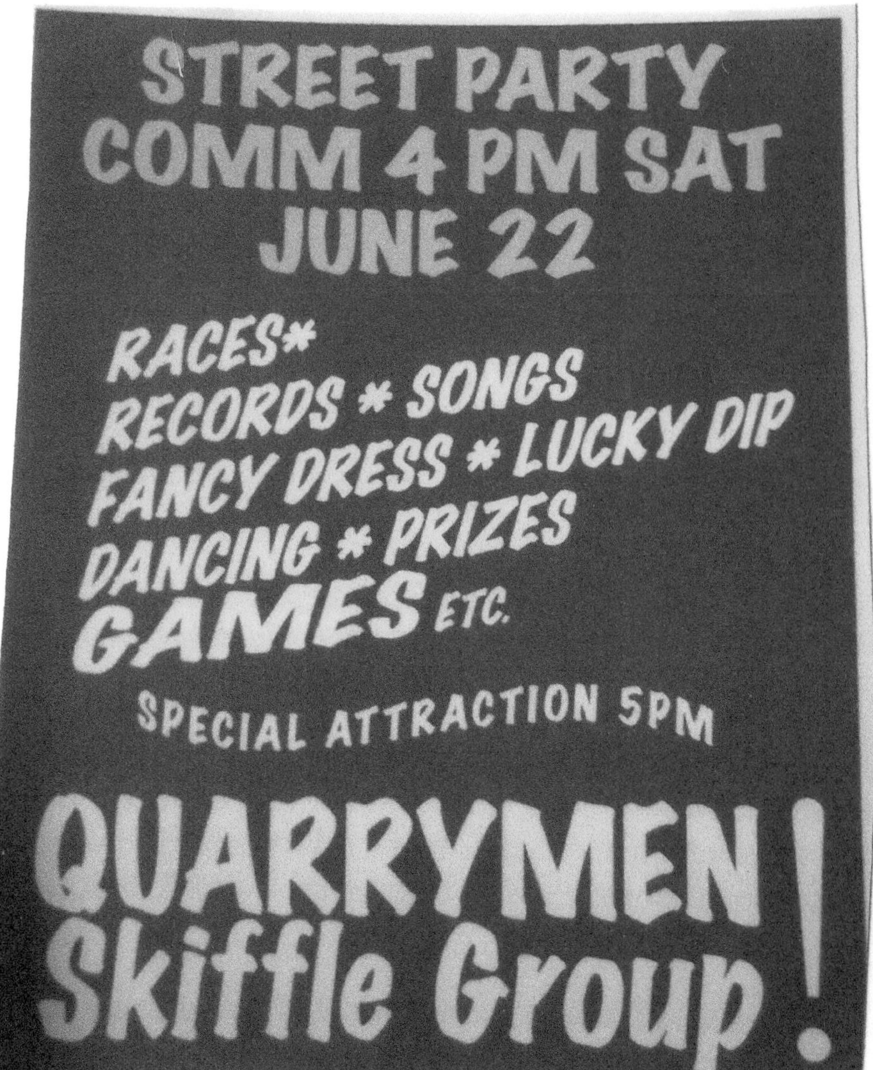

A reproduction of Charlie's Quarrymen poster displayed in his window

"At the time John and the others would have been strangers in a strange land whereas I'd spent at least one night sleeping on a settee at Charlie's after a night out drinking, so I was already familiar to some of the audience."

The Quarry Men turned up with time to spare and so the boys had time to kill.

"We arrived fairly handily before the gig and a couple of us went off down to the local pub, 'The Clock', on the corner of Beaumont Street and Kingsley Road, and enjoyed a couple of pints. As memory serves it was just John, Pete, Eric and I who went for a drink but we were not inebriated when we returned, just loosened up. And also – much to our pleasure we'd met some girls – more of which later."

Quite a crowd had built up by the time the four returned and, among those youngsters present, a noisy, excited buzz was building up ahead of The Quarry Men's appearance.

"Back then any sort of event boasting a skiffle band would have grabbed the attention of teenagers who had very little to entertain them. From the vantage point of sixty plus years away it's hard to explain just how big a deal a skiffle group like The Quarry Men playing on your street would have been – especially given how utterly unsophisticated skiffle music was by today's standards. But in 1957 music aimed at a teenage audience was all so new: the skiffle of Lonnie Donegan and the rock 'n' roll records of Bill Haley and Elvis were unlike anything else around – a million miles from anything our parents were listening to such as the Joe Loss Orchestra or Victor Silvester. That kind of big band dance music didn't rock the teenage boat: the kids deemed it to be 'square'."

More to Colin's point is that skiffle and rock were seldom heard on the radio because of radio's strict quotient of 'needle-time' (see the footnote at the end of this chapter). This limited the amount of time records could be played 'on air', so kids were starved of opportunitues to hear rock 'n' roll on the radio. To hear a real 'live' skiffle group playing the music they loved provided a compelling reason for teenagers to turn out in good numbers to hear it wherever it was being performed.

"I can't remember for how long we were booked to play, half an hour maybe or just a little longer. It was about 5pm when we climbed onto the back of the lorry to loud applause and cheers. We'd been playing for about maybe ten or fifteen minutes when the mood of the crowd began to darken. I'm not 100% sure what songs we would have played – maybe 'Lost John', 'Rock Island Line', 'Railroad Bill', 'Blue Suede Shoes' – they were the standard tunes we were doing at the time. We were going down well – in fact wherever we played we went down well, after all we were a teenage band playing teenage music to a teenage audience. You have to ask yourself – what could go wrong?"

However, John, being John, was attracting the wrong kind of attention.

"Things can get a bit tribal when you're that age and not locals. Lads are always on the look out for anyone they think is getting above themselves or attracting too much attention or fancied themselves just because they were in a group. It especially goes to another level if lads think some smart arse interloper is receiving too much attention from the local girls. And, in my opinion, that's exactly what was happening that afternoon on Rosebery Street.

I'd noticed some lads in the crowd I did know and others I didn't. They began putting their heads together, there was a lot of mumbling going on, so when we'd finished a song I leaned over the side and asked one of the lads I did know, 'What's going on?' His reply was terse: 'They're going to get the singer.' He didn't say who 'they' were. No reason was given, 'they' had just decided they didn't like him – as I say – probably because the girls were paying him too much attention. Charlie says John had been winking at some of the girls. All I knew was the lads meant business. Something had stirred them up.

I called over to John, nodded in the direction of the gathering hordes

The Quarry Men, Rosebery Street, 22nd June 1957

and said, 'They're going to get you.' He couldn't really see what was going on because he wasn't wearing his glasses but he certainly wasn't hanging around to get 'got'. Surreptitiously the word went 'round the rest of the group and with no warning whatsoever we abandoned the wagon: we simply stopped playing, grabbed our equipment, jumped off and ran. Remember – there was no amplification so no amps or anything to worry about, nothing to unplug – just grab our gear and run!"

In other versions of the story it is suggested that John's poor eyesight caused the problem, his squinting brought on by not wearing his glasses caused him to screw his eyes up in an attempt to see what was in front of him. Some say this had riled the lads looking on because they interpreted John's squinting as giving them 'the dead eye', a provocative look. Provocative in the sense of challenging them to a fight, trying to out-stare them, in other words looking for trouble. It sounds very feasible, after all it's not unknown for lads to try and stare each other down as the precursor to a fight. Colin takes the point but his feelings both on the day and all these years later is that this was not the case.

"In no way would John have been trying to provoke the boys in the audience: what possible point would there have been in doing that? John was no fool: he was not about to take on a gang of lads in a fight. Anyway, he wasn't there to fight; he was there for the music (and maybe the girls!) – that's what it was all about for him.

John's squinting could certainly have been mistaken for trying to look 'hard', which in turn would seriously rankle the local 'hard cases'. However, I'm convinced it was because of the girl attention he – and quite likely Eric – were attracting. (Eric was always a great favourite with the girls, who reckoned him as 'handsome'.) It wasn't uncommon. Charlie's memory of John's winking further suggests this was the crux of the matter."

Fortunately for the band sanctuary was only a few doors away.

"We barricaded ourselves inside Charlie Roberts's house. Once inside although we were shaken up we didn't feel too threatened. The others went directly into the back room out of sight while I remained in the front living room folding my drums away into their suitcase. I could see what was happening outside in the road and those outside could see me, consequently a lot of the kids outside looking in began banging on the window pane. As far as I remember they weren't the lads I'd clocked plotting to get John, just kids joining in, wondering what was going on.

Charlie's dad was anxious a window was going to get broken and he urged me to vacate the front room and join everyone in the back dining room. Which I did.

We were all excited, anxious as we talked about what had happened, debating the reasons why we were going to 'get it'. As we did so we calmed down. The conclusion was it was definitely John they were after because he was the singer, the focal point for the local ladies and then the local lads who weren't happy about that situation. John was a bit shell shocked but took it in his stride as just one of those things: it was a learning curve."

Stranded and surrounded in Charlie's house escape now became the boys' priority.

"How we effected our escape was quite interesting. As I said before the gig some of us had gone down the local pub, The Clock, for a couple of pints. In the pub one or two of us had tapped off (Liverpool slang for 'meeting a member of the opposite sex'). I'd met Norma Hanson, who lived in Rosebery Street and had very quickly become attached to her. I remember giving her quite a big sloppy kiss in the pub. Well, after we'd been chased she'd followed us inside Charlie's house and was sitting with me in the back room. (Although I would go to the cinema with Joan, at this point we were not officially 'going out' with each other; we weren't boyfriend and girlfriend yet, so me dating another girl was still okay.)

Somebody telephoned the police to help us make good our escape and a lone bobby was dispatched to escort us safely to the 'bus stop. When he arrived I had my bass drum in one hand and suitcase in the other ready to go. I said to Norma, 'When we get outside instead of turning right with the boys I'll turn left and come home with you.' She was agreeable. I was on a date – no way was I going home!"

So, that's what Colin did. Bidding goodnight to the other boys he and Norma headed down to Norma's house on Rosebery Street where Colin stayed for the evening partying with her and her mum and dad who were the sort of people who liked to get up, sing and party.

"Ultimately I had a good day whereas John and the band's day was spoiled by having to hightail it out of there.

Apparently the bobby didn't walk The Quarry Men all the way down Rosebery Street; he turned right, right again across the top road and right again down the next avenue to the 'bus stop on Princes Avenue. This was the long way round but he did not want to risk walking them down Rosebery, where the gangs might still have been lingering."

The memory of the occasion causes Colin to muse on the changing times between then and now.

"It sounds ridiculous that only one bobby came to rescue us but the police were perceived differently in those days; people weren't going to mix it with a police officer, not back then. If they even tried they'd have been in real trouble."

A little known postcript to The Quarry Men's adventure on Rosebery Street provides a happy ending to the story for two other boys in the group.

"Of course I wasn't the only one who met a girl in the pub earlier that day. John and Eric had both tapped off and for a while after the gig the three of us would go down in the evenings mid-week to Rosebery Street on a joint date. We weren't too nervous to return. To our way of thinking the event had attracted a big crowd and the ones who had wanted to cause trouble hadn't been locals but outsiders, so no one was waiting there to 'get' us."

So, emboldened, the three Romeos felt safe to return.

"John, Eric and I would spend time in one or the other of the girl's houses just having a laugh and a joke, playing records, a bit of kissing and cuddling, that kind of stuff. We were very innocent in those days: that's all we ever did, a bit of kissing and cuddling!"

ENDNOTES

Needle time

This was a time restriction placed on the amount of commercially recorded music the BBC could broadcast each week. It was a device created by the Musicians' Union and Phonographic Performance Limited to ensure the livelihood of professional musicians employed by the BBC by restricting the amount of commercially recorded music that could be played. The main source of recorded music in the 1950s was gramophone records, which were played on gramophone players using a needle, hence the term 'needle time'. In the 1950s the playing of records was limited to below 30 hours per week. By the 1960s this rose to five hours a day. All other music had to be performed 'live' by musicians (although this could be pre-recorded).

24

AS FETE WILL HAVE IT

With the hindsight of sixty years Colin reflects that with every booking The Quarry Men learned something new about being in a group and being 'entertainers'. One thing was certain: you attracted attention, some good, some undesirable. There was some 'mystique' about being in a group that people – especially girls – found interesting if not exciting and attractive. You met people, people were introduced to you. You were being 'observed'.

"Rosebery Street had been eventful. On a personal level I had rather enjoyed myself but professionally it had made us aware that audiences could be hostile. We needed to be alert, to 'read' the mood of a crowd if we could."

The Quarry Men's next gig was another outside event involving a lorry: this time it was the St. Peter's Annual Church Garden Fete in Woolton. It was, after all, summer. Come rain or shine the British like to celebrate the season. In the Fifties, very much as it is today, it was the season for picnics, garden parties and garden fetes so beloved of the British. Like cricket, Wimbledon, gymkhanas, cream teas and trips to the seaside, fetes (which quite often involve much standing around in, or seeking shelter from, the rain) are woven into the fabric of British summertime and the British psyche. They are to be enjoyed – or endured.

GARDEN FETE

ST. PETER'S CHURCH FIELD

WOOLTON PARISH CHURCH Rector: M. Pryce Jones.

Saturday, 6th July, 1957

at 3 p.m.

ADMISSION BY PROGRAMME:

CHILDREN 3d.

PROCEEDS IN AID OF CHURCH FUNDS.

The cover of the programme
for the garden fete

PROGRAMME

STALLS — SIDESHOWS — ICE CREAM — LEMONADE

Teas and Refreshments in large Marquee situated behind the hut.

2-00 p.m. PROCESSION leaves Church Road, via Allerton Road, Kings Drive, Hunt's Cross Avenue; returning to the Church Field.
Led by the Band of the Cheshire Yeomanry.
Street Collection by the Youth Club during the procession.

3-00 p.m. CROWNING OF THE ROSE QUEEN (Miss Sally Wright) by Mrs. THELWALL JONES.

3-10 p.m. FANCY DRESS PARADE.
Class 1. Under 7 years.
Class 2. 7 to 12 years.
Class 3. Over 12 years.
Entrants to report to Miss P. Fuller at the Church Hall before the procession.

3-30 p.m. to 5-00 p.m. MUSICAL SELECTIONS by the Band of the Cheshire (Earl of Chester) Yeomanry. Bandmaster: H. Abraham.
(By permission of Lt.-Col. G. C. V. Churton, M.C., M.B.E.).

4-15 p.m. THE QUARRY MEN SKIFFLE GROUP.

5-15 p.m. DISPLAY by the City of Liverpool Police Dogs. By kind permission of the Chief Constable and Watch Committee.

5-45 p.m. THE QUARRY MEN SKIFFLE GROUP.

8-0 p.m. GRAND DANCE in the CHURCH HALL

GEORGE EDWARDS BAND also *The Quarry Men Skiffle Group*

TICKETS 2/-

REFRESHMENTS AT MODERATE PRICES.

The inner sheet of the programme for the garden fete

On the day of the Woolton Fete – Saturday 6th July – there were at least four other fetes taking place fairly locally including one at Quarry Bank High School itself which was opened by the chairman of the Education Committee, Councillor Mrs. Wormald. Not exactly a big draw loaded with the 'wow' factor. Indeed none of the other fetes were as big or promised as much fun as St. Peter's. Certainly, none of them promised anything as radical as a skiffle group.

"We were all Wooltonians – Len was only a bike ride away – and events like this were happening all around us. They were a big summer attraction and fun to attend. Among the attractions would be musical acts and so it was that the Quarry Men found themselves performing alongside the Band of the Cheshire Yeomanry who had also been invited to play at St. Peter's Church Garden Fete on Saturday 6th, July, 1957. In the evening St. Peter's followed up with a Grand Dance in the Church Hall featuring the George Edwards' Band and yet again – us, The Quarry Men!"

As little boys John, Rod and Pete had all attended services and Sunday School at St. Peter's in Woolton. John had even sung in the church choir. Now as teenagers most of them were members of St. Peter's Church Youth Club. Pete's mum, Bessie, was a member of the Church Committee who organised the fete. It was a very big event in the village involving rose queens, coronations, processions through the village, side shows, events, displays and a variety of entertainment, all of which was rounded off in the evening with a grand dance in the church hall across the road from the church itself. It took a lot of organisation and local businesses were always supportive – local merchants would lend their lorries for use in the parade. Local scout and guide troops, local Mothers' Union and marching bands would be involved.

"A skiffle band playing a church fete was a bit unusual but we had inside help in getting the booking. Pete's mum had the bright idea of suggesting

The Quarry Men to the fete's committee. The committee, the rector and Jack Gibbons who ran the youth club were persuaded and so we were set to play three times: twice in the afternoon on the church field during the fete itself and once in the evening at the grand dance."

The fete gave the boys in the group something special to look forward to as well as being a star turn on their own patch.

"We were very excited about it – it was a chance to perform and show off in front of family, friends and the people from the village. As everyone would know us it would be a less threatening atmosphere than Rosebery Street. And – we could enjoy ourselves into the bargain: there were lots of sidestalls involving games of chance or opportunities to win prizes by showing off your skills, throwing things like darts or balls. Most importantly it offered us the chance to meet girls.

Amazingly, I don't remember any specific rehearsals ahead of the day – there's no doubt we would have agreed to just play our regular set; in any case it was being held on our regular rehearsal day. By then we had started – at John's behest – to include some rock 'n' roll songs in our set such as 'Baby, Let's Play House' by Elvis. I think on the day of the fete we unveiled 'Be Bop a Lula', so we must have done some rehearsing, it was certainly a great favourite of John's that he would just spontaneously sing in front of us as he did with a lot of songs when we were sitting around at rehearsals or just talking among ourselves. He himself said it was on that day that he performed 'Be Bop a Lula' for the first time in public. That was how it worked in The Quarry Men: John sang, he chose the songs and we just tagged along. From the outset he led, we followed."

Colin can't remember if he wore his fluorescent socks on that particular day but he did take care with his appearance: after all, girls were on the horizon. Time to look sharp!

"When the day arrived I woke up feeling excited. I remember dressing up a bit for the occasion: a light grey suit and a white shirt – far out! Casual clothes

Single label for 'Be-Bop-a-Lula'/Gene Vincent

weren't quite the norm in those days. So a suit it was, but not one like my father would wear. I abandoned my tie on that occasion and wore my shirt open-necked. Later, during the parade, I also jettisoned my jacket and rolled up my sleeves because it was so hot and humid. Eric, Rod and Pete also turned up in white open necked shirts while John and Len wore their Rosebery Street Julia-bought checked shirts: ever the rebels!"

At 2 p.m. a parade was scheduled to precede the Fete which meant a reasonably early start for The Quarry Men. John arrived having had 'words' with Mimi. On leaving 'Mendips', she saw how he was dressed for the occasion. It was all a bit too Teddy Boy for her.

"Not long after my breakfast I got my drum kit together and walked up to where we were all assembled in the scout hut that was situated on the church field behind the church itself. It was about midday because ahead of the fete (and our performances on the church field) there was a parade around the village. The idea was we would perform sitting on the back of a lorry. Once Woolton's finest were all assembled aboard the convoy of trucks the grand parade set off from in front of St. Peter's on Church Road to follow a circular route around the village back to the church. After unpacking my kit I left my suitcase in the hut and along with the other lads boarded the lorry."

Spirits were high.

"We were all excited, our regular banter hiding whatever nerves we had. I can't remember what was actually said but as at the Carroll Levis auditions we were full of it: laughing and joking. After all this was home turf, because of work and family commitments our parents wouldn't be coming to some of the venues we hoped to play in the future, (such as The Cavern or the Wilson Hall) but they could come and hear us at the fete because it was a weekend afternoon, a family occasion and so their presence added to our sense of anticipation. John's mum and his sisters, his Aunt Mimi and cousins David and Michael would be there so, he was rocking – if not a tad anxious about Mimi's reaction to actually hearing and seeing him perform on stage."

The journey around the village proved to be an anti-climax.

"We began at full throttle but soon realised that as we were moving people would only catch a snippet of each song and of course we had an engine to compete with. Added to that it was not easy on a moving vehicle to play guitars, banjo and tea-chest bass whilst standing up as Len had to do and which John preferred. Swaying with the motion of the vehicle made them unsteady and it was a bit dangerous because there were no sides on the lorry to stop us falling off, so John just sat down – I clearly remember him saying, 'This is a waste of time…' Even so when we sat down we did keep going a bit for our own amusement – Len, Rod, Eric and I kept on playing and John would sing occasionally. In a photo taken by Rod's Dad on the day, we can be seen sitting on the lorry as we were driven down Kings Drive. It clearly shows John is singing. He's got his eyes closed and is concentrating. I have my left hand on the cymbal, which is what I would do to simulate a hi-hat. I would tap the cymbal and pinch it with my thumb and forefinger to shorten the reverberations, which produced the same sound as if I was hitting a hi-hat."

Once the lorries assembled back on Church Road outside St.Peter's the group disembarked to walk up the church drive to the big field behind the church where the fete was all set up ready to go after it was opened at 3 p.m. by Dr. Thelwall Jones.

"We walked over the field back to the scout hut on the opposite side to park our kit ahead of our performance on the field. I put my drums and jacket down and then all of us in the group went out to enjoy the attractions of the Fete: hoopla, hammering a nail into a very hard ('seasoned') piece of wood – which none of us could, a coconut shy, dropping pennies into a bucket of water hoping they'd cover the half crown (old money) at the bottom, throwing darts at cards and so on – all very typical garden fete attractions in those days. The scouts had built a zip wire along the quarry side of the church field but whilst we admired this I can't remember any of us trying it.

After a while we split up agreeing to meet back at the hut ahead of our scheduled appearance. I went back to the hut where I sat playing on my snare

The Quarry Men sitting on the back of the lorry as they travel around Woolton as part of the procession that preceded the fete, 6th July 1957.

drum. A scout was in there playing his bugle and so I rattled out a march rhythm to accompany him. These days they'd say we were 'jamming'.

Not long after, at the far end of the hut, I noticed John had returned by himself (I assumed the others Pete, Rod, Eric and Len had stayed behind playing the attractions). He was standing talking to another scout. It was at this moment that Ivan Vaughan walked in accompanied by this dark-haired lad whom I'd never seen before. I carried on jamming while the three of them stood talking. This carried on for about five or ten minutes after which John, Ivy and the stranger left the scout hut together."

Unaware – how could he be anything else at the time – that the boy whom Ivan has just introduced to John was Paul McCartney – Colin carried on regardless, jamming away until the other lads (including John) began drifting back to the hut.

"They arrived to collect their instruments before we made our way over to where we were going to perform on a low concrete permanent stage that had been built years earlier near the entrance to the church field. As we walked towards the stage we were all so focused on our performance and the activity of the fair going on around us that neither John nor I never mentioned the meeting with Ivan and his mystery companion.

We had been scheduled to perform twice that afternoon: once at 4.15 and again at 5.45 but events had overrun so in the end we only played once sometime around five-fifteen or just after. We played for about thirty-five minutes, which, in those days, was the regular length of a Quarry Men performance. After that we would run out of material. We were the last scheduled 'event' of the afternoon and so I can remember that as we played folks were walking past us on their way out and away from the fete, which was beginning to shut down. It was mostly the younger folks and children who'd lingered to watch us and some of them were climbing all over the stage. You can see this in the famous photograph Geoff Rhind – a friend of John, Pete and Rod's at Quarry Bank School – had taken. John's Aunt Mimi, his mum, sisters and assorted cousins were looking on, as was Ive Vaughan and his friend, all part of the audience who'd gathered to watch us."

Aged just fifteen at the time, Paul and Ivan were good friends from school, The Liverpool Institute High School For Boys on Mount Street in Liverpool 8, which stood almost in the shadows of Liverpool's magnificent Anglican cathedral. As Paul himself recalls Ivan had invited him to accompany him to the fete specifically to meet John.

> **Paul**: *"Ivan or 'Ive' as we called him came from Woolton. He was born on June 18th 1942, exactly the same day as me so we became great mates at school even though we weren't in the same class. He'd told me he had a mate in Woolton called John who played guitar. Knowing I liked rock 'n' roll and played guitar Ive said, 'You'd like John, he's great'. He then told me there was going to be a garden fete in Woolton featuring John's group and would I like to come. I said yes... the idea was I would see John and his band and that he, Ive, would introduce me and we would hang out. Ive had even been in their skiffle band. He'd played tea-chest bass: 'Jive with Ive, the ace on bass', that's what was painted on it."*
>
> *(The Day John Met Paul, BBC Radio 2, 2007; Bob Harris interview.)*

Paul has also commented that Ivan had mentioned that the fete was *"a good place to meet girls"*: another compelling reason to attend when you are just fifteen and the mysteries of life – especially girls – are irresistibly revealing themselves to you (or you hope they will).

Colin's memory of John standing talking to Paul and Ivan in the scout hut is not how the very first meeting between these two budding popular musical geniuses is usually depicted. The usual version of events as told – by others who were there, and by others who were not, plus countless commentators, authors, documentaries and biopic films about the early days of John and The Beatles — has Ivan and Paul arriving together at the fete

Ivan Vaughan, The Ace on the Bass

(sometime after it has begun), and almost immediately walking onto the church field where they see and hear The Quarry Men, who are already on stage playing.

Paul is described as having his hair slicked up into his best Elvis quiff and dressed to impress in tight black trousers or 'drainies' (drainpipes) and a white sports coat – in the weave of which there is a metallic thread that sparkled in the sunlight. He's dressed *a la* a hit song of the summer – 'A White Sports Coat' – which charted for both the King Brothers (number 6 in late May) and Terry Dene (number 18 in early June): he would have looked very trendy for the times.

After this historic first encounter with the boy whose talent will bond with his to become the creative hub of the greatest band in popular music, Paul accompanied Ivan to listen to the group perform on the church field before going into the church hall, where he will be more 'formally' introduced to a few other – but not all – Quarry Men.

> **Paul**: *"I remember clearly coming into this field where the fete was, going past the usual stalls – hoopla and then just over the edge of the field there was a stage and there was a band up there and they were playing 'Come Go With Me' which I knew as a song by the Del-Vikings. I don't remember the fete being packed, just little groups wandering here and there, trying this and that. There was a small group as I recall around the band. I remember it being a lovely sunny day and enjoying myself generally but mainly thinking this is a good little band and that singer's good."*
>
> *(The Day John Met Paul, BBC R2, 2007; Bob Harris interview.)*

At the top of the drive that ran alongside the church lay the church field itself. It was here that the attractions of the fete were situated. On the main body of the field there was a large open area on which the police dogs would perform. The oblong concrete stage where

The Quarry Men were due to perform was close to the entrance/exit to the field. Paul's memory suggests he and Ivan had arrived before it had begun to pack away and had wandered around the fete to check out what was going on and enjoy themselves on some of the stalls while checking out the girls who were around. This supports Colin's memory that he and Ivan visited the scout hut to see John before they listened to The Quarry Men in performance.

In Geoff Rhind's superb and very famous photograph of John, Colin, Eric, Len, Pete and Rod taken as they played on the small stage, unfortunately Paul in his trendy white sport coat was not caught in the frame. Just how he would have looked is captured in a photo taken by his brother Mike later that summer in August on the beach when they were holidaying at Filey, Yorkshire. In the snap Paul is wearing a white sports coat – most likely the very same one he describes wearing to the fete, his hair is Elvised into a quiff as he sits on a metal push chair belonging to his young cousin Ted. In Mike's photo Paul is strumming his brand new Zenith guitar. Cousin Ted is also in the picture, enjoying an ice cream cone while his mum, Bett, looks on. Bett's husband, Mike Robbins, was a Red Coat at Butlin's Holiday Camp where Paul and Mike stayed later that summer with their father, Jim.

Colin's abiding memory of that very brief pre-performance meeting in the scout hut between John, Ivan and Paul has been generally overlooked. Even by Paul and of course, none of the other Quarry Men were present to remember/witness it and sadly Ivan passed away in 1993. It's a memory not so much written out of history as sidelined for Colin has mentioned it to several other writers.

In Geoff's famous black and white photograph of The Quarry Men singing and playing that afternoon, John is wearing the red checked shirt his mum had bought for him for his Rosebery Street performance; alongside him there are some youngsters sitting on the lip of the platform, others standing on stage. John is looking directly at the camera, singing. Of the dozen or so tunes they

Saturday 6th July 1957: Geoff Rhind's photo of The Quarry Men,
St. Peter's Church Fete, Woolton

performed that afternoon it was, as Paul says, 'Come Go with Me' by the Del-Vikings, a song he already knew and liked, which caught his attention as he watched the group and listened to them play. Paul enjoyed it not just because of the way John sang but also because John was not singing the correct words.

> **Paul**: *"He was making them up. He was singing 'Come, come, come go with me down to the penitentiary' – I thought they're kind of bluesy but they're not the words. But that is enterprising. That was my first introduction to seeing them (The Quarry Men), liking them as a band and liking John's ingenuity, liking his voice and his stage presence."*
>
> *(The Day John Met Paul, BBC R2, 2007; Bob Harris interview.)*

What is not in doubt is that The Quarry Men's performance came towards the end of the afternoon's activities. As Paul remembers, he watched the rest of the set with Ive *"and that was the end of the fete"*, after which there was an interval before The Quarry Men played later in the evening in the church hall.

What is also not in doubt is that Paul's personal introduction to the Quarry Men as a group (or those of whom were around at the time) and not just to John came *after* the performance on the church field, by which time along with their equipment they had repaired to the church hall across the road ahead of their evening performance. Paul describes the meeting as very low key, which it was.

> **Paul**: *"We went up, sort of 'backstage' at the church hall where there was an old piano. A couple of the guys had their guitars and things and we just hung out for a bit, Ive introduced me to John."*
>
> *(The Day John Met Paul, BBC R2, 2007; Bob Harris interview.)*

On that day Paul impressed all those who actually witnessed the moment in the church hall when he borrowed a guitar and played a song.

> **Paul**: *"One of the guys had a guitar – it could've been John's – which I borrowed and because I was left-handed I had to turn it upside down. Nobody would ever let me change the strings around because they'd have to take them off and screw around with that and then they'd have to put them back so they're not going to allow me to do that. All my mates (like Ian James, George Harrison) were right handed so I'd learned to play – just about – upside down. And the song I could do was 'Twenty Flight Rock' by Eddie Cochran. I remember John being very impressed – I think mainly because I knew the words – that was like the currency in those days. It wasn't so much how you sang but it was 'he knows all the words!' So that was impressive and I was kind of 'in' the group now – not literally, but in spirit – I was included in the crowd now."*
>
> *(The Day John Met Paul, BBC R2, 2007; Bob Harris interview.)*

Up to now Paul had – by his own admission – felt intimidated by being younger than the other Quarry Men, the 'wrong side of the cusp' while the lads in The Quarry Men were the right side of it.

Without it being specifically stated as such at the time, 'Twenty Flight Rock' proved to be the audition/initiation with which Paul McCartney entered The Quarry Men's inner circle, where, particularly for its leader, a devotion to rock 'n' roll music was key. Paul could not have chosen a better song to sing. 'Twenty Flight Rock' would have grabbed John's attention immediately. It was an Eddie Cochran tune that he'd performed in a stand-out scene in the newly released rock 'n' roll film 'The Girl Can't Help It'. John had seen the film and the song was a

Single label for '20 Flight Rock'

favourite of his and he admired Cochran, so for Paul to know it would have been proof that he was a kindred spirit, a true soul brother.

> *As* **Pete Shotton** *observed: "After effortlessly serenading us with Eddie Cochran's 'Twenty Flight Rock' – which we'd thought too difficult for our band to even attempt – Paul further ingratiated himself by writing out from memory the complete lyrics to some of John's favourite rock 'n' roll numbers."*
>
> *('John Lennon In My Life', Shotton and Schaffner, p,55.)*

Paul could now relax a little, the difference in age less of an issue: he'd proved himself a fan, he'd proved himself worthy.

Paul had also realised he'd seen John before – on the 'bus one time where John had grabbed Paul's attention by being decked out in full Teddy Boy garb, which had equally ensured Paul had kept his distance and his head down so John would not notice him. Teddy Boys could be trouble: you didn't stare at them, however much you were tempted to do so. Little would Paul have realised that, without his spectacles, as he would have been in public in those days, John would not have known or noticed who or what was around him.

In the first volume of his peerless Beatles biography *Tune In*, on p.130, the world's leading authority on The Beatles, Mark Lewisohn, notes that Paul has said that on an earlier occasion – not long after he and his family moved in to 20 Forthlin Road, Allerton, in late April 1956 – he had also exchanged a few words with John outside a newsagent's on Aigburth Road, where Paul had a paper round. But seeing someone on a 'bus or exchanging a few words outside a shop barely counts as a formal 'introduction' so history seems secure in claiming 6th July 1957 as the day John truly met Paul when their mutual friend Ivan Vaughan brought Paul to the Woolton fete to check out his friends' group: this was the day they truly connected.

Having grabbed The Quarry Men's attention – particularly that of their leader, Paul's confidence was clearly 'up'. He'd seen and heard what they could do: time now to reciprocate.

> **Paul**: *"So then I started messing around on the piano: I knew a bit of 'Whole Lot of Shakin' Goin' On' by Jerry Lee Lewis so I started playing that. I remember John leaning over my shoulder. I remember his beery breath – I thought dear me, the state of him. Anyway I liked him a lot... he's a very witty guy, a big friend of Ivan's and obviously the leading force in this group. So I was impressed with him... and being one and a half years younger than him, at that age (I was fifteen, John was sixteen nearly seventeen) that's a big difference. I saw them in the evening and again they were good, a good band and again I was particularly impressed with John."*
>
> *(The Day John Met Paul, BBC R2, 2007; Bob Harris interview.)*

As for 'Whole Lot of Shakin' Goin' On', it finally hit the UK charts in September (climbing to number 8) although it had been released much earlier in April that year.

At the drop of a hat Paul could also sing and play Little Richard's 'Long Tall Sally', consequently he dropped a lot of hats in those days: in several accounts of that momentous afternoon he's mentioned playing 'Long Tall Sally' to the assembled Quarry Men.

The choice of Little Richard would have been hugely impressive for John Lennon to hear, even more so than 'Twenty Flight Rock'. Indeed Paul could not have chosen anything more incendiary to perform; it would surely have stopped John Lennon in his teenage tracks. Not only could Paul play and sing 'Long Tall Sally': he had that wild Little Richard vocal off to a tee.

As Nik Cohn wrote on page 32 his brilliant rock 'n' roll biography of 1969, 'AwopbopaloobopIopbamboom': Richard *"had a freak voice, tireless, hysterical, completely indestructible, and he never in his life sang at anything lower than an enraged bull-like roar."*

Hearing a kid from just a mile down the hill in Allerton who could replicate Little Richard – with all the vocal tics in place – would have been a seriously mind-blowing moment for John for, as he told music writer Ray Coleman in 1962, hearing Lonnie Donegan and Elvis for the first time in 1956 had already been life-changing moments in his life. Hearing Little Richard had been almost too much for him to to take.

> **John**: *"This boy at school, Mike Hill, had been to Holland and said he had this record at home by somebody who was better than Elvis. Elvis was bigger than religion in my life. We used to go to this boy's house and listen to Elvis on 78s. The new record was 'Long Tall Sally' (b-side, 'Slippin' and Slidin'). When I heard it, it was so great I couldn't speak. You know you are torn. I didn't want to leave Elvis. We all looked at each other, but I didn't want to say anything against Elvis, not even in my mind. How could they be happening in my life, both of them?"*
>
> *(John Lennon 1940–1980, Ray Connolly.)*

There could have been few times in John Lennon's life when he was rendered speechless but the impact of hearing Little Richard for the very first time was surely one of them. Presley, Donegan and Little Richard had so touched him he had discovered what he wanted to do with his life. He wanted to make music, to play rock 'n' roll. On hearing Paul he must have known intuitively he had met the person who could help him make this dream a reality.

Returning to Planet Earth, however, Colin has no memory of of Ivan introducing Paul to the group in the Church Hall or of Paul performing any songs because he wasn't there. He remembers taking his drums into the church hall and putting them in the room to the side of the stage but little else after that. That he can't is because he did not witness it.

"I wasn't there because ahead of The Quarry Men's evening performance I'd gone home for a bite to eat. I only lived a ten minute walk away and hadn't eaten since breakfast, so after coming off the church field and putting my kit in place ready for the evening's performance I'd nipped home for my tea and in the process I missed that historic audition."

He's not the only one for whom the historic moment did not register. Fellow Quarry Man Rod Davis also has no recall of that meeting.

> **Rod***: "Perhaps I paid a visit to the toilet because I have no memory of the greatest meeting in rock 'n' roll history."*
>
> *(The Quarrymen, Davies, p.59.)*

Neither did Eric Griffiths! Eric said he had no memory of Paul playing a guitar to the group at the fete – he thought he must have gone home for his tea during the interval.

> **Eric***: "I noticed Paul while we were playing. He was standing with Ivan… I can't remember him carrying a guitar."*
>
> *(The Quarrymen, Davies, p.58.)*

Eric recalls hearing Paul play guitar and sing for the first time at a later date when he and John visited Paul at his house

Pete Shotton, Len Garry, John Lennon, Paul McCartney and Ivan Vaughan were undoubtedly there, all eye witnesses to Paul's 'audition'.

These days it would be so easy for Colin and Rod to just go along with the story and say they remember Paul's singing and playing in the church hall but such is their honesty they will only say what they definitely remember as eye witnesses. Time has not persuaded them to do otherwise, so good on them. But it is a reminder that this event happened over sixty years ago and at the time Paul was introduced it was nothing very special in their lives. Like most bands they met a lot of new people every time they were booked to play. Often there'd be a lot of people hanging out with them before or after a perfomance. No wonder that in the interim exact memories faded, details disappeared. It would be many years after the event that The Quarry Men would be asked to describe this day in the forensic detail people now want from them. Therefore, pinning down exactly what did happen can never be an exact science.

Consequently The Quarry Men do not share a collectively rock-solid memory of the afternoon. They were not all present in the same places for some of the key moments. At the time it was a fun day but of no great significance to most of them beyond the moment of their performance; they were young lads who had other things on their mind: summer holidays, exam results, Sixth Form, careers, futures, work, girls… They were teenage lads out for some fun, maybe a date (or even more) and since that afternoon much time has flown under that particular bridge.

By the time the significance of it had dawned on everybody and all of the original Quarry Men were asked about it, lives had diverged, heads filled up with lots more personal memories, many other lifetimes lived, The Beatles had been, come and gone.

In the intervening years scant attention was paid to the day John met Paul. Early biographies of The Beatles got the date wrong: even the one and only, much-vaunted source of eye-witness memories, Hunter Davies's marvellous 'Authorised Biography' of 'The Beatles', published only eleven years after the event in 1968 stated the garden fete where John met Paul took place on 15th June 1956. A 1964 paperback biography entitled 'The True Story of The Beatles' by Billy Shepherd published by Beat Publications (who published The Beatles Book Monthly and consequently had direct access to the group), which sported many, many 'quotations' from John, Paul, George and Ringo, dated the fete as taking place on 15th June 1955, two years and a month earlier than it did!

So memories and details have fluctuated over the years as everyone has tried to recall what they'd long ago consigned to the back of their minds – or simply forgotten. Only a week after the event itself, on 11th July 1957, the *Liverpool Weekly News* published a feature article on the fete entitled 'All the Fun of the Fair at Woolton', which commented on The Quarry Men's performance and remarked on their earlier appearance in the Carroll Levis Discoveries. Surely, it would seem, this has to be considered a 100% accurate 'eye-witness' account. Not so – for while it named the members of the group it specifically noted 'Colin Hanton who is the drummer did not appear on the Saturday'. Oh really? Take a look at Geoff Rhind's photo!

So if, within a week of the event, history is being reported inaccurately what hope forty, fifty, sixty years later?

Moving beyond the events of that late afternoon meeting to their evening performance Colin recalls returning from home to the church hall to find it packed full of lads (many of whom were friends of the group) and lots of girls.

"The place was buzzing!"

Somewhere in that audience were Ivan and Paul and another lad called Bob Molyneux. Bob recalled that he turned up with his brand new Grundig tape recorder (the one with the flashing green eye!) to record the Quarry Men's performance. And this is something else of which Colin has no recollection. He doesn't remember Bob and his tape recorder on that particular occasion but says not long after the fete he remembers Bob turned up at a private function to record the group for what would have been a second time.

Bob was not the only one who recorded The Quarry Men. Colin's next door neighbour, a young girl called Geraldine Davies, recorded them in rehearsal at Colin's on her Grundig. Frustratingly, on discovering her old tapes years later, she found they had been taped over: such is life.

What Colin does remember is that almost before he could catch his breath he was on stage and The Quarry Men were rocking. He has a clear memory of the young people dancing in front of the group. While he does not wish to be pinned down to the exact repertoire they ran through that evening, for posterity's sake he has had a go.

"We would have played what by then was our usual set: 'Rock Island Line', 'Railroad Bill', 'Midnight Special', 'Cumberland Gap', 'Maggie May', 'Lost John', 'Come Go with Me, and of course the only songs surviving on Bob's tape (like Geraldine during the intervening years Bob taped over most of what he recorded that night and/or on the second occasion): 'Putting on the Style' and 'Baby, Let's Play House'. John himself said it was the day he first performed 'Be Bop a Lula' on stage and I have no reason to doubt that. We played two sets that day – one on the field, one in the hall. Len Garry has said over the two performances we played fourteen tunes and in his lists he includes 'All Shook Up', Blue Suede Shoes', 'Freight Train' and 'Hound Dog', which is quite a rocky set for a skiffle group.

A lot of the teenage girls who were there danced to the music but a lot of the boys just stood either at the front of the stage or down the side of the hall just watching us, taking it all in. Our music was new and very lively – we were not old-chaps-in-a-band churning out old standards, we weren't playing mums' and dads' music: this was something unique. Something different that connected directly to those kids in our audiences. They were really into it."

The gig in the church hall was, of course, acoustic.

"What is often lost on people is that The Quarry Men and most every skiffle group would be acoustic, unplugged, no electric guitars, no amplification. And of course, in those days we went to all our gigs on the 'bus – we carried all our own instruments everywhere. We would have to play above the noise of the crowd although most audiences were interested in watching and listening more than they do at rock music gigs today and so it may not have been quite

so noisy to play over. The singer might not even have a microphone – John certainly didn't when we played dances at St. Peter's Youth Club. So our focus was on playing loud and emphasising the rhythm – no one would attempt to play lead guitar because no-one would have heard them. On this occasion however John was singing through a microphone because the band on after us – the George Edwards Band – was a dance band who had a microphone of their own which they allowed us to use."

Prior to their evening performance a friend of Colin's, a boy called Peter Ashton (his parents owned a grocer's shop in Woolton), had tried to persuade Colin to play a drum solo with the promise that: *"If you play a drum solo I'm convinced you could have the pick of any of the girls here tonight."* Modesty prevailed and Colin refrained from testing Peter's theory – although he says he was tempted.

Later, not long after the fete, Colin recalls a couple of occasions when standing at the 'bus stop on Kings Drive some girls walking by on the other side called across to him: 'Hi Gene!' a reference to world famous drummer Gene Krupa – Colin's hero of course and proof he had been noticed that night at the grand dance. Now he had his own fans! Fame at last!

On the night itself almost as soon as The Quarry Men finished their set and left the stage Colin says he split.

"I just packed up my drums and headed home. I didn't hang around. The drums were a bit of a pain when it came to joining in any 'after show' activities. I had to get them home safe and sound. That was my priority. I didn't go on anywhere with the others – in fact I can't remember anyone going anywhere that night, at least – no one mentioned anything to me."

And so ended the day for Colin. As he or any of the boys in The Quarry Men fell to sleep that night he could have had no idea just what repercussions that day would have on his life or on John and Paul's lives, on the story of popular music and the world in general: who possibly could?

Colin also has no memory of a story that is occasionally told of all the boys including Paul and Ivan repairing to a local pub and then fleeing for their lives when news reached them of a rival gang headed their way looking for some trouble. Come to that he doesn't remember John or any of them having any beer that afternoon – although Paul usually comments that he could smell beer on John's breath, as he famously did in his 'Introduction' to John's first book *In His Own Write* published by Jonathan Cape in 1964.

Such is the stuff of memories: no wonder the truth is so hard to pin down. We all blink, but not at the same time, so we all miss something someone else saw (or says they did).

ENDNOTES

Tea-Chest Bass

The tea-chest bass is a UK variation on the American washtub bass often used in jug bands. It's a home-made instrument that originally used a washtub as a resonator. In the UK during the skiffle craze of the Fifties the washtub was replaced by a tea chest into which a broomstick would be placed, from the top of which a string would be stretched and attached to the tea chest and plucked.

Redcoats

Holiday camps were very popular holiday destinations for working class British holiday makers in the 1950s and beyond. Butlins and Pontins were two such popular chains of camps. At Butlins 'Redcoats' were staff who engaged directly with guests as adult or child entertainers or stewards. The cheerful redcoats they wore made them easily recognisable. Many went on to be popular entertainers of the day. Butlins and the Redcoats are still going strong to this day.

LIVERPOOL

Plans for The Show are being rapidly finalised

A FREE Continental holiday, a cash prize of £50, a 20-guinea mannequin course, and a handsome silver cup valued at £100 . . . Sounds like a dream? It isn't. Those are some of the prizes for the girl lucky enough to be chosen Miss Liverpool, 1957. Vital statistics and a pretty face are not enough in this competition. A panel of experts, including TV personality Jerry Desmonde, will be looking for a girl who combines an attractive appearance with an intelligent and pleasing personality.

The personality girl will be chosen next week on the last day of the Liverpool Show which opens on Saturday.

To be eligible for the competition, a girl must be over 16 years of age.

At the Liverpool Show office this week an official told the Weekly News that entries for the competition were continuing to come in, but will be closed on Saturday.

Many of those who have been successful in preliminary heats come from the south end of the city which certainly has its fair share of pretty girls. Their occupations? Nurse, shorthand typist, clerk, schoolteacher, hosiery repairer and housewife.

The girls? Theodora Ann Corton, of 8 Green Lane, Allerton (schoolteacher); Bernadette Cuerdon, of 7 Belle Vue Road, Gateacre (hosiery repairer); Jean Learney, of 29 Ridgeway Road, Wavertree (housewife); Teresa O'Hara, of Greenheys Road, Liverpool 8 (shorthand typist); Patricia Sloane, of 7 Salisbury Road, Wavertree (clerk); Joyce M. Bain, 33 Woodend Lane, Speke (shorthand typist); Barbara Birtles, 15 Childwall Crescent, Childwall (student nurse).

MORE ATTRACTIONS

The Personality Girl contest is by no means the only attraction at the Liverpool Show which is designed to bring the country to the city. At a Press conference on Monday, Mr. C. T. Colvin (assistant show secretary) said that because Liverpool was an industrial and shipping centre it was sometimes difficult to attract people to a show so closely connected with agriculture.

However, the emphasis is not only on agriculture. There is a full programme of entertainment. Most popular is the show jumping which has attracted enough competitions to warrant a five-day show. To solve some of the problems of stabling, 80 temporary stables have been erected on the show ground.

Among the well-known personalities who will be seen in this section are Wilfred White, Ted Williams, last year's Show Jumper of the Year, and John Lanni, the international rider.

Alderman J. L. Hughes, deputy chairman of the Horticultural (Special) Committee, who presided at the Press conference in the absence of Alderman Griffin, said cash prizes amounting to £7,500 would be competed for at the show.

The number of trade exhibitors who have taken stands at the showground is a record and one third higher than last year. Particular emphasis in this section is on domestic appliances which should be of great interest to the housewife interested in cutting chores to a minimum.

The floral marquee—always an outstanding feature—covers about 30 acres, nearly half of the showground area and will be under canvas.

There has been increased interest from local schoolchildren in the special section of the flower show reserved for them and there have been double the usual number of applications for entry forms from youngsters and schoolteachers in primary and secondary modern schools. Other favourite sections of the show with the children will be the competitions for the best ticket.

Since the show started in 1949 the attendance figure has doubled itself and last year, which was not particularly favoured with good weather saw 53,000 Merseysiders pass through the turnstiles. Last year's loss of £9,283—the lowest ever—will be considerably reduced if residents take advantage of a show which has something for every member of the family. It is estimated that the show will cost £23,000, and whole-hearted support from Merseyside residents could ensure that there is no deficit.

COMMITTEE

Tremendous organisation is involved in running a show of this kind. Some indication of this was given by Mr. P. W. H. Conn, Chief Parks Superintendent, who said that five miles of electricity cable and three quarters of a mile of water piping had already been laid on the show ground.

In addition all the committees of the Liverpool Corporation are to provide exhibits. For example, the Public Health Department has three exhibits showing: 1. The progress being made in dealing with infectious diseases; 2. Hygiene in the home; and 3. Model milk testing.

The Water Committee's section which will include a display of articles made from the timber at Lake Vyrnwy will also incorporate a children's play corner.

Last word on the Liverpool Show which promises, given the right kind of weather, to be the most successful ever, comes from Mr Colvin: "This will be a show for Mr. Merseyside, his wife and his youngsters. It has been the committee's policy this year more than ever to provide something of interest for every member of the family. The 1957 Liverpool Show will be unique. It will have more variety and interest than any other show on Merseyside or South West Lancashire has ever had.

ALL THE FUN OF THE FAIR AT WOOLTON

Gatekeeper Mr. John Moore and his assistant, Mr. Tuskley, were kept extremely busy at the annual garden fete of St. Peter's Church, Woolton, on Saturday. Hundreds of people passed through the gates into the church field to see the crowning of this year's Rose Queen, Miss Sally Wright.

Sally and her retinue, and the retiring queen, Miss Susan Dixon, arrived on decorated lorries, accompanied by children in fancy dress, Girl Guides, Boy Scouts, Brownies and Cubs, members of the Discoverers, the Youth Club and the popular Quarry Men Skiffle Group.

The procession, headed by the band of the Cheshire (Earl of Chester) Yeomanry, made its way from Church Road, along Allerton Road, King's Drive, Hunts Cross Avenue, and back to the church field for the crowning.

The Rev. M. Pryce Jones (rector) conducted prayers, and then Mrs. Thelwall Jones performed the crowning ceremony. Fair-haired 13-years-old Sally looked charming in her gown of white lace with a flowing train of pink velvet.

After a bouquet had been presented to Mrs. Thelwall Jones by Felicity Clegg, Mr. Thelwall Jones declared the fete open.

The queen's retinue included Jane Cuthbertson, Elizabeth Metcalfe, Elizabeth Rimmer, Jennifer Jones, Ann Dowell and Joyce Wright, who is the new queen's sister. The crown bearer was Harold Earp.

The retiring queen, 14-years-old Susan Dixon, was accompanied by her attendants, Marian Dobson, Edna Ward, Beryl Goodwin, Rosemary Ashton, Mary Gee and Pat Mason. Other small attendants were Pamela Cottrell, Alison Millett, Elizabeth Thompson and Anne Burgess. Soldiers were Anthony Pietka, Dennis Sowler, James Sowler, John Radford, Christopher Jones, Kenneth Edge, Brian Hall and John Dennis. The retinues were arranged by Mrs. O. Holdsworth, Mrs. A. Clegg, Mrs. C. E. Chappelle and Mrs. M. Ross.

After the crowning, the fancy dress competition was judged by Mr. and Mrs. Thelwall Jones. There were three groups in the competition, and all had quite good numbers of entries.

Many of the visitors were attracted by the balloon stall, where they could send up a hydrogen-filled balloon with their names and address attached. The sender of the balloon which is returned from the furthest place will receive a prize. A special children's attraction was the aerial car set up by the Scouts, and until early in the evening the children were queueing for rides.

Always a popular feature is a display by the dogs of the Liverpool City Police, and the people of Woolton showed their appreciation of the demonstrations by the dogs of obedience training and obstacle training.

Throughout the afternoon, musical selections were provided by the Band of the Cheshire (Earl of Chester) Yeomanry under their bandmaster, H. Abraham.

An entirely different type of music was provided by the "Quarry Men Skiffle Group." These five boys are members of the youth club, and some of them are pupils of Quarry Bank High School. Recently they appeared in the Carroll Levis Discoveries show at a Liverpool theatre, but unfortunately did not quite qualify for the finals. They are John Lennon, who plays the guitar and is the popular vocalist, Peter Shotton (washboard), Eric Griffiths (guitar), Len Garry (bass) and Rodney Davis (banjo). Colin Hanton, who is the drummer, did not appear on Saturday. Their songs included "Cumberland Gap," "Maggie May" and "Railroad Bill."

THE ORGANISATION

The organisation of the fete was largely in the hands of the committee, Mr. H. T. Forrest (chairman), Mr. H. Hilditch (secretary), Mr. H. P. Johnson (treasurer), Mr. F. J. Benson (sideshows), Miss A. Jackson (refreshments), Mr. H. L. Mercer (publicity) and Mr. H. Tambling (Sunday school).

Music for a dance in the evening was provided by the George Edwards Band and the Quarry Men Skiffle Group. Proceeds of the whole afternoon reached about £350 net and are to go to church funds.

Stalls and stallholders included: Hardware: scouts and cubs; general: Day School; flowers: Miss Leather and Mrs. Glynn Morris; fruit and vegetables: Brigadier and Mrs. Phelps and Mr and Mrs. Dwyer; sweets: brownies; biscuits: girl guides; groceries: Sunday school teachers; lemonade: Sunday school teachers; cakes: committee and members of Adult Fellowship; bran tub: committee and members of Adult Fellowship; refreshments: Youth Club (Miss Jackson and helpers). Sideshows included: treasure hunt, bagatelle, egg hoop-la, darts, pin bagatelle, aunt Sally, quoits and shilling-in-the-bucket. They were arranged by the Adult Fellowship, the choir, the Youth Club and other organisations of the church.

LEATHER BELTS WRAPPED ROUND THEIR HANDS

"THE police at Garston are having great difficulty with gangs of youths coming from the Dingle area every night and causing a great deal of trouble in the Garston district," said Mr. J. W. Bonner, prosecuting at Liverpool City Magistrates' Court on Friday, when two youths appeared before the Stipendiary Magistrate (Mr. A. McFarland).

Leslie Bowden, 17-years-old baker of Toxteth Road, Liverpool, pleaded guilty to having an offensive weapon, namely a leather belt, in Speke Road, Garston, on July 4th.

Mr. Bonner said that Constable G. Barker saw Bowden with a number of other youths near Garston public baths causing a general disturbance.

Bowden wrapped round his hand a heavy leather belt which was fitted with metal studs, and when asked about it replied, "I have no excuse."

Bowden was fined £5 and the belt was ordered to be forfeited.

Robert Frederick Atherton, aged 17, trucker, of South Street, Liverpool, pleaded guilty to having an offensive weapon, namely a belt, in Speke Road, on July 4.

Mr Bonner said that Constable G. McGuffie and Sergeant Hindley saw Atherton among a group of 20 youths at the corner of Speke Road and Horrocks Avenue. He had a large Army type belt wrapped round his hand and was shouting "Come on lads, get started on them."

DETENTION CENTRE

As they saw the police approach they broke up and walked away. Atherton was stopped and was asked for an explanation regarding the belt, which was then fastened round his waist. Atherton said, "It is only holding my trousers up." Mr. Bonner added that Atherton had another belt underneath this one.

When questioned about this, Atherton replied, "It might break." Told he would be arrested he said, "For wearing two belts?"

Atherton was sent to a detention centre for three weeks.

Copy of a page from the *Liverpool Weekly News*, 11th July 1957. A long report about the fete including the first ever media mention of John Lennon performing in a group.

25

YOU SAY GOODBYE...

Paul McCartney may have entered the story at this point but back in July 1957 this did not immediately affect The Quarry Men in terms of adding to their on-stage personnel, rather their numbers reduced. Rod left the group: *'sort of drifted away'* is how he describes his departure.

Rod was possibly more of a musical purist than the other boys in the group. He loved blues and country music and what, today, would be called 'roots' music. Of all The Quarry Men he felt the most uncomfortable playing rock 'n' roll down The Cavern when they were not expected to. By definition The Cavern was a jazz club, newly opened, but on Wednesday nights it relaxed its jazz remit to host 'open mic' nights. On these occasions skiffle would be accomodated but it most definitely did not tolerate 'rock 'n' roll'!

As well as his banjo-playing skills Rod was also an 'A' student for whom a glittering academic future beckoned. Once the O-Level exam results arrived Rod found he had passed with flying colours and returned to Quarry Bank Sixth Form and A-Levels. As a sixth former with two friends, a drummer and pianist, himself on guitar he formed a jazz trio. He became head boy at Quarry Bank, passed his A-Levels and went to Cambridge University (which placed him at the top of the educational tree). Educationally Rod was a class act.

On the other hand John Lennon failed all his O-Level exams and had to leave school. Fortunately for him – and to Aunt Mimi's great relief – John's prowess in art secured him a place at Liverpool Art College, even though he had conspired to fail his O-Level Art. (At least he was consistent.)

As a consequence of all of this, change was in the air. Rod's days playing in a skiffle group were most probably numbered anyway: it wasn't just the call of academia but partly because he played banjo, not the most rock 'n' roll of instruments, and with Paul in the group it was towards rock that The Quarry Men were irresistibly bound.

Colin remembers a night at The Cavern when Rod became concerned about the group deciding to play some rock 'n' roll numbers when the management at the Cavern insisted on 'skiffle only'.

"It was sometime before Rod's last performance with us, which was at the fete. We were down The Cavern playing possibly an unpaid 'open mic' gig – so not a full set, maybe twenty minutes max. The rule was, 'No rock 'n' roll'. Well we'd played a couple of skiffle songs and next on our set list – as we'd agreed before we took the stage – was a rock 'n' roll number. I can't remember which but I do recall before we went to the show that night Rod had voiced concern that we were going to play this particular tune. The rest of us weren't too bothered, John certainly wasn't. So we did, we played it and as we finished someone at the front of the stage handed John a folded piece of paper.

John held up the note for all the audience to see and with great glee announced, 'We have a request!' Opening it up he read it aloud to everyone (there were mics at The Cavern). It said, 'Don't play any more rock 'n' roll', signed, 'The Management'. I can remember that John was taken aback but not knowing what to do, he and the rest of us just carried on with our next and final song which I do believe was another rock 'n' roll number. So Rod had been vindicated: we'd been bad boys and suitably reprimanded.

Since then I have learned that this was not such a rare occurrence – several bands got just such a note passed up to them at The Cavern when they attempted similar acts of rebellion. Rory Storm's group was one."

As for the aftermath? John and the group's determination to play some rock 'n' roll songs and the management's reaction to John's act of rebellion did not incur any back stage 'I told you so' outbursts from Rod. Rod was not that sort of chap. He just took it in his stride.

"When we got backstage into what they call the Green Room, although there were no arguments John was concerned, like the rest of us, that we might now be banned from The Cavern. We didn't want that to happen because we liked playing there. Equally we didn't wish to be barred from playing rock 'n' roll because we liked playing it. We were facing a bit of a dilemma.

Sitting alongside us in the Green Room on that occasion was a singer from another band who shared our sentiments. He was adamant that we should just tell 'the management' to 'get lost'. It wasn't just us, he said, there was already a wider rebellion among other groups against the ban. The times were changing, skiffle was fun, jazz was 'cool' but rock 'n' roll was where the future lay. No one from the management ever did speak to us about our act of rebellion – it was just that note and nothing more. We weren't banned or anything like that, in fact we got booked for subsequent gigs for which we even got paid. All in all it was just a storm in a teacup."

In Hunter Davies's biography of the group, Rod says his last performance as a Quarry Men was at The Cavern on Wednesday 7th August. He'd checked the listings in the *Liverpool Echo* for that evening which placed The Quarry Men on the bill alongside Ron McKay, The Deltones and The Demon Five Skiffle Group. Since the publication of Hunter's book, Rod has corrected this. It was not the date of his last gig because he has since discovered his father's old passport in which date stamps reveal he and his family were actually abroad on holiday by then and so he could not possibly have been on stage in Liverpool on 7th August which confirms the fete as his last appearance with The Quarry Men.

"It just happened, there was no falling out, Rod just left and we lost touch. After the fete I don't recall him being around, suddenly he just wasn't there. Even though he lived close by I wouldn't see him again for forty years until we met as Quarry Men at the Fortieth anniversary of the opening of The Cavern Club."

26

... I SAY HELLO

Paul's entry into the group stalled after the fete.

The fete was early in July and John, Pete and Eric would most probably have left school by then after completing their O-Levels exams. All they had to do now was await the results. Younger than them, with a year to go to their O-Levels Ivan, Len and Paul would still be attending lessons, breaking up for the long summer holiday in mid-July.

'We had no gigs that week after the fete and so the next time we all met up was the next Saturday – July 13th at my house. Saturday afternoon was by then our designated regular group practice. As he often did – especially after introducing us to Paul – Ivan turned up. I remember how we used to arrange ourselves around the room at my place: John and the other lads would stand by the front window that overlooks the garden where my brother's radiogram was situated underneath the window. I was at the back of the room. We set ourselves up this way because when my neighbour Geraldine Davies used to come to record the group she always placed her tape recorder on top of the radiogram consigning me as far away as possible from the microphone to the back of the room because of the noise my drums made. On this particular Saturday I do not recall Rod being there and Ivan was sitting in the armchair to the right of the fireplace.

During an interval we began chatting about Paul and his appearance at the fete and whether or not he would be a good addition to the group. It was at this point that Ivan became quite agitated, cutting in to comment quite sharply, 'I don't understand you lot. I introduce you to the best guitarist in Liverpool and you can't make your minds up whether you want him in the group or not!'"

Ivan's intervention took The Quarry Men aback because it was so unlike him. For a minute or two they were silenced by the strength his opinion.

The first to react was Pete Shotton who, as Colin recalls, turned towards John and said: *"He's right, John, we need Paul in the group. If he's not in our group he'll end up in someone else's."*

John listened, taking it all in, looked towards Colin and asked: *"What do you think, Col?"*

Colin nodded, *"That's fine with me, John; you and Eric are the guitarists, I'm just the drummer."*

Ivan's intervention had most certainly focused their minds – especially John's.

"Paul was Ivan's mate so he was as loyal to him as he was to John and to us as a group. Most of the time Ivan was a very relaxed, likeable lad but on this occasion he was quite irate – adamant in fact, frustrated I think by our lack of response towards Paul's appearance at the fete. Being with Paul in the church hall, Ivan was one who had actually witnessed Paul's 'audition'. He'd seen and heard the impression Paul had clearly made on those present. I had certainly never heard him raise his voice before. He clearly felt very strongly about this issue. It startled us, or should I say John, not so much into making a decision – which I believe John had already done – but into doing something about it.

It was not the group who would have made such a decision anyway, it would have been for John to make up his mind for the unspoken rule among us was that The Quarry Men were John's group. So, ultimately, although he might ask us our opinion it was his decision, not ours, we would simply follow his lead. Make no mistake John was always aware of his position as the leader, the decision maker. Now his hand had been forced, we were as one when John agreed with Ivan: Paul McCartney should be invited to become a Quarry Man."

Colin says that after this momentous decision had been taken it was business as usual: rehearsal time. With their focus turned to practising it meant when they left Colin's that evening no one had been specifically tasked to convey the decision to Paul. Maybe they just assumed Ivan would do so, but he hadn't been personally asked to do so; no one had.

"The Quarry Men who had witnessed Paul play and sing in the church hall – John, Pete, and Len – had commented on how assured Paul was as a musician and performer. He had been un-fazed by performing in front of lads he'd never met, lads who were established friends, who were older and already a gigging unit. It took some bottle to do that. However polite and charming he'd been, Paul was clearly confident in his own ability. He was more accomplished and confident musically than any of us and had been happy to let John, Pete and Len see and hear that."

One thing was for sure: if he agreed to join, as Pete had been quick to note, Paul's presence in The Quarry Men would be a positive move.

"I hadn't witnessed Paul play but I could tell he'd made a big impression. In hindsight, from John's own comments that I have read, I personally think John was concerned as to how much of a challenge to him as leader it would be to have a lad like Paul join the group. John was our accepted, unchallenged boss. Paul was an unknown quantity and from John's point of view his presence in the group may have posed a threat. At the same time John was desperately keen for The Quarry Men to progress, to go beyond skiffle, to play rock 'n' roll and it was clear a talented lad like Paul McCartney could help John achieve that goal. Paul could also help John play better guitar by teaching him proper guitar chords. John wanted it so much. Paul was a natural. He just had it. He could sing like Little Richard. Nevertheless John sat on the decision."

Colin believes part of John's hesitation involved another crucial aspect of group politics. Someone would have to go. Paul's presence would expand The Quarry Men into a seven-piece. There would be three guitarsts. John knew seven performers on stage would be unwieldy and some of the lads not quite up to the mark as players would have to go.

"John would have recognised that one or more of us might have to leave the group to accommodate Paul. Ivan's outburst may have forced his hand but he knew Paul's presence would change the dynamic of The Quarry Men. These were John's friends and he felt a loyalty to them, especially Pete; booting one of them out was not something he would relish but inside he desperately wanted the new reality. He instinctively knew Paul was special; with him by his side John knew he'd move a mighty step closer to achieving his ambition of making rock 'n' roll his life. Ivan's outburst made it so much easier for John to incorporate Paul because it was backed by a consensus of opinion. As for the tricky decision of who to jettison, that, for the moment, could be put to one side."

John himself muddied the waters of how Paul joined the group when, in one of his very last interviews, he said: *"I turned round to him right then on first meeting and said, 'Do you want to join the group?' And he said 'yes' the next day as I recall it."*

John's version of events truncates what actually happened after the fete but confirms his mind was set from the moment he heard Paul play. Walking home with Pete from the fete that night, Pete says John talked about Paul and was clearly mulling over asking him to join The Quarry Men to the point of seeking Pete's thoughts. Pete, who himself had never felt too comfortable perfoming in the group and was looking for a way to leave, said John should ask Paul to join.

> **John**: *I had a group, I was the singer and the leader; I met Paul and I made a decision whether to – and he made a decision too – have him in the group: was it better to have a guy who was better than the people I had in, obviously, or not? To make the group*

stronger or to let me be stronger? That decision was to let Paul in and make the group stronger."

(John Lennon In His Own Words, Miles, p. 18.)

The mechanics and sequence of how Paul learned of John's decision became protracted.

According to both Pete and Paul it was Pete who actually extended the invitation for him to join the group, not Ivan. It happened on Vale Road in Woolton where Pete Shotton, Nigel Walley and Ivan Vaughan all lived. Vale runs directly behind Menlove Avenue where John lived at 'Mendips'. Ivan's house, 'Vega', is almost immediately behind John's. It appears that Pete spotted Paul as he cycled along Vale – possibly on his way to call at Ivan's. 'Vega' was just up from Pete's home, number 83, on the corner where Linkstor Road joins Vale.

Pete: *"Another fortnight went by (after the fete), and… I was the first to see Paul again, cycling through our neighbourhood. Spotting me on the roadside, he stopped his bike to chat. 'By the way', I ventured, '… we'd thought maybe you'd like to join the group.'"*

('John Lennon, In My Life', Shotton and Schaffner, p. 55-6)

Paul recalled: *"And then (after the day of the fete) I didn't really hear much from anyone. What I remember was cycling along Vale Road just behind Menlove where Pete Shotton, John's mate, also lived. Pete saw me and told me that all the guys loved 'that' (i.e. Paul's playing the guitar and piano in the church hall) the other day. I can't recall his exact words but the point was The Quarry Men thought I was good. I was glowing in the praise when he went on to say, 'They want you to join the group.'*

(The Day John Met Paul', BBC R2, 2007; Bob Harris interview.)

Paul says the invitation to join The Quarry Men stopped him in his tracks, which suggests Ivan had definitely not yet said anything to him about the group meeting he'd attended.

> **Paul**:*"I thought, 'Oh? Well I'll have to think what does this mean?' So I said I'd give them a ring. So I did, I had a little think about it – not very long. I thought this sounds a bit terrifying being in a group, because I'd just played at home on my own – they were seasoned professionals! But I thought 'maybe' and ended up joining The Quarry Men… and things progressed from there."*
>
> *(The Day John Met Paul, BBC R2, 2007; Bob Harris interview.)*

So sequencing these events together we find Paul was introduced to John and some of the other Quarry Men on Saturday 6th July at the fete and, the following Saturday afternoon the 13th at Colin's house, Ivan attended a group rehearsal to remonstrate with them. Shortly afterwards Pete saw Paul riding on his bike and asked him 'officially' to join the group, which leaves the question: when did Paul McCartney actually sit in with the boys for the very first time as a bona fide member of the group?

Here Rod's memories of his final days in the group possibly help to approximate that date. Rod never played on stage with Paul, his own tenure in the group ending soon after the fete early in the school summer holiday of 1957. Yet he has a memory of being at Mendips not long after the fete when Paul arrived at the back door and Aunt Mimi escorted him into the front room – most likely during one of those rare instances when John hosted a practice. Rod says this was the very first time he became aware of Paul and it was to be the only time he ever met him while he was still a Quarry Man.

Rod being introduced to Paul at Mendips would have to have been before he and his family went on their summer holiday which, if it was a rehearsal day, makes Saturday 20th July 1957 possibly the day/date Paul and John first convened together as members of the same group. No one can be 100% sure that this was the date but it fits the eye witness memories. Paul recalls cycling to Mendips for the first time and being met by Aunt Mimi at the back door and of her escorting him via the kitchen and 'Morning Room' into the front or 'best' room where the group were waiting.

According to Colin all six members of The Quarry Men being at Mendips was a rare event, although it did happen occasionally in the very early days. He has surer memories from much later on, when the other original members had left, of just himself, John, Paul and George rehearsing in that front room

Rod clearly remembers sitting in Mimi's front living room as being the first and only time that, as a Quarry Man, he met Paul. When he asked John who the lad was, Rod remembers John replied that he was just a lad who was interested in the group. Such a question also confirms Rod's own lack of any memory of meeting, being introduced to or seeing Paul at the fete (or of attending the post-fete meeting/rehearsal with Ivan at Colin's).

"In those early days we certainly only practised at Mendips on a very few occasions as a full six-piece group. Although she was more relaxed about things than you might expect, Mimi was concerned about the noise we made and possible complaints from either the neighbours or of distracting the student lodgers who were studying next door in the dining room. As an alternative we'd often meet at my house for instance because Mum and Dad were both out working on Saturdays so we could be more relaxed – and make more noise! Until Paul joined the group we rehearsed a lot at mine – and Eric's. We also practised occasionally at Julia's house. She would grab her banjo and join in. Her's was always a good place to rehearse, so while Mendips was not somewhere we practised on a regular basis having said that when we did Mimi was very hospitable – she always served us tea and biscuits in the tiny Morning Room next to the kitchen."

Aunt Mimi inspired genuine respect in Colin.

"She had the ability to terrify everybody – a cross between a headmistress and a chief librarian. Yet she was also the first adult I recall who would hold a conversation with you as an equal. She didn't talk down to you or treat you like a silly teenager like a lot of parents would. She would talk to us about the group and the music and other subjects, about life in general. She paid us respect – for which, in turn, I respected her."

A particular conversation remains etched in Colin's memory.

"Believe it or not but in those days I had a passion for wearing rings, it must be a drummer 'thing'. They were cheap rings, nothing too posh or expensive, after all I was only on an apprentice's wage. I had a silver lion's head ring with stones for the eyes and a gold ring that was like a snake wrapped around my finger. One time we were sitting in the Morning Room at Mendips having tea and biscuits when Mimi noticed my rings. Having caught her attention she asked from where I'd got them. I didn't like to say Woolies (Woolworths), which is where I had bought them, because it was considered to be a cheap shop (which it was) so I said Lewis's, which was a bit posher and I thought would be more impressive. Mimi agreed with me that Lewis's was a good shop so I'd definitely said the right thing as far as my choice of retailer went. As for the rings, although she was polite she no doubt thought they looked too cheap for Lewis's, (which they were) and even at the time I suspected she'd seen straight through my white lie. No doubt those rings were just further evidence for Mimi of how tacky rock 'n' roll was. How she must have despaired for what was to become of her nephew."

Lion's head rings aside, Mimi seemed to approve of Colin. She even let him use the front door, which was usually reserved 'for best', for visitors such as the vicar or doctor or someone she considered worthy. All the other boys were directed to the kitchen door at the back of the house. Colin thinks it was because of his drums that she made an exception for him.

Mimi would no doubt have raised an eyebrow to learn that this new boy, Paul, lived on a council estate, a fact which John would no doubt have taken some delight in telling her. However, like Colin, Paul also won Mimi over sufficiently to make it into Mendips – albeit via that back door.

After their delay in inviting Paul to join their group the boys would have another wait before Paul actually rehearsed with them or appeared with them on stage for he was off on his holidays. From 29th July–7th August he and his younger brother Mike, as members of the 19th City School Scouts Troop, went on summer camp to 'Callow Farm', Hathersage, Near Sheffield, Derbyshire, departing from Central Station at 11 a.m. on the 29th.

This particular scout camp is etched in Mike and Paul's memory because events did not go to plan. The very first evening in Hathersage Mike proceeded to break his left arm and such was the complex nature of the fracture he remained in hospital in Sheffield for the next four weeks.

27

TROUBLE DOWN THE CAVERN

Whilst Paul was away with the Scouts, The Quarry Men continued to perform. They'd played The Cavern on several occasions before he'd met them at the fete but the first one they played without Rod and before Paul joined them remains etched in Colin's memory.

"Wednesday 7th August 1957 was a bit special for us because it was the first time a gig of ours at The Cavern was advertised in The Liverpool Echo. Our line up was John, Len, Eric, Pete and myself. Paul missed what would have been his group debut because he was travelling home from Scout camp. It turned out to be an eventful night because when we were on stage Pete and I fell out big time and got involved in a bit of a fracas."

What actually happened was that Colin stood up and tried to grab Pete by the throat. Fortunately he was thwarted by the presence of his drum kit that got in his way as he lunged at Pete. The subsequent delay brought Colin to his senses and he returned to his drum seat to carry on drumming: like true professionals for whom the 'show must go on', the group carried on but throughout their performance John, Eric and Len were fully aware of the tensions between the other two Quarry Men.

"Pete had turned to me during the group's performance of 'All Shook Up' to tell me to stop playing a rim shot on the snare after the brief pauses in the song

just ahead of the chorus. I could be a bit precious about my playing so I certainly wasn't taking instructions on how to play the drums from the washboard player. I mean, who did he think he was? I simply saw red. My view was, I was the drummer; I was setting the beat not Pete. What I couldn't see was that John was kicking his leg out each time that pause ended just as he began to sing the lyric 'I'm all shook up', consequently he and I weren't in sync. I couldn't see what he was doing and was actually blissfully unaware he was doing anything – this 'kick' hadn't been rehearsed, it was a touch of spontaneity on John's part. I just thought Pete was being awkward and bossy, neither of which I was going to take: I did have a bit of a short fuse in those days.

Obviously when we came off stage the other boys in the band were eager to know what had gone off.

When Pete told them, they just laughed about it, no more was said and we carried on packing up ready to catch our 'bus. But between Pete and I it was far from over. We had both gone quiet and didn't speak to each other: we just smouldered. On the journey home nothing more was said but Pete and I very definitely kept our distance.

On buses home from gigs The Quarry Men always went up stairs to the top deck where the smokers hung out and if they could would spread out, each to their own seat. John would sit with his guitar, strumming. It was a similar situation that evening. Pete was on a seat behind me. When the 'bus got to Menlove Avenue and the stop where John and Pete would get off, as Pete passed me to go down the steps he poked me on the shoulder and said, 'Don't ever do that again!'. Immediately the red mist descended yet again, I jumped up and leaned over the top of the stairs and again tried to grab him by the throat as he was going down. As on stage I couldn't quite reach him, so he challenged me. I ran down the steps after him, grabbed my drums from under the stairs and leaped off the 'bus ready to confront Pete. By the time I had done so John had already split to go home – Mendips was just a few steps from the stop. He'd left us to sort it out between ourselves, so we did. Pete and I squared up to each other, each looking to throw the first punch."

How long this impasse went on for Colin is unsure but long enough for tempers to ebb, although the anger remained.

"The longer we squared up the less likely we were to actually fight but we certainly traded insults. I accused him of not coming to rehearsals and not knowing that was the way we'd practised that song, me playing the rim shot. John hadn't said he would kick his leg, so as far as I was concerned I was just playing it as we'd agreed as a group. And then suddenly came the curved ball: out of the blue Pete changed the subject and mentioned a girl called Sheila whom we had both dated. She lived at the top of my road. His gripe was that if he'd taken a girl out then we, his friends/rivals in the group, apparently weren't allowed to do so. I was flabbergasted for it dawned on me that here was the true cause of his picking on me: revenge for moving in on his territory."

As a diversionary tactic it worked. Colin's impulse to fight totally abated.

"To be fair I think I'd actually dated her before she dated Pete. So I couldn't really see what was bugging him. I couldn't exactly go back in time and un-take her out. It all seemed crazy to me. However, taken aback by his outburst I dropped my guard and said words to the effect of, 'Pete if you think I'm going to fight you over a girl, you are crazy.' He pondered for a bit and agreed. I think he realised this was really a non-situation, one that gave us both a way out of our ridiculous impasse over the rim shot and avoid any physical stuff between us. Inadvertently he'd given us both an easy way to back down."

However, even as the tension ebbed Pete wasn't quite ready to let things go. He still had enough stuff going round inside his head to fire off one final insult.

"He rounded the evening off by telling me that the other lads in The Quarry Men didn't really want me in the group anymore because they thought I was a rubbish drummer. He said they only put up with me because I had a set of drums with the group name on. I was astounded, most definitely upset and very hurt. This was news to me. I didn't like to think they'd been talking behind my back, criticising me, that they were just tolerating me. I said, 'If that's how it is, if I'm not wanted, I'll go. I'll see John at rehearsal at Eric's

on Saturday and sort it out.' And that was it. We stopped arguing. I think we both saw how absurd the whole thing had become. Maybe he felt bad about what he'd just said about me. I know we went very quiet. Now here's the daft part. After all this venom between us, can you believe Pete stood with me until another 'bus came along to help me on with my drums: a gentleman to the end."

A point to remember is these were two teenage boys: pride was at stake, but while the testosterone was flowing neither Pete nor Colin were fighters; they didn't go looking for trouble. True Teddy Boys/gang members might well have done – and when they did, they fought dirty, carried flick-knives or chains, or had razor blades sewn into the inside of their lapels – truly vicious and nasty, but lads like Colin, Pete, John, Rod, Len and Eric were essentially benign and would have run a mile at the very thought of arming themselves or hurting one other. Essentially they were friends. John had not hung around that evening because he wanted nothing to do with Colin and Pete's falling out. Among each other in The Quarry Men their greatest weapon – especially in John's case – was their tongue: repartee, banter, wit. That's how they sparred with each other. Of them all no one could match John when it came to verbals. His wit was sharp and his tongue a rapier that could cut to the quick. So Pete's broadsides were the verbal equivalent of landing some punches.

For Colin, however, although no blood was spilt that evening, it left him feeling upset. Already lacking confidence in himself as a drummer Pete's remarks sowed new seeds of doubt into his mind. As he sat on the 'bus he couldn't stop mulling over that word 'rubbish'. It needled him and upset him. No punch had been thrown but he'd taken a hit, he was wounded.

28

BROKEN DRUMSTICKS AND A BROKEN WASHBOARD

Rattled by Pete's comments, Colin was determined to resolve the issue.

"When Saturday (August 10th) came around and we gathered at Eric's for our rehearsal John was there ahead of me, Pete had not arrived. As soon as John saw me he asked how I'd got on with Pete. I told him he had brought up this thing about this girl Sheila whom we'd both taken out. John gave a little laugh – it was almost as if he knew Pete wasn't happy about him and me seeing the same girl.

In truth what was really bugging me were Pete's comments about my drumming and my place in the group so I repeated what he'd said. John listened carefully and was adamant: he had said no such thing. Even so I still gave him the option to sack me: 'If you want me out all you have to do is just say and I'll go'. John shook his head saying quite firmly, 'No, we want you in the band.' He even went one further by commenting, 'Drums are better than a washboard'."

John's words gave Colin something to think about. Was John hinting that if anyone's position in The Quarry Men was in the balance it was Pete's? This stopped him in his tracks because knowing how close John and Pete were Colin had just assumed that John's loyalty would always be to Pete. Apparently, it now seemed, maybe not when it came to matters affecting the group.

As the conversation gradually turned to their next gig at The Cavern the tension inside Colin remained. He now realised John was wrestling with a true dilemma: loyalty to a long-time, close friend or to progressing the band which with each day was becoming more and more important to him.

"By now Pete had arrived and spotted John and me talking. He could see that we had not fallen out, I was still around. I think he also realised at that point that John had a genuine problem. Pete knew that John certainly wasn't going to sack him, his best mate and right hand man, but on the other hand he clearly wasn't going to ditch his drummer. Having a drummer in those days was a bit special because a kit was so expensive whereas a washboard wasn't – to be truthful a washboard was more of a novelty than a necessity. If a group was to make the transition from skiffle to rock 'n' roll then drums won out every time. Pete, being Pete, probably knew his days were numbered. In truth he had never been particularly comfortable playing washboard or being on stage and was ready to go. However, just up and quitting was complicated by the fact he didn't want to hurt his best friend's feelings by saying so. As for John he had enlisted Pete's support in forming the group in the first place so he was not going to find it easy to ask Pete to leave. The problem was to find a way to make this decision easy for both of them."

No one likes to tell someone they are surplus to requirements. More than many other boys his age John knew how much it hurt to be rejected by those really close to you and this possibly lay at the heart of his pulling back from personally sacking Pete or any of his old pals from the Quarry Men.

On (or about) 24th August the situation was resolved much sooner than either John or Pete might have expected when The Quarry Men played a private function, the wedding of Dawn Hanson, the sister of Norma, the girl whom Colin had met in the pub on the day of the infamous Rosebery Street Party.

After her wedding, Dawn and her new husband – whose

name Colin can't recall but can remember was in the Royal Navy (because he got married in uniform) – held their reception in a venue on Upper Parliament Street (just around the corner from Rosebery Street).

"This was one of our last bookings without Paul. We were invited to play and did our first set early in the evening. When we took a break the immediate family went off to the pub for a drink – most probably 'The Clock', their local. I had spent a fair bit of time with the family after our street party gig in June, they always had a few bottles of beer at home because they enjoyed a drink and a sing-song so I accompanied them to the pub. It seemed like a good idea – I knew it would be fun and that there'd be beer on tap!

I was right. I soon found myself, pint in hand, sat at a table with Mum, Dad, bride and groom and other members of the immediate family having a great time. I began to enjoy myself too much in fact, which I was prone to do when I'd had a beer, so when Mr. Hanson mentioned to me on a couple of occasions that I was wanted back at the venue to play drums I was having too much fun drinking and laughing with the family to pay close attention, hence my return was considerably delayed. But return I did, whereupon I was met by Pete Shotton who told me that as I had not come back from the pub in time he'd sat in for me on drums. He was very wary and apologetic because he knew I didn't like anyone touching my drums."

Rather than get uptight Colin quickly grasped the situation: The Quarry Men had obviously been under a lot of pressure from the wedding guests to play. They simply couldn't wait any longer for Colin, who was lost in the pub. The guests wanted to dance and were getting impatient. As they were the wedding band, The Quarry Men's function was to play: with or without their regular drummer, the show must go on. And so it had with Pete deputising on drums. Feeling quite 'mellow' by the time he heard all this, Colin did not raise any objections, indeed he was happy with the arrangement, which must have surprised Pete given their recent falling out and Colin's protectiveness towards his kit.

"Even when Pete told me he'd broken one of my drumsticks I didn't get too upset. That's how mellow I was. Normally I would have been angry but not on this occasion. It was a stick from the two pairs I'd brought along with my kit (they had the name 'John Grey' printed on them – the manufacturer). It takes some doing to break a drumstick, so quite what Pete had done to snap it I can only imagine. But I was enjoying myself and there was the prospect of more fun ahead so I was happy and my attention was sufficiently diverted."

Not diverted enough however not to notice that The Quarry Men had clearly finished playing for quite a while before he'd returned and in the interim a lot of drinking had gone on, Pete in particular had clearly imbibed more than usual.

"He was quite ill with it. John had also had a lot but most probably not quite as much as Pete. He certainly wasn't sick like Pete. This is the only occasion on which I can remember the pair of them being inebriated to this extent. What also remains in my memory is that finding himself in this state Pete took the opportunity to retire from the group and John seized the chance to help him on his way. It's my belief that John was relieved. It solved a problem he and Pete had both been avoiding.

In other words, this was the night that John famously broke Pete's washboard over his head to symbolise his exit. I stress it was a purely symbolic gesture and done very good naturedly – they were both in stitches of laughter when it happened. John just said, 'That takes care of that!' It was not an aggressive act in any way and in truth Pete's washboard was literally on the point of falling apart anyway, as John well knew. The corrugated tin body was already loose so it came out of its frame very easily: not much force was necessary to make it do so."

> **Pete:** *"The washboard frame slid neatly round my neck and the tears of laughter rolled… down my face. Not only was I feeling no pain: I knew the destruction of my washboard (which I certainly wasn't about to repair or replace) had effectively released me from all further obligations as a Quarry Man."*
>
> *('John Lennon, In My Life', Shotton and Shaffner, p.58.)*

Being sick and then having the washboard brought down upon his head had the effect of sobering Pete up and by the time the reception ended both he and John had further recovered.

Following on from the reception everyone – family, friends and Quarry Men – convened to the family house, where a party was in progress.

"We looked set for a good time. Norma took my drum kit upstairs but we were only in the house a very short while before she reappeared with them and told us we had to go. We hadn't done anything wrong but her dad had told her it was a private party, she shouldn't have invited us back: we had to leave. I suspect he didn't want us drinking all the beer or being 'ill' all over the place. So before we knew it we were out on the street and headed towards the 'bus stop. On our way we passed a house where a ladder was propped up against a bedroom window and John quipped: 'Look, lads, someone's eloping!' Not that funny I admit but it seemed so at the time and soon had us all rolling around in fits of laughter, which in itself suggests just how tipsy we still were."

29

PAUL'S FIRST PERFORMANCE WITH THE QUARRY MEN

By September 1957 The Quarry Men had undergone several changes. Rod and Pete had departed their ranks.

Equally important, now only Len and Paul were still school boys. John and Pete had both failed all their O-Levels and could not return to Quarry Bank as sixth formers. Eric had passed some but not enough to remain at school.

John's Aunt Mimi was particularly anxious as to what was to happen to her nephew, reminding him quite frequently that, *'The guitar is alright as a hobby, John, but you will never earn a living with it.'*

Fortunately John managed to avoid the world of work by the skin of his teeth when his prowess in art – despite failing the exam – secured him a place in Art College. Mimi was relieved more than impressed: for her and countless others of her generation, 'art' as a career offered poor future prospects. It was deemed almost on a par with playing rock 'n' roll for a living – i.e. there was no long term future in it: no job for life, no security. *"What can you do with art?"* Even so she supported him in this endeavour by agreeing to fund it. This was a very generous thing for her to do and reflects how much she cared for him and his future well being. To her way of thinking it bought John time and a second opportunity to acquire what she considered to be some all-important 'qualifications'. As she shrewdly observed, *"Any port in a storm."*

Pete became a cadet at Liverpool's Police College, which, by his own admission was an 'arbitrary' choice: the college brochure depicting cadets playing pool and enjoying themselves in a large heated swimming pool being a highly persuasive element in his decision rather than any public-spirited intention to protect the public from unscrupulous criminals!

"Although Pete left The Quarry Men he remained very much a part of the group's 'scene'. He was always there backstage with us as a friend, helping to carry equipment, reporting on audience reaction at gigs, which songs got the best reception, things like that. He remained close to John. Being off the stage when we performed and not the focus of attention of jealous boyfriends meant he was now in a better position to actually chat up the girls, which he enjoyed. With Rod also gone that left just John, Eric, Len, myself and the new lad, Paul McCartney."

Eric's three passes at O-Level were not enough to allow him to enter Sixth Form so he also left Quarry Bank. Just ahead of his seventeenth birthday he joined Napier's as an apprentice engineer. Like Colin he was now a working man, his future clearly mapped. Napier's made aeroplane engines. Unfortunately Eric quickly found the work repetitive and boring. Sent to college on day release each week he hated that as well. It was clear he wasn't going to last in this 'career' but, whilst he did, The Quarry Men provided escape from the drudgery of work as he experienced it – and, as they improved so bookings picked up and promoters started to pay them which put a little extra cash in Eric's pocket.

Not long after Pete left the band Nigel Walley had some calling or 'business' cards printed for The Quarry Men.

"It was at The Milk Bar in Woolton Village in 1957, not long after Rod and Pete had quit the band but before Paul was performing with us. For some reason Nige was not at the booking that evening and had passed a bunch of these cards to Pete to hand to me and the others. We were walking to the Milk Bar in Woolton – a favourite haunt of ours – when Pete put his hand into

his inside pocket and handed them to me. It wasn't long after the wedding gig and so I actually thought he was reaching into his pocket for some money to pay for the broken drumstick and I was about to say, 'No thanks, it's alright' when I realised he was actually proffering business cards.

We were regulars at the Milk Bar. The owner, Jo, was friendly with us; she knew we were a group and always made us welcome. She had a big flat above the Milk Bar and so when she was arranging her 21st. birthday party we were invited to play. The party carried on to midnight at which point Jo's mum intervened to say the party could go on a while longer but there could be 'no more band'.

As things quietened down Bob Molyneux, who was there with his tape recorder, played back what he had been recording that evening. When he put it on I recall saying, 'That sounds awful Bob what is it?' To which he replied, 'That's you lot!' which made us all laugh."

Even though they'd lost two original members The Quarry Men were on the move: reduced to a five-piece (once Paul returned from his various summer excursions to join them) they now had their own business card, which they all admired as a very 'professional' touch.

So, what Colin is often asked is: when did this new, slimmed-down, revamped, business card equipped Quarry Men skiffle group tread the boards for the first time with Paul McCartney in their ranks?

Like the day John and Paul first met, for historians this is an important date in the history of rock 'n' roll. However, while the Fete can be dated exactly, the first time Paul performed *in public* with John and The Quarry Men is more problematic.

Colin says after his various summer excursions Paul sat in with group several times to rehearse before he actually appeared on stage with them. As Rod recalls he met with them as a new group member briefly at Mendips a couple of weeks after the fete before Paul went off on scout camp followed by a family holiday. During this period he missed a booking at the Cavern, the 'wedding' gig and the party at the Milk Bar.

A Quarry Men business card, signed by Nigel Walley.

Some of the first rehearsals Paul attended to learn The Quarry Men's set were held at Colin's house. And, while Colin recalls Paul performing with The Quarry Men at some St. Peter's Youth Club dances, Colin is convinced Paul actually made his debut at the Wilson Hall, Garston, at another 'talent' contest.

"It wasn't billed as a dance night but as a 'talent contest' so there were no names on the bill. This means adverts in local papers didn't carry names so we can't trace the date that way. But I do clearly remember Paul being there. As a dance venue the Wilson Hall could be a bit of a rough house but on that particular evening I don't recall any outbreaks of violence so he did not have to endure a baptism of fire. As ever we had turned up convinced we were going to win."

If John had had his way The Quarry Men would never have set foot inside the venue to participate that night for the lady on the door was adamant: *"Everyone who comes in has to pay, contestants as well."*

This stopped the boys in their tracks for the way they saw things The Quarry Men where there as part of the evening's entertainment; surely they shouldn't have to pay to get in!? John saw this as an attempt by the organisers to have their cake and eat it, although organiser Charlie McBain, or 'Charlie Mac' as he was known, viewed the situation somewhat differently and Colin could see Charlie's point.

"Charlie was, after all, a business man looking to make money, he wasn't running open house, he wasn't a charity. Charlie's reasoning was that if four or five groups turned up to enter the contest together with girlfriends and assorted hangers-on, the dance floor would be filled with people who hadn't paid, leaving less room for those who would. Also if word got around you could get in for free if you said you were a contestant, soon everyone who turned up would do so professing to be a singer or member of a group. So Charlie McBain insisted that everyone had to pay, irrespective of whether they would

be performing or not. That was the house rule. In Charlie's mind he was doing us a favour by opening a door of opportunity. And, of course, the winners would receive a cash prize."

Even so John was unmoved by McBain's logic to the point he was ready to walk.

"He didn't like it one bit: paying to play did not sit right with John Lennon. And it is this that convinces me that this was Paul's first performance as a Quarry Man. You see we did eventually pay to go in – John included – and it was Paul McCartney who convinced John we should do so. Paul's reasoning was we were more than good enough to win the prize money. In Paul's mind it was a foregone conclusion. He argued that as we would soon be walking off with the cash prize anyway we could afford to pay to go inside. He was very persuasive. His conviction was simply irresistible. (I think, more than anything, having come this far to play with us for the very first time, Paul really wanted to play.) So we all did cough up and in we trouped, set up, performed and of course proceeded not to win. It was undoubtedly a reality check for our new super-confident guitarist. We all came away out of pocket but steeped in admiration for Paul's enthusiasm and blind faith in The Quarry Men's ability. He had impressed us all."

Paul persuading the group not to walk away from that talent show at the Wilson Hall registers with Colin as Paul's debut with The Quarry Men but he also recalls that around the same time the group – with Paul in their ranks – played several unpaid bookings at St. Peter's Church Youth Club. So Colin is unsure whether the Wilson Hall gig or one of the youth club performances came first, but turning up for that talent contest registers most strongly in his mind. What is certain is that, within The Quarry Men's career trajectory bookings at the Wilson Hall quickly eclipsed those at the youth club.

In essence the youth club was a launch pad, a place in which to find their feet as a group surrounded by (mainly) friends. It's where they built their first fan base.

"We drew larger crowds every time we played. My next-door neighbour and good friend Geraldine Davies was a particular fan who encouraged all her friends from school to come along every Saturday night for a bop. And by word of mouth we were also attracting more and more young people besides just our friends to the youth club.

Geraldine was one of our very first fans who came not just to dances but to rehearsals. She had a brand new Grundig tape recorder and when we rehearsed at my house she liked to come around to record us. Of course we encouraged her to do so – the novelty of hearing what we sounded like really impressed us – but Geraldine insisted she pressed the buttons, which was her way of getting into our practices. It also ensured we didn't mistreat her precious tape recorder. Not many people had one in those days…

I remember during one recording session my sister Lynn who was aged about eight wouldn't keep quiet. John asked her several times to 'please' keep quiet because up to that point she had succeeded in spoiling every recording we were trying to make. Try as she may Lynn just couldn't stay quiet long enough. John had been very patient and very gentle in the way he spoke to her but finally enough was enough. Without raising his voice he told her, 'That's enough – you are going out!' He put down his guitar, walked over and very carefully gathered her in his arms and – accompanied by her girlfriend who was in the room with her – carried her into the hallway to deposit her on the bottom step where he instructed her to 'stay' and 'keep quiet!' He didn't close the door on her, we could still see her, but it worked, she and her friend did keep quiet. It was done in such a gentle way we all smiled to see John in this unfamiliar role of 'big brother'."

One Quarry Men youth club booking that they were scheduled to play but definitely *didn't* would be the one that ended The Quarry Men's tenure and their welcome there.

"Over several weeks an issue had been brewing between us and the chap who ran the dances. It was over the provision of a microphone for John, or should I say the lack of provision of one. Jack Gibbons, a very nice chap who helped run the youth club was always promising he would get one. He made the same

promise every week but never acted on it, which had really begun to bug John. He didn't like straining his voice so hard to be heard over the noise of the audience. Finally on this particular Saturday it all came to a head. A good size crowd had gathered – including Geraldine and quite a few of her school friends.

When we arrived at St. Peter's Church Hall it was the same old story: still no microphone. For all his promises Mr. Gibbons had failed to deliver. Jack said they were far too expensive and John would have to manage without. For John that was the final straw. He said he wasn't going to strain his voice singing and shouting over the ever-growing crowds that our popularity was pulling into the dances. Paul chipped in to say he reckoned Mr. Gibbons had never had any intention of getting a mic and such was John's mood I'm afraid no spirit of 'the show must go on' descended upon us. John was really narked, so we packed away and walked out. The place had really filled up by then and it must have been a very tricky situation for Mr. Gibbons to deal with, poor chap.

I immediately split to take my drums home – I couldn't cart them around the village all evening. The others, guitars in hand, wandered off into the Woolton night. When I returned I was unable to find them so called into the youth club to see if they had possibly returned. I should have known better. They weren't there and I was informed – in no uncertain terms – by a quite fractious Mr. Gibbons that not only was John not there he would not be welcome if he ever did deign to show up in the future. And for good measure neither would the rest of the group. Effectively, The Quarry Men were barred."

In reality this did not cause the group too many heartaches for by then The Quarry Men had outgrown the youth club and discovered the Wilson Hall. Like all good things that come to an end so had this particular chapter in their lives.

30

20 FORTHLIN ROAD

Once Paul became a Quarry Man he began to take his turn to host group practices. He was anxious that we should meet his dad, Jim McCartney, who was a great self-taught pianist, a former band leader and someone who encouraged both his sons with their musical and artistic endeavours. They could learn from Jim. Paul's was a home where the group became assured of a warm welcome so, once Paul settled into the group, an invitation to rehearse there was quickly forthcoming.

"I remember our first rehearsal at Paul's. It was a Saturday and those of us who lived in Woolton met up with Paul in the village. He came up to escort us to his house down in Allerton on the Mather Avenue estate, number 20 Forthlin Road. Mather was a road running parallel to Menlove Avenue, Forthlin led off Mather and backed on to the Police Training Grounds. We rehearsed regularly at Forthlin, initially on Saturdays but later on Sundays. That very first time I went down with Paul and the others I had my drum kit with me, John and Eric their guitars. For once Paul did not have his guitar with him. That was kind of strange because like John he usually carried his guitar with him so it was odd to see him without it. As far as I remember Pete did not accompany us – he would have left the group by then but did often attend rehearsals. I also have no memory of Len being with us although he would still have been in the group.

We took the 66 'bus to Allerton to the bottom of Mather Avenue, where we got off – just across from where Liverpool Parkway Railway Station now stands (the 66 did not stop at the end of Forthlin Road, where Paul lived, like the number 86 did, which was the 'bus George Harrison would catch to Paul's). In those days where the 66 stopped there was a big pub on the left hand side of the road just behind us.

Simultaneously as our 'bus dropped us off, on the opposite side of the road a bus had deposited a middle-aged man who was struggling with a rather large and obviously heavy suitcase festooned with stickers. As we crossed the road we could see the stickers were from around the world. In Liverpool a suitcase decorated in this way immediately identified the person lugging it around as a seafarer.

As he crossed towards us so we met on the central reservation that runs down the middle of the road. Those central reservations on Mather and Menlove are where trams once trundled. From the drums and guitars we were carrying it was obvious to him that we were a group. This realisation made him very excited – he couldn't believe he'd met a group. He quickly informed us he was indeed a sailor returning home and immediately started to pepper us with questions about who we were, why we called ourselves 'The Quarry Men', what songs we played. All the time this conversation went on we were standing in the middle of the road.

We were quite surprised by his level of interest because he was of the generation who usually saw skiffle and rock 'n' roll groups as the enemy – the agents of the devil – something to avoid not celebrate."

As The Quarry Men stood answering his questions he told them that as he'd been sailing the seven seas he had heard all about the advent of rock 'n' roll and the popularity of something called 'skiffle' in his hometown. So much so he couldn't wait to get home to hear what all the fuss was about. He was desperate to hear what this new music actually sounded like and simply could not believe that the very moment he'd stepped off the bus to walk home he found himself immediately confronted by a teenage skiffle group that he'd read so much about. Such was the level of his excitement he insisted on buying the boys a pint in the nearby pub.

It was an offer the boys could not resist although Paul's face immediately dropped. This was the last thing he needed. He was reluctant to accept the invitation because he knew his dad was waiting to meet The Quarry Men for the very first time. To turn up at home with a bunch of lads about whom he'd told Dad so much – and whom Jim was keen to meet – but who were now likely to arrive 'half cut' was Paul's worst nightmare.

To his credit, outwardly at least, Paul kept his cool and went with the flow. It was hard not to: as Colin remembers it, the sailor was very persuasive and he and the other lads were easily persuaded. Before they knew it they were standing at the bar waiting for a beer, not exactly an everyday occurrence for a group of underage teenage boys on the streets of Liverpool.

But it was not all plain sailing: from the moment they entered the pub the boys' euphoria had quickly dampened.

'While John, Eric and I gratefully accepted the sailor's offer of a pint and Paul politely declined, the situation had gone from being a bit of a laugh to something quite awkward for, facing us from the other side of the bar, was a barman whose withering look made it blatantly obvious we were unwelcome. His gaze fixed on our guitars and my bass drum as if they were the implements of the devil – he was virtually snarling with disgust. The sailor, however, was not to be deterred. Good-naturedly he worked hard on the barman, pleading with him, vouching for our good behaviour until, with great reluctance, the barman agreed to serve us and pulled four pints, one for the sailor, one each for us, nothing for Paul.

Cautiously we all moved to sit at a table to sup our beer, well away from the bar and the simmering barman. I placed my drums on the floor either side of me but as usual John and Eric had their guitars slung around their necks, hanging in front of them (they never carried them in cases). Like gunslingers always quick on the draw, they were for ever ready to play.

As we chatted the sailor began to insist we play him a tune – he so wanted to hear some of this 'skiffle' he'd read so much about. Throughout all of our exchanges the barman had not taken his eyes off us, just waiting for the slightest excuse to pounce. Consequently we knew exactly what would happen if John or Eric so much as played a note: he'd be over in a flash to throw us out. We didn't want the trouble he was offering.

John tried to explain this to the sailor but he was having none of it. He'd bought us the beer and so, in return, he expected to be entertained. He'd paid for us to play. The pressure from both sides became almost unbearable, so we downed our drinks and stood up as if to leave, at which point John and Eric went straight into 'Rock Island Line'. The inquisitive sailor man beamed with absolute delight as his feet began to tap. Across the floor space the barman was absolutely outraged and right on cue he rounded the bar and headed towards us, a curse on his lips, real purpose in his gait. Immediately the sailor's smile vanished as he realised what was afoot and watched as we walked towards the door, our pace quickening with every step. Even so John and Eric continued to play and sing, the bar man screaming at us to, 'Get out, get out'!"

Refreshed but not chastened by their excursion into the badlands of rhyme and reason, outside the pub the boys regrouped, dusted themselves off and resumed their journey to Paul's.

"Paul was clearly anxious that his dad would smell the beer on our breath and frustrated that there was nothing he could do about it. John reassured him we would be alright: it was half a mile at least to number 20 and the walk in the fresh air would take away the smell of the pub and beer. Reassured but not entirely convinced Paul walked ahead of us while we followed.

Once we arrived at the house Paul welcomed us inside into the living room, which was immediately to the left of the front door as we entered. On the opposite side of the room from that door were glass double doors leading into another area, which we learned was the dining room. As we began setting up, Paul's dad, Jim, accompanied by Paul's younger brother Mike, entered the living room from the dining room. Up until this point I hadn't realised Paul had a brother. Paul introduced us to his dad, who was friendly and chatted to us while I finished putting my kit together. Once I had done so Jim excused himself and told Mike to go with him back into the dining room, closing the glass doors behind them as they did so. Later I learned that Mike was two years younger than Paul, so he was about thirteen, which in those days was quite a gap from we lads in the group, he certainly seemed much younger than Paul. We also learned that their Mum, Mary, had passed away."

The rehearsal that day was to run through familiar tunes not to learn any new songs.

"We began rehearsing: 'Rock Island Line', 'Railroad Bill', 'Lost John', 'Maggie May', 'Baby Let's Play House', 'Putting On The Style', 'Come Go With Me', 'Be Bop A Lula' and so on – our standard set, but by now we were also doing 'Twenty Flight Rock' – a favourite of both Paul's and John's. We had also started playing 'All Shook Up' by Elvis. This visit must have been after my near fight with Pete Shotton at The Cavern and his exit from the group. Already Paul's prowess on guitar had sharpened us up as a band, our repertoire was expanding. By the end of 1957 it included the above tunes plus 'Blue Suede Shoes', 'Mean Woman Blues', 'That's All Right', 'Worried Man Blues', 'Midnight Special', 'Long Tall Sally' and 'That'll Be the Day'.

The way it worked either John or Paul would introduce a song they wanted to perform. Most probably they would have heard this first on the radio or in a listening booth in a record shop. They didn't buy too many records themselves because they were expensive. So, for example, in the very early days before Paul joined us, John would stand in a record booth and as the disc played he'd scribble down as many words as he could. He'd figure out some chords and in front of us he'd sing and play. Eric would follow John on guitar and Len and I would just join in. I just had to pick up a beat. As a group we'd decide whether that was too fast or too slow. Then, when Paul joined he would organise the guitar parts, teaching John and Eric guitar chords in place of banjo chords. Eventually John would do this himself. Paul would introduce a song in the same way."

John and Paul did buy records but they took a lot of pocket money to do so. John had purchased a copy of 'Rock Island Line', which he later sold to Rod. Julia bought Elvis records and introduced him to Buddy Holly's 'That'll Be the Day' so had most probably bought that one for herself as well. Paul says 'Be Bop a Lula' was the first record he bought.

A collection of 78rpm records kept in a briefcase belonging to John was donated to charity by Mimi after John was killed and this later came up for auction at Sotheby's in 1999. Inside were six discs by Elvis: 'Heartbreak Hotel', All Shook Up', 'Hound Dog', Got a Lot o' Lovin' to Do', 'Blue Moon' and 'Jailhouse Rock'. Maybe some of these had originally belonged to Julia before John. There were three Lonnie Donegan singles: 'Cumberland Gap', 'Lost John', 'Don't You Rock Me Daddy-o'. The others were Little Richard's 'Lucille', Buddy Holly's 'Peggy Sue' and The Goons, 'Ying Tong Song'.

'If they had bought a record they would play this over and over, constantly lifting the needle to jot down the words before trying to place it in the same place in order to catch the next set of lyrics. It was not always easy to work out what the words were.

After about an hour – as would become the norm for our many rehearsals at Paul's – the glass doors opened and Jim popped his head round to ask if we were ready for a cup of tea. He was very obliging like that and always struck me as a very pleasant, sociable and friendly man. After Jim served us our tea we carried on for another half hour before calling it a day. I think, despite the beery breath, we had passed the audition. Jim certainly didn't throw us out or make any comments about the smell of beer; he couldn't have been more hospitable, indeed we were invited back many times to rehearse. Being a musician himself and a former band leader, Jim understood the importance of a good rehearsal space in which you felt at ease. Rehearsing at Paul's was always enjoyable, Jim was always encouraging – his warm welcome allowed us to relax and focus on the music.

My impressions of Paul, as I knew him back then, was that he was a very polite lad, very clean, well dressed, well presented. He was also very diplomatic – he didn't like people to think badly of us or of himself. He also spoke very well for a lad off the council estate.

For Liverpool lads all of us were quite well spoken; none of us had a heavy Scouse accent, far from it (I remember after one gig some girls commented on how well spoken we all were). George was the first Quarry Man with a pronounced accent: very nasal, very Scouse."

John's Aunt Mimi certainly took exception to George's accent. Whereas she offered mild approval of Paul, George proved more challenging. His accent was just one of the many attributes she disliked about him. Mimi, being Mimi, ensured that not only was John fully aware of her disapproval but so was George himself. As he said himself, she would go so far as describing him – within his earshot – *as 'That scruff from Speke'.*

In those days regional accents were generally frowned upon by many middle-class parents – Scouse was considered 'common', and people who lived on council estates were 'not good enough', so much so that both Paul's parents and John's Aunt Mimi had made sure their boys spoke clearly and well – none of that dreaded 'Scouse'. They wanted their boys to be understood beyond the confines of the city. They were, after all, grammar school boys. (So was George, but that counted for nothing with Mimi in the light of his accent and dreadful Teddy Boy attire.)

"Paul was very pleasant. I think he and John were a tad wary of me because I was older, and in their eyes a working man – John never took the piss out of me like he was inclined to do with others (and which he could do very effectively). Maybe because I could be a bit short-tempered back then, I escaped that sharp edge of his tongue for which he was renowned and which I heard employed on many occasions. He was very quick-witted. John also didn't make fun of Paul. If John didn't like someone it was face to face; he never talked about people behind their backs."

By his own admission, in those days where certain things were concerned, for such a generally friendly and sociable lad Colin had a short fuse. A dead certainty to set him off was someone telling him how to play the drums. He particularly remembers his fuse being lit one time at Paul's, in 1958, some time after the early rehearsals described in this chapter.

"One time in 1958 at Paul's he tried to tell me what to do on the drums. By this time Eric was no longer in the band and on this particular occasion George wasn't there; it was just John, Paul and me. We were rehearsing 'Peggy Sue'. Paul came over and started tapping on my snare drum asking if I could repeat the pattern he was playing. I couldn't. Unfortunately this immediately put me into a bit of a sulk the like of which I was inclined to slip into in those days and especially if I felt threatened, which I did right then.

John immediately caught the look of discomfort on my face and said to Paul to leave me alone. Immediately Paul backed off; he didn't push it, I guess he'd made his point, he simply went back to playing his guitar. John was defending me. I was grateful for that. He knew what I could do and could not do and he was happy with that. He didn't want Paul upsetting me by telling me how to play the drums. John's intervention also reminded Paul – and me – just who called the shots in this particular band."

Paul also had issues with manager Nigel Walley, which came to a head in the autumn of 1957 when the group had reduced to just four: John, Paul, Eric and Colin.

"Paul wasn't happy with Nigel taking an equal share of the Quarry Men's earnings. When the group had reduced to a four piece, Charlie McBain paid the group £2, ten shillings (£2.50) which included Nigel's take. He would dole it out in ten-shilling notes. I remember one time Charlie coming into the Green Room and saying to Nigel, 'I owe you five'. I was taken aback, thinking £5 – that's a lot of money – but it wasn't like that: Charlie meant he had five ten shilling notes to give to Nigel. I watched as he reached into his wallet and carefully counted five ten-bob notes into Nigel's hand. As band memebers we never actually received any money from promoters: Nigel always received it and passed it on. Nigel always retained the fifth note for himself: equal shares all round. John, Eric and I had no problems with this arrangement but it bothered Paul.

He would regularly bring it up, saying Nige should receive less. John would always remind him that if it wasn't for Nige we wouldn't be getting the gigs in the first place and so it was fair."

It was Colin's generosity that resolved this particular issue.

"One time at 20 Forthlin Road when it was just John, Paul and myself rehearsing, the vexed subject of Nigel taking an equal share came up yet again. John made the point that we all had expenses and that he'd just had to pay 4/6d on new strings but recognised that Nigel would have telephone calls to pay for, and so on. I listened with interest. In reply I said that I was a working man while they were still at college and school and so the money I made from playing with The Quarry Men was just extra pocket money. Eric would have been in a similar situation to me by then, having just left school and working as an apprentice. My solution to the problem was to offer Paul and John my cut from future bookings if that would help them with expenses and take the pressure off Nige. John and Paul looked at me open-mouthed, especially John. They clearly could not get their heads around the fact that I was willing to give up my fee to them. After a short moment of silence during which they digested my offer, they both said, 'Thanks, Colin, that's really good of you', and accepted the deal. And so it was. I didn't get paid from then on: my cut went to John and Paul."

ENDNOTES

Paul's guitar was an acoustic hollow bodied six string Zenith Model 17. It was manufactured by Framus, a German company. It was an archtop, like Eric's Egmond, non-cutaway with f-holes and a white scratchboard. It was built for a right hander and so, as Paul was left handed, he had to restring it to play it. Consequently photos of him with the instrument show it being played 'upside down', with its scratchplate above the strings, not below.

Initially Paul persevered with it being strung for a right-hander but his wrong hand was playing the rhythm so he was stuck for a while. Seeing a picture of left-handed Slim Whitman playing his guitar made Paul realise it was okay to play left-handed although when he restrung it it took a bit of amateur guitar-teching to get the sixth string to sit right.

Gerry Marsden (Gerry and the Pacemakers) played in a skiffle group and his guitar was a Zenith.

(**Source**: Beatles Gear, Babiuk. Author's own research.)

31

GOOD AND BAD

Looking back Colin believes being banned from the youth club and attending that 'talent' contest at the Wilson Hall was a pivotal moment in the group's history. It allowed The Quarry Men to move beyond the 'schoolboys enjoying a laugh/youth club' scene onto the fringes of the professional circuit. And it coincided with Paul's entry onto the scene.

From playing to friends in a protective environment it took them into a world where the safety net had been removed, to places where audiences did not know them and so would be less forgiving and very quick to let you know what they liked and most definitely what they didn't: not only about your music but about you personally – your clothes, your face, your personality. If the mood was right – and it often was – these messages would be delivered by hand, more precisely the knuckles of said hand.

Pete Shotton remembers the Wilson Hall was a magnet for fights between individuals and gangs, although the neighbouring Garston Swimming Baths was much more violent and known locally as the 'Blood Baths'. The Quarry Men became regulars at the former but studiously avoided playing the latter.

Once the school summer holidays were over in 1957 and life settled down into its new patterns of college and school for John, Paul and Len, while Eric and Colin were at work – so Nigel's efforts as manager really began to pay dividends. Gigs were not just more plentiful but some even paid. Or at least they did once

Nigel secured gigs that weren't talent contests (to which the group continued to be irresistibly attracted) and The Quarry Men were booked in their own right. Talent contests only paid if you won. Which the group didn't, never, ever.

Colin says it was Nige who pointed them in the direction of the Wilson Hall.

"The first show we did that Nigel suggested we do was that one when John had not wanted to go in because we had to pay to do so. It was the first of a number of talent contests we played at the Wilson Hall as well as paid bookings. The Wilson Hall's real importance to The Quarry Men was that it introduced us to the owner/promoter Charlie MacBain, who was eventually impressed enough to start paying us. He ran regular Saturday night dances and we'd play the half hour interval slot when his house band would take a break.

What we didn't know to begin with was that he also had a place on Back Broadway in Norris Green called the New Clubmoor Hall (right off Queen's Drive on the 81, turn right into Norris Green – onto another 'bus and you're there) where, later, he would also pay us to play. I remember he asked us if we would be prepared to travel that far to perform and we agreed to do so. We got ten shillings (fifty pence) each to perform. It wasn't much but useful for those among us who were still at school or college. I remember it also tickled us somewhat to think, as Paul quipped, we would be playing 'Broadway' so early in our career."

It could be argued that the fee they received was really danger money. That ever-present threat of violence was no joke. Saturday night out in Garston was not complete without someone somewhere got punched – and punched hard.

"We were open to the possibility of violence more so in Garston than anywhere. To say the least as a band you were always a bit of a target. Of course we'd already discovered that, that afternoon in Rosebery Street and so we knew from early on the best thing was to keep your head down, play and avoid eye

Mr. Charlie McBain at the mic

contact with the audience. That could be a problem for John because he refused to wear his glasses and so never knew just whom he was looking at. We never went looking for trouble but it had a habit of looking for us."

Paul was fast learning the game.

"During one of our paid gigs at the Wilson Hall I remember a drunken Teddy Boy at the front of the stage became fixated on the group, haranguing us and eventually managing to engage Paul in conversation. This was a learning curve for Paul: don't engage in conversation with the audience if you can at all avoid it, especially if they were Teds. Especially big, mean, drunken Teds. Paul was shaking his head in the direction of the Ted saying, 'No, no' but the more Paul shook his head the more determined the Ted was to get Paul to do what he wanted. Eventually he climbed onto the stage, all the time demanding that we perform 'Long Tall Sally', which Paul was refusing to do. As a group at this stage we hadn't planned to do this number because we hadn't rehearsed it. Paul certainly knew it well enough; it was one of his 'party pieces' from before joining us. Paul knowing it was not the same as us having rehearsed it as a group.

Anyway this Ted was having none of it. He refused point blank to leave the stage. With one hand tied behind his back he could have made mincemeat of the lot of us if we'd tried to make him do so. Tempers would not hold much longer. His temper I mean. Realising this, Paul relented and agreed to sing the song provided the Ted left the stage, which to all our relief – especially Paul's – he did. Needless to say, the moment the guy left the stage Paul launched himself into 'Long Tall Sally' and I remember he really gave it some wellie. Fortunately for us, this satisfied our customer to the point he didn't come back with another request."

There was no doubt that the arrival of Paul among their ranks moved The Quarry Men up a notch or two musically but it was a slow process, they were still far from being the finished article.

"I worked with Charlie McBain's son, confusingly also known as Charlie McBain, although at work we called him 'Chas'. His dad had two jobs

– he was running a milk round as well as running dances, really pushing himself physically, and sadly only a few years later after these gigs I'm describing, in December 1960, he passed away. When The Beatles were happening Chas Jnr brought into work an old Quarry Men business card to show me that he'd found in his Dad's belongings. Written on the back were the words, 'Good and bad'. He asked me what I thought his dad had meant by this comment. I could only assume that it was a critique of the group as we were, i.e. a mixture of talent and ability. But he must have thought the good outweighed the bad because he was prepared to pay us to play. No-one – especially Charlie McBain Senior – was going to pay a group if they weren't any good."

Charlie McBain Senior certainly recognised The Quarry Men's potential and even had an idea how this could be possibly better harnessed.

"One time when we were backstage in the Green Room at the Wilson Hall he introduced us to a young girl singer with whom he'd been taken. Her name was Jill Martin. She was already playing the circuit as a member of a skiffle group (I think it was the Darktown Skiffle Group of which Ringo would briefly be a member in 1958 after the Eddie Clayton Skiffle Group folded). Charlie thought she would be better singing with us; he wanted us to back her, telling us she would be good in our group. A fair amount of discussion ensued but really it was a non-starter: there was no way John and Paul were going to let this happen. They were the lead singers, our front men; they weren't going to take second billing to someone else. So, as politely as was possible without damaging The Quarry Men's prospects of future bookings at the Wilson Hall – they said, 'No'."

This story is not only testament to The Quarry Men's potential but more significantly one of the very first instances Colin can remember of Paul openly exerting his muscle within the group, albeit alongside John.

"This was Paul and John determining what happened inside the group. Not just John on his own, but John supported by Paul. It was the first time I can recall them acting in tangent to make an 'executive' decision on our group behalf, one that we others would be expected to follow/accept regardless. Throughout the discussion Len, Eric and I were merely bystanders. We said not a word. The group hierarchy was clear. The Quarry Men was now their band: John and Paul's. John still the undoubted leader, but now Paul his confidante and right hand man. The rest of us were on borrowed time."

Expanding further on the changing dynamic within The Quarry Men, Colin gives a rare insight into life inside the group.

"Almost as soon as Paul started turning up to rehearsals he became on a par with John not only musically but in making decisions with John for the group which the rest of us were expected to follow. The group had become something more serious. The choice of songs we'd perform is an obvious example I noticed almost right away, because Paul would be doing some of the singing. Up to now John chose the songs because only he would sing – none of us even sang harmony up to this point. That changed right away with Paul's arrival. So the conversation with Charlie McBain Senior was further evidence of the changes that were afoot. We had not been expected to contribute, just to listen, our opinion was not sought. Equally those outside the group were picking up on this. It was John and Paul to whom Charlie and the girl addressed their comments and deferred, not us. They presented it as a decision for them to make.

John was always the undisputed leader but from almost the moment Paul joined The Quarry Men became a joint project. Different personalities for sure, but joined at the hip musically. The rest of us accepted this, it was how it was, we didn't feel put out or annoyed. And if we had, there was precious little we could have done about it. We certainly weren't going to challenge it.

As well as the regular Saturday group rehearsal as the weeks passed, independent of the group, John and Paul began meeting at each other's homes. There they would learn tunes to play in the group, play records, talk music – and unbeknownst to us were also beginning to collaborate on tunes they had either written individually or together. They were into the music in a different way to the rest of us. John was impressed with Paul's musical ability and prowess on the guitar – Paul could teach John to play proper chords without John having 'to learn the dots'. He wouldn't have to learn scales or how to read music etc., but could go straight into learning songs. That suited John, who liked things to be immediate and instant. John respected Paul for that; he respected his musical ability, so naturally Paul was pretty soon John's collaborator. Paul was impressed by John's personality, his voice, his way with words and wit. John was different, spontaneous and sharp. It was a case of mutual attraction, their individual strengths rounded them off musically, and of course – it was John who had the band. Paul was always very diplomatic, however: he always deferred to John. He knew where the boundaries lay."

Colin is convinced Pete had seen this coming, so tuned in was he to John.

"I think Pete knew intuitively Paul was going to be a rival for John's attention, especially if he remained in the group because Paul was musically totally in tune with John. It not only suited Pete personally to leave but it also meant it avoided clashing with Paul for John's attention. The group could be their territory. The music their bond. Outside the group, socially, Pete could remain John's best friend."

On another occasion at the Wilson Hall when The Quarry Men were playing Charlie had become embarrassed by a skiffle group whom he'd booked and so he turned to The Quarry Men to help him out of a tricky spot.

"When this other group took the stage – just after our set – it was apparent from the first song that the singer was tone deaf. I was impressed by how Charlie took charge of the situation. He went on stage after their second number, seized the mic and thanked them – very politely – for their endeavours and asked the audience to give them a big hand before ushering them off stage. He had already been backstage to speak with John and ask if we would go

back on stage almost immediately to fill in. As leader, John had agreed to do so. We were being paid that night but the group Charlie kicked off stage were being auditioned."

This small incident reveals how much The Quarry Men had improved, so much so that Charlie McBain was booking them to even headline some of his dances. It also reveals how well Charlie knew his audiences, a singer who couldn't sing could draw the wrath of an audience, and, as has been said, the atmosphere at Wilson Hall could be volatile – it could change in the wink of an eye. A tuneless singer was the perfect excuse for some 'bother' – so Charlie had to be ruthless. Get them off stage as quickly as possible, get The Quarry Men on, keep the audience sweet.

Alongside their gigs at the Wilson Hall The Quarry Men began to play that second venue Charlie had mentioned – the New Clubmoor Hall on Back Broadway, Norris Green. Initially they were the interval act there, booked and paid to play while the main band took a break.

32

THE NEW CLUBMOOR HALL ON BACK BROADWAY

A purpose-built venue in Norris Green, the New Clubmoor Hall was almost identical to the Wilson Hall. Constructed just after the war, it was a single story building with a front door and cloakroom at one end, the stage at the other. No curtains. There was a small room at the side and back of the stage which acted as the Green Room. All bands were expected to keep the noise down when in that room and another was on stage.

Despite having played previously with The Quarry Men at both the Wilson Hall and the New Clubmoor, Paul McCartney usually refers to his appearance with them at the New Clubmoor on Friday 18th October 1957 as his debut. He certainly has good reason to recall that particular booking because of what happened when that evening he launched into the guitar solo in the instrumental tune, 'Guitar Boogie' which he hoped would confirm his position as lead guitarist.

> **Paul**: *"It was upstairs at the Conservative Club on Broadway, just above a bank or something, I'm not sure, one floor up. They had done it (played in public) and I hadn't. I'd been allowed, I think on the first time I played with The Quarry Men, to play lead. In private I wasn't bad and the guys thought great, you could play lead but I totally froze that first time. Suddenly it*

The Quarry Men, Colin, Paul, Len, John and Eric
on stage at the New Clubmoor

came to my solo and I just couldn't squeeze a note out. I just froze, the guitar froze and time just stood still. I just said, 'I can't do this, never again.' So what with one thing and another I said to John, 'There's this mate of mine, he's a bit young… but he's really good'."

(The Day Met Paul, BBC Radio 2, 2007; Bob Harris interview.)

Of course 'this mate' was George Harrison and Paul's mention of him to John presages the next phase of The Quarry Men's evolution.

Why Paul refers to this as his 'first' gig with The Quarry Men and not those he'd played previously with them at the Wilson Hall, the New Clubmoor itself or before that at the Woolton Youth Club could be because his memory of those fluffed notes have subsequently eclipsed his memories of those earlier shows. Clearly this incident has left an indelible mark on his memory. Paul also describes it as as the first time the group got paid, although Colin remembers otherwise.

"The first time we got paid a set fee to play as a group was at the Wilson Hall. Our manager Nigel Walley collected the money and distributed it among us. We had actually played the New Clubmoor previously to the 18th, October – and been paid.

There could be a thousand reasons why Paul describes it as his first performance with us. Most likely several memories have morphed into one. Just like the church fete it was a long, long time ago… and in his case many thousands of gigs ago!"

That this is a case of memories merging is further suggested by the fact that there is no upstairs at the New Clubmoor. It's a single-storey building much the same as the Wilson Hall. That aside, what overwhelmingly convinces Colin this show came later in Paul's tenure with The Quarry Men is logistics.

Single label for 'Guitar Boogie'/ Arthur (Guitar Boogie) Smith

John and Eric (New Clubmoor)

"It came after Wilson Hall because it was owned by Charlie McBain, who owned both venues. He first heard us at Wilson Hall at a talent contest in which Paul was very definitely involved – if it hadn't been for his insistence we would have walked away that night. As a result of hearing us there on that night and a few more occasions (for which he paid us) Charlie McBain then offered us a paid gig at the New Clubmoor. The only venue where we went upstairs to play was Woolton Village Club in January 1959. Right next door to Woolton Village Club was/is a bank. I think Paul has simply confused shows and run them together in his memory but I agree it was at the New Clubmoor where Paul tried out as lead guitarist."

Despite Paul's embarrassment the other boys in the group took Paul's fluffed notes in their stride.

"I don't remember it being a major disaster. We simply laughed it off. It was no big deal in our short experience, worse had happened. But I guess for Paul who was undoubtedly out to impress it would have been embarrassing. It's the sort of thing that really stings and bugs you in the moment it happens, especially when you are young – and from the outset he was a perfectionist. But, of course, as the years roll on perspectives change, and – especially if you go on to enjoy the unparalleled success and acclaim Paul has – your youthful embarrassments often fade to become a great story to tell, one in which you can laugh at yourself to the amusement your friends."

Colin remembers that John made light of the incident, nothing too acerbic.

"John just commented to the audience words to the effect, 'Oh you'll have to excuse him, he's our new boy'. We were still a young band, amateurs in reality – freshly semi-professional, we made mistakes on a regular basis. No one was pointing any fingers."

Maybe the real significance of this show and Paul's reaction to his mistake was that it pulled George Harrison into the frame – at least in his mind as he looked to correct his error and make the group stronger. What he needed to do now was to get John to hear George play.

In that very moment ley lines were being drawn and planets aligned.

"How Paul knew George was through school (The Liverpool Institute High School For Boys). Before he moved to Allerton in 1956 to 20 Forthlin Road where he was living when he met us at the fete, Paul and his family had lived out in Speke, where George was also living on the same huge council estate. George and Paul shared the same 'bus into and back from school each day: the number 86. They continued to do so even after Paul moved to Allerton. Despite Paul being older than George – which mattered when you were teenagers – they'd apparently become bonded by a shared passion for guitars."

Paul says the McCartney family moved from Speke to Allerton in late April 1956 although his younger brother Michael clearly remembers celebrating his twelfth birthday in number 20 Forthlin Road. That would mean the McCartneys were living in Allerton as early as January '56 because Mike's birthday is 12th January. (He was born in 1944.)

Paul remembers that it was when he was still living out at Speke and travelling on the 86 that he and George had become acquainted. They became friendly despite the fact Paul was a whole eight months older than George. The age difference really mattered because it meant they were in different years at the Institute – Paul one year ahead of George. At the 'Inny' the protocol was that boys from the year above didn't speak to the boys a year below. It was a hierarchical thing.

What would lead Paul to break that all-important protocol was George's appearance. Indeed it wasn't just Paul who took note when George boarded the 'bus to school; all the lads did, for whatever their ages they were equally amazed by the incredible quiff George sported. According to McCartney it looked *'like a fucking turban'*. All the boys were transfixed. Paul also observed that this younger lad's school books – similar to his own – were adorned by drawings of electric guitars: like Paul, the boy was clearly an obsessive. Intrigued and wanting to know more, whenever the amazingly bequiffed youngster sat next to Paul on the journey to 'the Inny' the age barrier was gradually broken down as conversations began and a shared obsession drew them closer.

33

ABANDONED TEA-CHEST BASSES AND CONFISCATED DRUMSTICKS

As the summer of 1957 turned to autumn The Quarry Men found more and more opportunities to perform in public. The number of skiffle groups in Liverpool was increasing all the time and competition for places to play was keen. The growth in number and popularity of 'talent contests' throughout the city during the Fifties provided an important and fairly regular platform on which such nascent stars could strut their stuff. Such events allowed several groups to appear on the same bill at the same venue on the same night. They also allowed the punters to stretch out and dance. As Colin has explained they were economically very attractive for club owners to stage because they they did not have to pay the artists and groups to perform and – even better – as each act would be accompanied by a posse of friends and fans *who had to pay* to get in, club owners/promoters were assured of a full house nearly every time.

Herein lies The Quarry Men's apparent propensity for talent contests – they were what was available fairly locally. Plus, who knows, one time they might strike lucky.

'These contests provided a great opportunity for us and other young skifflers such as The Crossrocks, The Sunnysiders and The Connaughts to play regularly. A loose kind of camaraderie built up among us, and it was always good to know what the opposition was up to, what songs they were performing,

what was attracting fans to their cause and who might change allegiances to us. We weren't driven by any desperate desire to win although to have done so – just once – would have been great. It was the chance to play in front of an audience that really mattered to us. That doesn't mean we were blasé: not winning did irk us at the time of each show – because we believed we were the best. We just didn't allow failure to dampen our spirits, we always bounced back in time for the next one, our resolve to succeed even stronger."

The popularity of these shows meant that clubs did not have any headline acts to advertise/publicise in advance only that a 'contest' was being staged. Consequently individual group names were not recorded on posters or in the local newspaper adverts of the day because the promoter would not know for certain who was going to turn up. This – plus the absence of any member of The Quarry Men keeping a diary – means compiling a full chronology of where and when the boys performed is nigh on impossible. There are a few advertised bookings that help compile a 'selective' chronology but this cannot be in any way considered 'definitive'. There were a lot more bookings that were not advertised/recorded but are definitely remembered.

In working with Colin to compile his memoirs many hours, days… weeks, months… I have been spent attempting to accurately weave into the 'list of known bookings' approximately when some of the other 'unrecorded' performances occurred. It has been largely defeating. Memories of the shows have grown clearer but the dates remain elusive. The personnel of the group for each show provides an approximation of when they occurred.

The early Wilson Hall bookings would have occurred during the autumn of 1957 after Pete had left but ahead of the departures of Len and Eric and the arrival of George Harrison. Len and Eric left at different times during the autumn and early winter and so some of the shows Colin recalls occurred when one or other of them were no longer Quarry Men.

A feature of the early shows was usually their aftermaths.

The Quarry Men often found themselves in tricky situations confronted by local Teddy Boys from whom they were forced to run for their lives. One such narrow escape occurred after a talent contest staged at the Belle Vale Labour Club. The group personnel that night was: John, Paul, Eric, Len and Colin.

"As per usual it had been a fairly unsuccessful night, i.e. we didn't win. Somewhat downhearted, John, Paul, Len, Eric and I packed our kit ready to exit but just as we were about to do so we were confronted in the club's reception area by a rather large and unpleasant Teddy Boy accompanied by another, much smaller, but equally mean-looking Ted trying his very best to look as intimidating as his mate. The big Ted and his weasly mate had taken a real dislike to John. This was not an unusual feature of our performances, John seemed to attract ugly, nasty buggers like this on a regular basis.

This particular thug was goading John, trying to provoke a fight but John was doing what he usually did in these situations – attempting to talk his way out. Paul had already made his way to the front door, clearly concerned that there might be a fight, wanting to quit the venue as quickly as possible to avoid such an eventuality. I was going backwards and forwards from the dance floor to the reception area each time making eye contact with John just so he knew he hadn't been abandoned, that we were there should he need us. Actually, I'm not sure what we would have done had violence erupted. As I've already mentioned, The Quarry Men were not built to fight!

Eventually word got around that we had a problem and a committee member approached me to ask, 'Are you in lumber?' It wasn't a term I was familiar with but I knew exactly what he meant. My answer was a very positive, 'Yes' – followed by an equally positive plea that, 'It wasn't us, we didn't want any trouble!' He smiled and told me that when we left he would accompany us to the 'bus stop.

As a wave of gratitude flooded over me I replied we were actualy packed up and ready to go right that moment. In fact if he would just hang on I would go and tell John. Returning to where John was still being harangued, I boldly interrupted the big Ted and informed John, 'We have to go now or we will miss our 'bus'. As I did so I caught a threatening look from the Ted's smaller mate.

As I paid more attention to this aggressive little sod it dawned on me that I actually knew him: he was a work colleague, a young lad who had recently joined Guy Rogers where I worked.

Suddenly I felt empowered: a possible way out of our tricky spot had opened up. I immediately engaged this lad in conversation, reminding him we were actually workmates – my hope being that this connection would bring him up sharp, make him think of the possible consequences and end the confrontation. To an extent it did – at least enough to divert his attention from John on to me.

It also succeeded in distracting his mate, the big Ted whose venomous look now became focused on me. As he fixed me in his glare he asked his partner, 'Is he alright?' He definitely wasn't inquiring as to my health. To my immense relief the smaller gangster said, 'Yes'. That was all I needed: a break in concentration. Seizing the moment I emphatically told John that we really did need to go and began edging him towards the door where Paul and the other lads were nervously waiting.

True to his word the committee member was also there not only to see us safely exit the club but he even joined us to walk to the 'bus stop to catch the number 66 back home to Woolton village. As soon as one arrived and the chap bade us good night, relieved and desperate to escape into the 'bus's welcoming sanctuary, The Quarry Men raced upstairs to enjoy a smoke – never thinking to look behind.

The first one to get off the 'bus at the bottom end of Kings Drive was Eric Griffiths. My stop was next, halfway up Kings Drive. So keen was I to retrieve my drums from under the steps and scuttle home like Eric before me I didn't notice the nasty bastard Ted, his ugly mate and a few of their cronies had slunk onto the 'bus after us and were quietly sitting downstairs waiting in ambush. As Eric and I had alighted they'd said not a word because we were not their prey; we were allowed to leave safely without alerting us into sounding the alarm: their target was John.

John told me later when he and the others got off in Woolton village so did the army of Teds lying in wait on the bottom deck. In the ensuing melee the big Ted punched John on the cheek. John said the blow really startled him but once he'd been hit instinctively he and the others had immediately begun to 'leg it' home to avoid a real beating. It was a close-run thing. Such was the suddenness and fury of the assault, in order to affect his escape Len had been forced to abandon his tea-chest bass in the middle of the road where it would remain for the next week or so. During that time whenever we ventured onto the High Street Len's tea chest bass would be in a different place, moving up and down the street as if it had a life of its own, desperately seeking refuge or rescue. Then, one time, it was gone, disappeared. We never did find out what finally became of it."

Len did not retrieve his instrument because in those days tea chests were easily obtainable and so the loss of such a piece of kit – which would undoubtedly have been damaged in his pursuit of personal survival – was not unduly concerning.

This was the second Quarry Men tea-chest bass to be so abandoned. The first had also been relinquished during another desperate manoeuvre to ensure survival.

"The first time Len ditched his tea-chest bass was after a show at the Wilson Hall in Garston. As The Quarry Men left the venue I was with my drinking buddies Kevin and Charlie just ahead of the other lads in the group. Charlie was carrying the bass drum.

There were a gang of mean-looking Teddy Boys standing menacingly just outside the club and so we'd got our heads down, eyes averted – the standard non-combat strategy for exiting the Wilson Hall. Suddenly, behind us, we heard a blood-curdling battle cry ring out. As ever it wasn't Charlie, Kevin or myself who they were after – it was John. The moment he emerged the gang roared, 'There's that f-in' Lennon! Let's get him!'

John, Paul, Eric and Len instantly took to their heels. Len, encumbered by his tea-chest bass, was almost caught immediately by the pursuing posse of hooligans, so he just dropped it in their path and sprinted hell for leather with the others towards the 'bus stop. By sheer good luck a 'bus pulled up the moment they reached the stop and by an even greater stroke of good fortune as they clambered aboard it pulled away leaving the marauding Teds behind, cursing and swearing, stranded at the stop. Luckily Charlie, Kevin and I completely escaped the attention of the Teds and slipped unnoticed into the nearby pub, 'The Alexander'. Those thugs only had fists for John."

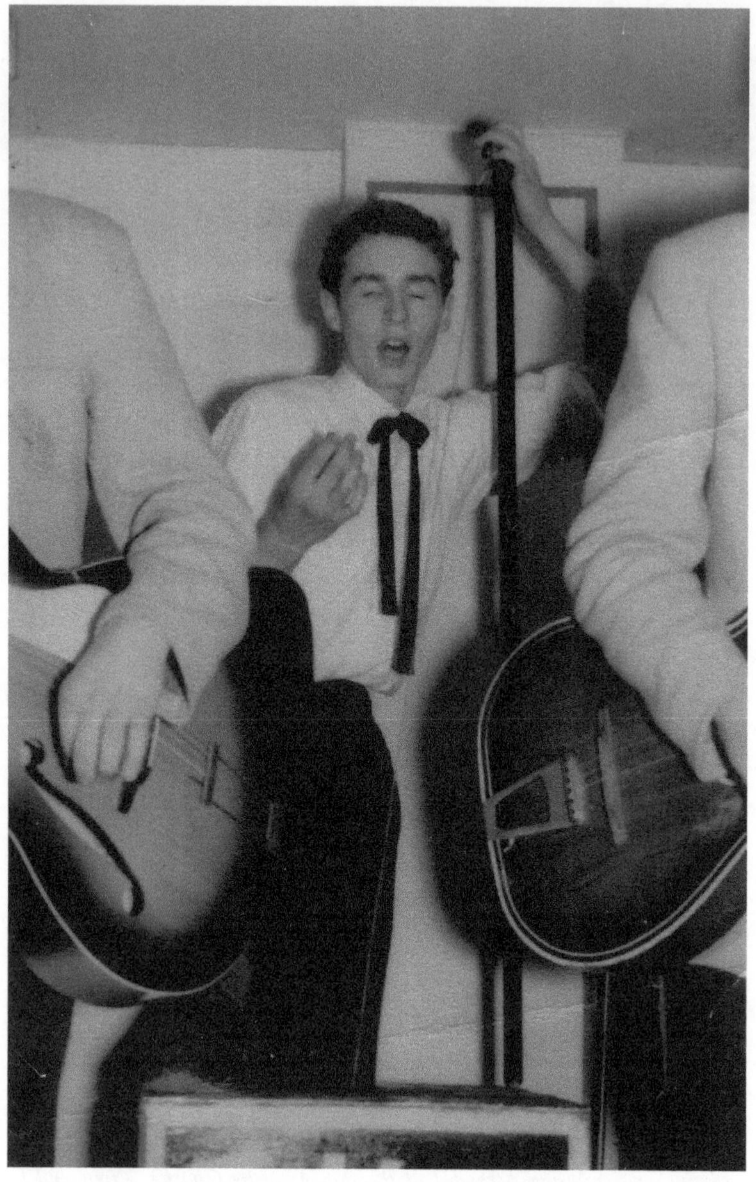

Len Garry on a different night to the photos of the New Clubmoor – and on a different tea-chest bass

As ever survival proved the better part of valour for all The Quarry Men and by the time Colin and his drinking buddies emerged from 'The Alexander' the Teds had long gone.

"All was quiet but just ahead of us silhouetted on the path was Len's tea-chest bass now in complete tatters, no doubt having taken the kicking intended for John."

Another moment of tension Colin recalls from those early days when Paul had just joined the group came from within the group itself, not from without.

In this instance Nige Walley felt compelled to use direct intervention to sort a problem that had first surfaced among The Quarry Men when they played the St. Peter's Church Youth Club dances. The lack of a microphone at St. Peter's meant Colin's drums had a tendency to drown out John's vocals (and Paul's). It became a bone of contention within the group. To resolve the issue the boys and their manager Nige had started to ask Colin to play quietly. Not only was he not moved to comply with their request Colin also resisted their suggestion of using brushes instead of sticks. He says he wasn't being contrary; he just wasn't comfortable doing so. He played loud, that was his style. It wasn't his fault the youth club didn't have a microphone.

Strangely, it was at The Cavern that Nige took this situation in hand and exerted some managerial muscle to resolve the impasse. (Even though The Cavern always provided a microphone for artists to use.)

On this particular evening as The Quarry Men assembled on stage ready to rock, instead of being situated in his usual place among the audience to listen to their feedback, Nige was just to Colin's right on stage. He was standing half way in, half way out of the doorway leading from the Green Room directly onto the stage. As John began to announce their first number Nige leaned forward, grabbed Colin's sticks and swiftly disappeared back through the Green Room into the audience, leaving the errant drummer on stage with just his brushes.

Colin being Colin – as Pete Shotton had already learned – could only be pushed so far.

"I did not enjoy being told how to play my drums – especially by the manager of all people, who did not play any instrument. I certainly wasn't going to put up with this sort of treatment. Instead I just sat back, folded my arms, ignored the brushes and made no attempt to play. After finishing his introduction and hearing only silence where the drum roll should have been John turned to see me sitting in silent protest. I'd descended into one of my infamous sulks. Immediately sussing the situation John simply leaned forward and, peering into the audience, instructed Nige to hand me back my sticks. Without hesitation or protest Nigel did so. From that moment on the subject was dropped, I was never asked to 'play quiet' again; our 'leader' had spoken."

34

EYE-LEVEL TUTU

Around the same time as the New Clubmoor gig, Nige Walley pulled off a real coup: he got The Quarry Men an audition for a television talent show. Despite their previous experiences with such shows, The Quarry Men's enthusiasm remained rock solid.

"Ever hopeful, we went into this as as starry-eyed and convinced as ever that we would win. The auditions were held at ABC Television studios in Didsbury, Manchester. Being an audition for the TV there was no way I wanted to miss this but it was a mid-week gig so I had to ask my boss for a whole day off work in order to attend. He was not impressed, quite grudging in fact. When he asked why I needed the day off and I told him what it was I was up to, he looked me squarely in the eye and told me straight I should make my mind up. Was I going to be in a group or be an upholsterer? I hung my head and tried to look suitably abashed. However, he did – reluctantly – give me the day off (without pay, of course)."

When the great day arrived the boys met at Penny Lane opposite the 'bus shelter in the middle of the roundabout.

"John was already waiting at the stop when Eric and I arrived at the same time. When Len arrived he said he'd decided he didn't want to skip school and so he wasn't coming – he didn't want to 'get done' for 'sagging' school. In those days truancy was a big deal. A serious misdemeanour for a boy at a prestigious grammar school like the Institute. John was not impressed and I

quickly pointed out to him that I was losing a day's pay to come and so, with pressure from John, Len was 'persuaded' to reluctantly come along. Paul was last to arrive, with no such qualms about cutting school, and so we jumped onto a bus to Central Station in Liverpool from where we caught the train into Manchester."

Once in Manchester the boys had to find their way to Didsbury. They had not realised it was nearly five miles out from the centre of the city.

"We were directed to a 'bus, hopped on and, as ever, trooped upstairs, sat down and got our fares ready to pay. As we did so Paul had a major panic attack: like the rest of us he hadn't expected to have to make this additional 'bus ride and immediately realised that once he paid his fares to and from Didsbury he wouldn't have enough money to get back home to Liverpool.

He was sitting on a seat ahead of me towards the front of the 'bus: he and John always took a seat to themselves if they could because they had their guitars. He immediately appealed to John who was sat in front of him and as he was still panicking a chap walked down the aisle towards the steps at the back ready to disembark. As he passed Paul he pushed some money – a florin (two shillings) – into the palm of Paul's hand. The chap said nothing, just carried on his way down the aisle.

For a moment Paul was stunned; he just sat looking at the coin in the palm of his hand, amazed at the kindness of strangers. Remembering himself just in time he ran to the back of the bus and shouted down to the chap below waiting to get off, 'Thank you very much. I love you'. To this day I can hear him shouting those words. We all just burst out laughing and as Paul returned to his seat John said, 'You daft get, fancy telling a stranger you love them.'

"As teenage lads we weren't used to hearing or in the habit of telling someone – especially a complete stranger – we loved them. But Paul didn't care; he was simply relieved, as he said, 'He's given me some money – it means I can get home'. It certainly amused us and took a weight of Paul's shoulders and he was right, that chap was most definitely a Good Samaritan worthy of his gratitude."

Arriving at the studio The Quarry Men were directed across the road to a 'big' hotel where the auditions were being held upstairs.

"We went into a cloakroom which acted as a dressing room. Once we were ready we joined the other 'hopefuls' sitting on chairs in the hall outside the cloakroom. I remember as I sat there my attention was completely diverted when a young lady ballerina wearing a tutu came and stood next to me. She couldn't sit down because of the tutu and so her bottom was at my eye level. It was just too much for a young boy to endure! Try as I may I couldn't look the other way."

Valiantly Colin maintained his composure and avoided eye contact with the other lads in order to avoid any embarrassing comments or outbursts of laughter.

At the end of the hall where The Quarry Men were sitting were double doors through which hopefuls such as they – and the young woman in the tutu – would disappear for their audition. In most cases contestants re-emerged minutes later, sad-faced and downhearted, even tearful, to report that they had been unsuccessful.

"Eventually one chap dressed like a clown emerged with a smile on his face to say, 'He can say yes!' So just before it was our turn our hopes were renewed. My immediate concern was that I didn't have a stool on which to sit to drum and didn't know if there would be one inside the audition room. Fortunately, as we went in I noticed a dining room chair by the door so I positioned myself and my drums there. But that didn't go down at all well with the producer or whoever he was in charge; he was quite grumpy and abrupt and although I tried to argue my case, he simply cut across me and commanded, 'Get yourself over here!' pointing to a designated space (which I hadn't noticed as I'd entered the room) where all the acts had to stand. I stopped protesting and carried my drums and the chair over to where he wanted us. He was quite severe and so I remained silent for the rest of the audition. His grumpy manner soured

the occasion. None of us felt comfortable. And, of course, we got the thumbs down."

Down but not out! All that way and nothing to show for it. By now The Quarry Men were talent show-hardened. By the time they got back to Liverpool they had bounced back and were already looking forward to their next booking. In the meantime, word got around amongst friends and followers that they had failed yet another audition because Colin had lost his composure and told the producer to 'fuck off!' Colin absolutely denies saying anything of the sort. It wasn't his style: it was just a very miffed John and Paul's way of saving face and glossing over yet another rejection.

35

DARK HORSE ON THE HORIZON

Paul's earlier gaff at the New Clubmoor may have set him thinking about George becoming a Quarry Man but, although he's edging into the frame, before he actually did so two more of the original line-up would leave.

The first one was Len, whose departure had nothing to do with personalities or musical ability; it was simply down to plain bad luck. Eric would be the next, more of which later.

"It was at a booking at the Wilson Hall that Len first failed to turn up for a show. He'd already gone when we played Dovedale Towers on the 11th October and wasn't there for our first 'advertised' booking at the New Clubmoor on the 18th October. I do not recall him being on stage with us for either of those bookings. We had played the New Clubmoor before this date but always unadvertised; that's what is forgotten in most books – we played many bookings at these venues but our name was not always used in the advertisments for the shows.

It was at one our first bookings at the New Clubmoor that along with the rest of us Len had been caught on camera wearing our new stage uniform but not long after at a booking at the Wilson Hall he failed to turn up. As I say, he did not play those two dates in mid-October that I've mentioned which means he left sometime in late September/ very early October. To not turn up was so unlike him. He never missed a practice or a gig. I remember asking Nige Walley if he knew where Len was and he replied that Len was ill.

That first night without Len, his place on tea-chest bass was taken in turns by Nigel and Ivan. They must have received word in advance because they turned up with Len's tea-chest bass. Very early in the group's existence, Ivan had played tea-chest bass in The Quarry Men, his place being taken by Len, whom Ivan himself introduced to John and the boys before he brought Paul to meet them. (Len was an Institute boy.)

During our set Ive and Nige took it in turns on bass. Nige was less comfortable on stage than Ivan, who jumped up and down a lot, which amused the audience and so after a few songs he remained on stage for the rest of that evening."

After this Colin does not remember Len playing with the group again or turning up to rehearsals.

"I don't recall seeing Len again after this. I'm not sure why he stopped turning up at this particular time but I never saw him again until the late 1990s when we got together at a Cavern anniversary. I know he contracted tubercular meningitis but he says this was in 1958, so this must have been something different that afflicted him. Tubercular meningitis is a hugely nasty and serious illness: they call it a 'killer' disease. Apparently Len collapsed at home, fell into a coma and was rushed to hospital and placed in isolation. Fortunately he was made of strong stuff and did not succumb although he spent seven months in hospital."

Len was not replaced in The Quarry Men.

"Nigel did not play again with the group – he stuck rigidly to his role as manager. Ivan stood in for a couple more shows at the Wilson Hall but not long after The Quarry Men dumped the tea-chest bass altogether and became a four piece: John, Paul, Eric and Colin. Banjo, washboard and now tea-chest bass had gone: instrumentally we were no longer strictly a skiffle band, more of an acoustic rock 'n' roll band. Rock 'n' roll numbers, including some Buddy Holly songs, now formed the majority of our set. Indeed there is a newspaper advert for a gig of ours at the Wilson Hall in which we are described as 'rockers'!"

Len's sudden departure directs Colin's thoughts to the famous photograph that appears in many books depicting Colin, Len, John, Paul and Eric on stage at the New Clubmoor Hall. The picture is often dated as being taken on Saturday 23rd November 1957. The boys are decked out in white shirts and long bow ties, with John and Paul also wearing 'white/light coloured' jackets. Colin's memory is that this photograph was taken much, much earlier than 23rd November.

"It had to be because Len had departed the group well before then."

In the very short time Paul had been in their ranks he had clearly not only raised the bar musically but professionally as well. With him in their ranks The Quarry Men began to also *look* the part.

Being left- and right-handed, John and Paul brought symmetry to the way The Quarry Men now lined up but it was at an early appearance at the New Clubmoor that the whole group appeared for the first time on stage in matching attire.

"Paul wore a 'light coloured' jacket (I remember it being an 'oatmeal' colour), which was matched by John – goodness knows from where he got his – but there was no way he'd have let Paul upstage him by drawing more attention to himself on stage in the way he dressed. More to the point, John would have had to agree to this 'uniform' before either of them wore it. The other boys including myself were expected to follow their lead by wearing white shirts, but not jackets, and long bow ties – a little touch of Country & Western apparel to which, later in my story, I will return. (Country was very popular in Liverpool.) Nige most probably helped us source those bow ties. For the audience the wearing of the jackets by the two central singers visually established John and Paul's ascendancy over the rest of us on stage . We didn't mind that; after all it looked good and, they were the front men, it gave us a bit of style.

Not too long after that photograph was taken Len left the group. He was not with us by late November. I don't know who decided that was the date of the picture. People like to accrue this kind of information even if they don't know if it's correct. So many people want it to be a photo of the first time Paul performed with The Quarry Men but wanting it to be doesn't mean it was.

Not all Quarry Men dates were advertised. I believe this specific 'dating' of the photo as 23rd November, 1957 happened when the New Clubmoor was reopened earlier in the 2000s and it suited their purpose to quote that date in publicity for the club but in truth there is no written evidence that it is correct. I have never believed it was."

Other 'advertised' dates around this period are another at the Wilson Hall on Thursday 7th November and a date at Stanley Abattoir Social Club, Old Swan, Liverpool, on Saturday 16th November. By all accounts they played a raucous show at the Abattoir but were never asked back.

36

DOVEDALE TOWERS AND THE HOLE IN THE WALL

11th October 1957 The Len-less Quarry Men played the Dovedale Towers on Penny Lane – just John, Paul, Eric and Colin: a four-piece. It's a venue situated about half way down Penny Lane right on the junction with Dovedale Road close to Dovedale Primary School, which John, Ivan and George had attended as young boys. Colin has good reason to recall this show.

'The main attraction that evening was a big dance band, we were just the interval 'turn', the token skiffle band for the younger ones in the audience. We turned up in the late afternoon minus Len and soon settled into the band room ready to go on stage later in the evening. With time to kill we decided to go off for a pint. The other lads headed to the Brook House on Smithdown Road while I was off in the opposite direction to the Rose of Mossley on Rose Lane to meet with my drinking buddies, Kevin and Charlie.

At that point John remembered I'd told him I was attending my sister-in-law Sheila's (Brian's wife) 21st birthday party later that evening after the show and so he became concerned thinking that that was where I was now heading for some fun. He clearly didn't think that was a good idea because I might not return and if I did I'd be already 'half cut', which would not be good news for the group. He'd forgotten that I'd said the party was after our show and wasn't local. Seeing alarm registering on the other boys' faces I tried to calm their fears by pointing out John's error – the party started much later and was being held at a private house near the 'Hole In the Wall' in Huyton, not locally, so, like them, all I was doing was just nipping out for a swift pint. This more or less put their minds at rest.

I was good to my word: accompanied by Kevin and Charlie I was back at the Towers in good time for our performance. We three were regulars at The Dovedale Towers because it was a good place for dancing and for a while became 'our local' dance hall. In those days it was known as 'Barney's' because it was owned by St.Barnabas church (where Paul had been a choir boy), which stands at the top of Penny Lane (facing the now famous roundabout). Kevin, Charlie, myself and Eric Griffiths were all adept at the waltz and the quick-step – the jive came later (Joan taught me) – and regularly stepped the light fantastic at Barney's in the hope of tapping off."

After what Colin calls 'a sweaty half hour' The Quarry Men finished their set, came off stage to no great acclaim and only grudging congratulations from the big band. Good naturedly remarking to the drummer of that band that he didn't know how he had the stamina to play all night in such heat Colin was met with the taciturn reply, *'You get used to it'*. The chap made it clear that bands like his had scant regard for a bunch of jumped-up teenagers playing that ridiculous 'skiffle music'. To blokes in professional dance bands in the Fifties The Quarry Men were mere amateurs playing something that was an apology for 'real' music. Little did they know that in The Quarry Men they'd come face to face with their nemesis.

Rapidly packing his drums away Colin caught the 4 or 5 'bus to Woolton, dropped his kit at home then embarked on a two-bus trek all the way to Huyton.

"As for the party I was not at all familiar with Huyton where it was being held so had presumed that the 'Hole in the Wall' to which I'd been directed was a pub. I asked to be dropped off as close to it as possible. Imagine my surprise when the conductor told me I was there and I stepped off to find myself face to face not with a pub but literally a huge hole in a very large

sandstone wall that surrounded the housing estate that was also directly in front of me. Through that very real hole stood a brightly lit private house from where I could clearly hear the rockin' sounds of my sister-in-law Sheila's 21st birthday party.

It being Sheila's 21st is why I remember that particular booking so well and know that, by then, Len had dropped out of the picture."

As a group, whenever they could, The Quarry Men were party animals and around this time the boys still socialised together quite a bit. One particular party Colin remembers attending was held by girls who were fans of the group. The house where the party was held was in north Liverpool and the idea was that the group would perform sometime during the evening.

"The house was too small: so we couldn't play a full set, it was too cramped, there was no room to move or properly set up. We played a couple of songs and then the rest of the time relied on the record player for musical entertainment. As the party unfolded we realised we'd missed the last 'bus home, which was not difficult to do in those days because last 'buses home would have run just after eleven. As the party flagged and the music stopped and the drink ran out, those who remained started to settle to sleep on chairs, settee and the floor. At some point John and Paul decided they needed some cigarettes. In those days there were cigarette machines outside most newsagents and so having ascertained if there was one locally they popped out to buy some. Half an hour later they returned with their ciggies and along the way had called into a nearby building site (as you do) and collected a cocky watchman's lamp. (Security in those days would be an overnight watchman.) The lamp was illuminated with two red and two white lamps and much to everyone's amusement they passed it around. It seemed a crazy thing to have done at the time but it amused us all. Eventually however, as best we could, we all settled to some fitful sleep.

The following morning the girl whose home it was discovered that the front door lock was full of hard cement. The problem was that, although she could get outside, trying to put a key in the door to get back in was no longer possible. She was not amused and demanded to know who was responsible. Of course no one owned up. Tempers became frayed. The only two who had been out during the night (and who had coincidentally visited a building site) were John and Paul so they were the obvious culprits. However, they were adamant that, cocky watchman's lamp aside, they were not responsible. They simply refuted the suggestion: 'How dare people even think it?' was their attitude. None of us were very helpful, instead we just quietly drifted away leaving her to sort the problem for herself. Needless to say I don't remember ever seeing her again at any of our shows, but it was a good party."

37

SIGNING ON THE GIGGLE BAND

As Colin says, almost from the moment Paul joined the group The Quarry Men became a different unit. Paul's level of musicianship seriously upped the ante. With him among their ranks they moved from being a loose conglomeration of school friends out for a lark into something approaching a 'proper' band. John had always been serious about The Quarry Men and rock 'n' roll. From the moment he had heard Elvis sing 'Heartbreak Hotel' and then Little Richard's explosive 'Long Tall Sally' he had known, instinctively, intuitively that somewhere inside this mighty beast they called rock 'n' roll, his future lay. In Paul he had met his musical other half. To paraphrase **Cynthia**, John's future wife, *'Although as people, John and Paul were as different as chalk is to cheese, musically they were joined at the hip'*.

From the get-go Pete Shotton had recognised this musical 'oneness'. Similarly Colin clocked Paul's influence, noticing how the band quite quickly became very much John and Paul's 'joint' baby. John remained the undisputed leader and Paul was careful not to rock the boat but John was clearly listening closely to Paul's ideas just as much as Paul was tuning into John's.

'Paul told us he was going to wear this oatmeal coloured jacket to gigs and not to be outdone John also got himself a jacket. Brian Epstein wasn't the first one to smarten John Lennon up. The rest of us however were not asked or encouraged to wear jackets. In fact we were told not to,

that we should wear white shirts and long western-style bow ties. Visually it worked well, it 'smartened' us up and established an on stage group identity. None of us, least of all John, objected to this idea. The first time we wore this 'uniform' was the first time we were invited to play the Wilson Hall as a paid gig. In Paul's view of things such an auspicious occasion demanded we looked the part, that we smarten ourselves up. He was right, it was a shrewd move, it not only made us look like a unit, it made us feel more like a 'proper' group: that was important. It made us feel like 'stars'."

Another Paul 'idea' that he and John were already road-testing in their private meetings at each other's homes, and which would have huge impact much later in the story of The Beatles, was reinforced at yet another talent contest that The Quarry Men didn't win.

"It was at the Grafton Ballroom on West Derby Road – a big dancehall – another talent contest gig of which I am uncertain of the date. John, Paul, Eric and I played this show. We were the fifth of six skiffle groups to perform that evening. By the time we hit the stage the audience had heard five of what we considered our better songs performed several times already by the preceding acts. Among ourselves back stage as we heard these tunes being played over and over we felt it put us at a disadvantage. Our spirits dropped accordingly. We had nothing new or different to offer.

However that was par for the course: most bands The Quarry Men encountered on the circuit played pretty much the same set. What I specifically remember at the Grafton was Paul bending John's ear about the fact that as a band we really needed to be performing our 'own' songs so that wherever we went we would be performing tunes that no-one had heard. He reasoned that in this way we would have a great advantage over the opposition because our set would be fresh and original, more likely to grab an audience's attention and so we wouldn't have to worry about repeating what audiences had already heard several times over. This would set us apart, give us an edge, an identity. John saw the logic in Paul's argument and agreed. Whether he meant them to write their own songs or to dig deep to cover more obscure records or both I can't say for sure, but I believe he actually meant they should write their own material."

By this time, the autumn of 1957, Paul had been in the band for a month or more and John was now a student attending the Liverpool College of Art right next door to Paul's school, The Liverpool Institute. They were already convening regularly at each other's houses independently of the other boys in the group and while they would be learning cover songs to introduce into The Quarry Men's set we now know they were also dabbling with writing their own tunes and sharing these with each other. So Paul's comment to John at the Grafton reinforces what they were already beginning to do*. Colin can remember much later in his time with the group rehearsing and performing 'One After 9.09' and rehearsing 'I Lost My Little Girl' although he says they never performed the latter because Paul was never quite happy with it.

(*In '*The Paul McCartney Encyclopedia*', *p.644*, its author, *Bill Harry*, says their songwriting partnership had begun after Paul fluffed guitar solo at the New Clubmoor Hall. Apparently Paul thought to impress John by playing him a tune he'd written himself – 'I Lost My Little Girl'. John responded by playing Paul some tunes of his own and things progressed from there.)

"Paul's observation aside, The Grafton was a disappointing night all round performance-wise. Yet again we hadn't won and as we began to leave were feeling quite down – but not for long. Every cloud has a silver lining and this night certainly did."

As The Quarry Men prepared to leave, as had become the norm, Colin gingerly peered around the door to check that their path was clear. To his great relief there wasn't the expected posse of local Teds waiting to beat them to pulp.

"In fact I couldn't quite believe my eyes. There were definitely no Teds, but nevertheless a gang of sorts was waiting: four young teenage girls. Our luck had changed. Four girls who clearly thought we were a bit special: they were waiting to get our autographs."

It didn't take the boys long to warm to this new phenomenon.

"John and Paul asked if the girls had a pen and paper. Of course neither they nor us had these items. Rootling around in her handbag one of the girls showed genuine enterprise when she produced an eyeliner stick and said we could use that.

Warming to the subject John then inquired what the girls had for us to write on. Even he was stopped in his tracks when with no further ado one of the girls pulled down her top and said: 'You can sign here!'

The Quarry Men were in new territory here.

"This was a truly exciting moment for us. So far we had had the rock 'n' roll but for the Quarry Men, apart from a kiss and a cuddle with the girls on Rosebery Street, there'd been very little approaching 'sex' and the drugs were still a very long way off. The girl revealed only the upper part of her breast but for us lads this was something a bit special. This was most definitely not our everyday request and we almost fell over ourselves in our eagerness to oblige."

The fun had only just begun.

"No sooner had we signed our names than a second girl did the same. Again, we happily obliged. I think by now we all wondered just where this night was leading us. Our minds went into overdrive when the third girl was even more risqué: instead of pulling down her top she hitched up her skirt and offered the flesh between the top of her stockings and the bottom of her knickers for us to sign: the 'giggle band' as we called it. We nearly fainted at the sight of naked female thigh. Our minds were now running wild but somehow we managed to compose ourselves and comply with her wish."

High on anticipation The Quarry Men turned to look goggle-eyed at the fourth girl.

"At that very point when we truly believed we'd struck gold our evening came crashing down around us. The fourth girl was not going to up the ante and only pulled the sleeve of her blouse higher for us to sign on her shoulder. Instantly we all calmed down; it was like a bucket of cold water being poured over our collective fantasy.

Suddenly we all became a bit self-conscious. There was clearly not going to be any after-show party and after some embarrassing shuffling about we said our good nights and despite the girls asking where we were playing next, our evening ended. We never saw any of those girls at any of our subsequent shows. But in a young man's life in the late Fifties this was not the usual behaviour of girls as experienced by The Quarry Men. This was a little walk on the wild side. It made us feel special and the memory of it was a much better prize to take home to bed than winning a crumby talent contest."

Lurching from booking to booking from girls to gangs The Quarry Men's show at The Locarno (situated right next door to the Grafton, which it predated) was, on paper, just another gig, another talent contest. In reality it was something else: another chance for Colin to observe the internal dynamic of the new-look Quarry Men, especially the evolving relationship between John and Paul.

"The Locarno was just fifty yards from the Grafton on West Derby Road. On this occasion the group personnel was just John, Paul and myself. Len had already departed and on this particular night Eric was ill. Sitting in the Green Room waiting to go on we noticed a poster on the wall advertising another talent contest scheduled for the next weekend. It was a bit different from usual however in that it was specifically for male singers – either as solo acts or duets, not groups."

Colin remembers that the poster clearly excited Paul's interest, who immediately drew it to John's attention, commenting, *"We could do that – we could enter that as a duo."*

Without hesitation John emphatically replied, *"No, I'm not doing that, we're a group."*

Colin looked anxiously to see what Paul might have to say about John's rebuttal but he didn't say a word.

"That was the end of that discussion. In my presence Paul never suggested it or anything like it again. This was a sign to me that for all Paul's growing influence John was still most definitely the leader of The Quarry Men. It signalled John as a group player whereas Paul might possibly be persuaded otherwise. Paul had the confidence to go out on his own. I thought he would have dropped the rest of us quite easily if John had been up for it but John was less comfortable on his own, he liked the support of his band around him. This is why he struggled with asking Pete Shotton to leave; he liked people he trusted around him. It's most probably why I survived for so long – and why, later on, in my opinion George was recruited in the way that he was and Nigel handed the job of actually sacking Eric."

Needless to say, the performance that night at the Locarno was desultory.

"Back on the 'bus, back home. Not much to say between us and in this instance nothing had been ventured and, most definitely, nothing had been gained."

38

DOES THIS 'BUS STOP AT THE WILSON HALL?

Charlie McBain clearly liked The Quarry Men. He booked them regularly to play both his clubs and – more importantly – paid them.

Their last documented show of 1957 was at McBain's Wilson Hall on Saturday 7th December.

"At the time, for me, it was just another regular Quarry Men performance. It was enjoyable but not eventful in terms of stuff like fights, gangs, threats, girls, being chased by Teds, there were no fallings out or musical differences: nothing of note like that."

And yet as Colin focuses on what happens next in the story of The Quarry Men the booking becomes hugely significant.

"By the time of that December 7th booking, my regular destination after a show at the Wilson Hall was not to go immediately home but to nip into the nearby pub, 'The Alexander', with my mates and regular Quarry Men supporters – Kevin and Charlie. We'd grab my kit and slip into the pub for a pint. That was our usual routine. We were working men with enough money in our pockets to afford a round or two – especially on a Saturday night.

On other occasions at the Wilson Hall, if Charlie and Kevin weren't around, Eric and I would get the 'bus home together. It would be a different one to that taken by John, Paul, Nige (and Pete if he had turned up to a show). In other words, when a show ended the various group members went their seperate ways. We were reliant on the 'buses to take us home."

Eric and Nigel weren't part of Colin's drinking circle. Neither were Paul nor John. As a schoolboy and a student, they were not only both underage but had little money to speak of. If, once he'd joined the Quarry Men, Paul had started rolling home after shows smelling of alcohol Jim McCartney would undoubtedly have had something to say (and would no doubt have blamed John's influence).

John and Paul had a different mindset; they hung out a lot, music was their driving force and bond: they moved in tandem. As 1958 approached, paths within The Quarry Men were dividing, different social circles forming: worlds colliding, worlds falling apart.

Eric and Nige didn't hang out with John and Paul either, although Nigel caught the same 'bus home as they did.

As per their usual routine on 7th December, after they'd finished and packed up, Nigel had divided the money in the Green Room (Colin's share now going to John and Paul anyway) and the boys dispersed.

It's what happened next that is crucially important.

As Colin, Charlie and Kevin entered 'The Alexander' and Eric made his own way home John, Paul and Nige were also jumping onto a 'bus home accompanied by George Harrison, Paul's mate from school. At Paul's request George – plus his guitar – had been at the show. Now he was sitting next to them on the top deck sharing their journey home.

From the night at the New Clubmoor when his fingers froze on his guitar fretboard, by Paul's own admission he had had it in his head that George could join the band to play lead. His instincts were good and he knew George was a better guitarist than Eric, but the other boys didn't because they had never heard George play. They needed to be convinced. Technically The Quarry Men didn't need another guitarist – and four in a group would surely be too many, so for George to join Paul knew Eric would have to leave – or possibly switch to play bass (in the unlikely event he could be persuaded). For this to stand any chance of happening Paul knew it was John Lennon he would have to win over to George's cause.

To achieve this he needed John to hear George play. Word of mouth was not enough. Dislodging Eric would not be easy because Eric was an old school friend, a founding member of the group and the same age as John. Expecting him to buy a bass was a real long shot for they were so very expensive. By comparison to Eric, George was just a 'kid' – and looked it. Age-wise John would have a difficulty with George. Paul recognised this and knew George had to do some persuading: he had to play for John. Hearing would surely be believing. But first Paul had to get George and his guitar in front of the group's leader.

7th December, was the night this happened. At Paul's request George Harrison came to the Wilson Hall with his guitar specifically to hear The Quarry Men and to play for John. And so it was that atop a Liverpool 'bus travelling back from the booking alongside Paul, Nigel and John, George Harrison got to play 'Raunchy' for John Lennon. As he did so the world once more shifted on its axis.

> **John**: *"I listened to George play, and I said, 'Play 'Raunchy''... and I let him in. That was the three of us, then. The rest of the group was thrown out gradually. It just happened like that: instead of going for an individual thing, we went for the strongest format, and for equals."*
>
> *(The Beatles In Their Own Words, Miles, p.17.)*

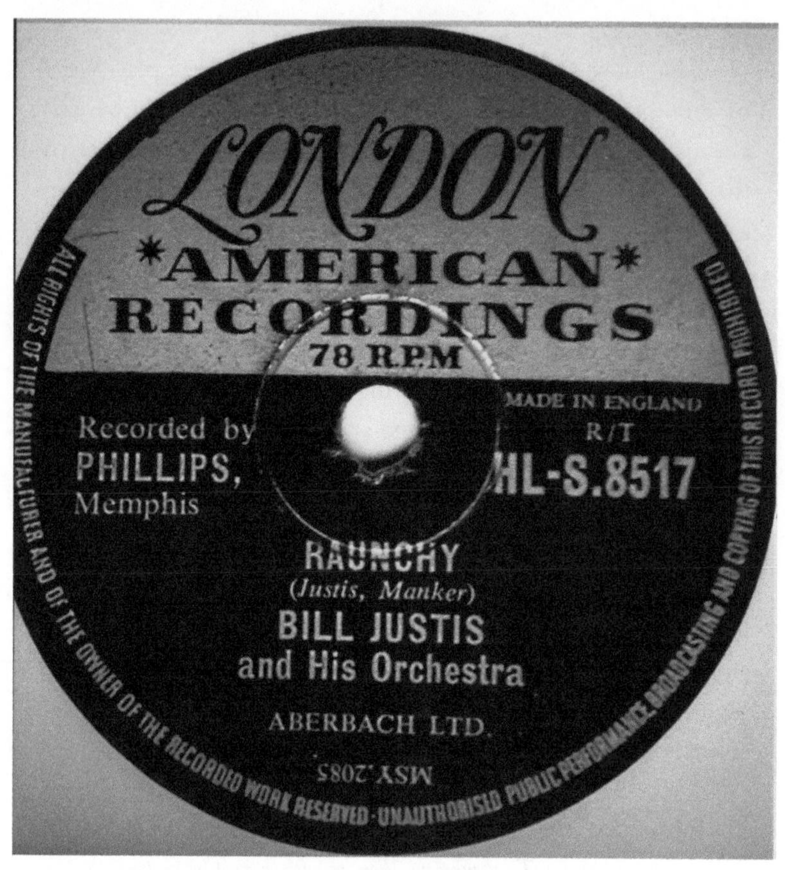

Single label of 'Raunchy' / Bill Justis

John, Paul, George and Nigel all recall witnessing this moment. That's four solid coinciding memories from the very people who were there. In the history of The Quarry Men that's so rare it's indisputable.

As with Paul's 'audition' in the church hall, Colin also missed out on George's famous audition because once again he was elsewhere: this time he was supping pints with his mates in 'The Alexander'.

39

A MEETING AT THE MORGUE

After his audition on the 'bus the only Quarry Men to whom George Harrison had not been personally introduced were Colin and Eric. In the grand scheme of things meeting Eric was not essential, in fact it was most probably better that he didn't because it was Eric's place that was at stake. But Colin was the drummer and they were hard to come by and so keeping him on board for the moment was important.

George did not have to wait long to meet Colin.

As Paul hoped – and expected – John had been more than impressed with George. Whatever reservations John may and did harbour concerning George's youthful appearance, they were outweighed by his excellence on lead guitar. With George in the group, The Quarry Men would move ever closer to John's (and Paul's) ultimate goal of becoming a fully fledged rock 'n' roll band. Musically this was the next big step. So George was in. This, however, left the tricky problem of what to do with Eric. The Quarry Men had no need for four guitarists. Eric would have to go, but before that happened he would be offered the lifeline of staying in the group provided he bought an electric bass. The odds of him agreeing to do this were very slim given how expensive they were.

Before they moved to remove Eric, John and Paul must also have agreed that Colin should be made aware of, and hopefully be agreeable with, what they intended to do. They knew it was

Eric who had introduced Colin to The Quarry Men and so maybe thought Colin might feel a group loyalty towards him which could be tricky. Whatever Paul's reservations about Colin's drumming he agreed with John: better a band with a drummer (who played loud) than one without. Hearing George play would surely prove to Colin their point that George would be a brilliant addition to the Quarry Men. More to the point he'd understand that Eric would from then on be superfluous to requirements.

There was no reason to hang about and so a meeting was quickly arranged.

"Had I heard George on the 'bus that night of December 7th, John and Paul would have had no need to introduce me to him or for me to hear him play. But I hadn't and so, just a few days afterwards I was invited to join them on a visit to Old Swan ostensibly to check out the possible premises of a new 'live' venue for skiffle groups where we could pick up some bookings. Anyway, that was what I was told we were going to do – there was no mention whatsoever that we'd also be meeting Paul's friend from school who played guitar. I guess they wouldn't have wanted me to mention this to Eric."

John and Paul had learned that a lad called Alan Caldwell, who lived with his parents (Violet and Ernie) and sister, Iris, at number 54 Broad Green Road was considering opening a 'live' skiffle music venue for teenagers. Al was known to the boys because of his skiffle group called the Texans or the Raving Texans, which he'd formed with his neighbour Johnny 'Guitar' Byrne in 1957. (In 1959 Ritchie Starkey aka Ringo Starr began to play drums with them and stayed when later that year Al changed his name to Rory and his band became known as Rory Storm and the Hurricanes.)

Through Johnny Byrne, Alan had gained access to a large, detached Victorian property in Oakhill Park just around the corner from where he lived on Broad Green Road, number 25 Oakhill Park to be exact, also known as 'Balgownie'. Johnny lived just a few doors away at number 37 Oakhill Park. 'Balgownie' was owned by a Mrs.Thompson, who lived there with her daughter. Apparently some nurses also had rooms there. It was her daughter who had persuaded Mum to let Johnny and Al practise in the house's cellar and to open a club there. 'Balgownie' could easily have passed for the set of a haunted house in a Hammer horror film. Inside and out it looked very neglected. Johnny 'Guitar' Byrne's girlfriend Pat Hesketh described it as *'decrepit'*, adding, *"You wouldn't have wanted to place even your worst relative in that place."*

Al and Johnny's club eventually opened on 13th March, 1958 and was called 'The Morgue'. In December '57, when Colin first heard about the club as he journeyed with John and Paul to check it out, he recalls it was already being referred to as 'The Morgue'. Maybe initially that was its nickname given the house's spooky appearance. In early 1958 in his diaries, Johnny Byrne referred to it as the 'cellar'. Nevertheless it all sounded very exciting and almost unheard of at the time – a coffee club/'live' music venue especially for teenage fans of skiffle… and rock 'n' roll.

"Although Old Swan/Broadgreen was in a completely different part of Liverpool to where we all lived, Alan had apparently invited us to see the premises with a view to us eventually playing there. By that I mean it was reachable by 'bus. So, as pre-arranged, we all met up in Woolton village. I say 'all' but it was actually only John, Paul and myself. As far as I was aware Eric was still a Quarry Man; he just wasn't there on that night. At the time I was slightly surprised he wasn't but thought little more of it, after all it wasn't a gig and maybe he was doing something else so it did not seem that important. None of us had our instruments with us because we weren't going to a gig and before long we were sitting chatting on the 81 as it made its way out of the village and along Queens Drive.

We got off somewhere just past 'The Rocket' public house to walk towards Broad Green Road where Alan lived, near to where this club was going to be. It wasn't familiar territory to us at all. We had an address and had been instructed to look for this 'derelict-looking house' a.k.a. 'The Morgue'. Of course we knew it wasn't abandoned; people were living in it, apparently it just looked run down. On the way and unsure of exactly where we were going but now feeling we were becoming lost, John spotted a club, either a Labour or a Conservative Club, I can't remember which, it didn't matter much to us. The lights were on and it was obviously open so in we went to ask if anyone knew the whereabouts of either 'The Morgue' or Oakhill Park. It sounded like a bit of a landmark, the sort of place locals would know about. It was worth a shot…"

Passing through the front door of this club The Quarry Men found themselves in a large foyer with a desk on the far side sitting behind which was an elderly gentleman. Bald with dark hair round the sides, Colin recalls he was wearing a white shirt, dark tie, dark waistcoat but no jacket. The appearance of three potentially 'unruly' 'Teddy Boys' in such a decorous establishment would have been most unusual and had clearly grabbed his full attention.

From the look of utter disgust on the fellow's face Colin could tell that he was not impressed by what he saw.

"He couldn't have made his disdain more obvious. His nose literally turned up at the sight of us. John immediately clocked the old chap's revulsion, but resisted what must have been an almost overwhelming temptation to say something cutting. Instead he kept his cool and politely asked if he knew of the whereabouts of 'The Morgue'. The chap seemed taken aback by John's politeness, no doubt further disconcerted by the fact that John didn't have that broad 'Scouse' accent he would have expected someone dressed like him to have. No doubt he also interpreted John's request for directions to a 'morgue' as taking the Mickey. There was no way he would have helped us even if he could, but momentarily he became flustered and stuttered, 'No, no'.

He wasn't wrong-footed for long. Within seconds his glare had returned and his cheeks reddened in anger. The look on his face told us all we needed to know: we were not welcome, so we turned around and headed for the door. By then the chap had regained his courage sufficiently to emerge from behind his desk and begin shouting and gesturing at us, 'Clear off, clear off, go on, get out!'

That they had done nothing wrong and were now being shouted at quite so vehemently stopped the boys in their tracks.

"We were really taken aback. We couldn't work out what we'd done to make him react so aggressively. We stopped and looked at him as if to say, 'We are actually going, so what's the big deal, why are you shouting at us?' Again, somehow we resisted the urge to shout back and outside just looked at each other in disbelief, shrugged and carried on with our quest to find 'The Morgue'."

Such reactions from adults were not unusual for teenagers who looked a bit too teenage for their own good. For The Quarry Men it was a reminder of just how hostile some adults could be, that this new-fangled 'generation gap' sometimes had teeth. Seeing lads like John or Paul with their quiffs and narrow trousers would more often than not put older folk immediately on their guard, fearing them to be juvenile delinquents. Rock 'n' roll was in its infancy and seen as something threatening by older generations, something at odds with the moral standards of the day, especially as flick knives and violence appeared to go hand in hand with it.

"No doubt that old chap thought he'd fought the war for future generations like ours and seeing a group of outrageously dressed teenagers such as us walking in off the streets he would have been wondering if it had been worth it."

The boys continued to wander the neighbourhood until eventually by sheer luck John (who Colin says had his glasses on) found the road and the house.

"It was a large, dark Victorian house that lived up to its spooky reputation. Four or five steps led up to the front door on which we all began to knock until it was answered by Al who immediately invited us inside. It felt very creepy and unlived in, which made it all the more incredible to think that it was

someone's home. No sooner where we inside than we found ourselves standing in a long, gloomy corridor. The walls were bare, no paint, no paper. A couple of metres down the corridor on the right was a door leading into a black, empty room with one little blue light in the corner. Alan told us it was going to be the room where he would put a stage.

Other than the light there wasn't really much to see and so after a brief look around we carried on down the long corridor to where there were two doors, one immediately in front of us, one to the right which had probably been a kitchen. Standing inside this room were two young lads, one of whom I soon learned was George. Indeed Alan, not Paul, who knew George from school, immediately introduced George to me. The other boy was Arthur Kelly and I soon discovered he and George were almost inseparable. On the way there neither John nor Paul had mentioned that George would be there and now we were, they were not at all surprised to see him. More to the point George was not surprised one iota to see them; it was clear he expected to do so.

George had a guitar with him. He was holding it in front of himself as if he'd been playing it to Alan and Arthur. Encouraged by Paul he was asked to play us something and without further ado George effortlessly reeled off 'Guitar Boogie', which was quite impressive to say the least. I recalled it was the very same song Paul had fluffed. But that was it, I don't remember much conversation between us or that he played anything else. In a nutshell I'd met George who hardly spoke more than a few words. I'd heard him play, had been suitably impressed, we'd seen the house, been suitably unimpressed; what else was there to do? The rooms we had seen were just shells. In reality there was virtually nothing to see, the house was a miserable, cold place. There was nothing to hang about for so we said goodbye and left."

Brief and almost as cursory as it is in the retelling the three Quarry Men's evening excursion had nevertheless given them much to mull over on their journey home.

"We certainly had a lot to say. As a prospective venue we all thought the house was a dump. There were no facilities at all. From what we'd seen it was going to need one heck of a lot of work to get ready for opening as a club. Painting,

decorating and Alan had mentioned he was going to build a small stage in the room with the blue light. We didn't envy him any of that. Mainly we talked about George and his ability on the guitar, how good he was for one so young. Amazing really. We had a laugh about the old chap in the club we'd gone into, but, without a doubt, meeting George and hearing him play had been the definite highlight of our trip, he was the focus of our conversation on the way home."

As the years have passed so Colin's thoughts on this outing have taken on a different perspective as he has learned more of the background to their visit. It's place in the general scheme of things has become clearer to him.

"At the time I knew Paul knew George from school because he'd mentioned him previously to all of us in the context of the group. He'd told us what a good guitarist he was. What was not mentioned at all as we travelled to Old Swan was that he was actually going to be there at our rendezvous with Al. There had been plenty of time for Paul and John to tell me. With the benefit of hindsight I believe the trip to the old house and the meeting with George was a bit of a set-up. It killed two birds with one stone, the primary one of which I now believe was for me to meet George.

Back then, even though I dismissed it as coincidence, it seemed to me like George was primed, ready and waiting. I can clearly see him standing in front of me, guitar in hand, reeling off 'Guitar Boogie'. (I'm convinced about that as well – he didn't play 'Raunchy' that I later discovered was his usual 'party piece' and which he'd played on the 'bus for John.)

More to the point, Eric wasn't with us. Now I understand why. He purposely hadn't been invited. At the time I was slightly surprised he wasn't there, but once we were on the 'bus headed for Old Swan it didn't seem important so I didn't give it too much thought."

Colin believes Paul learned about 'The Morgue' from George, who was friendly with Alan's family at this time and regularly spent time at the Caldwell's home. When Colin met George, George was dating Alan's sister, Iris, and was often at their house. Their mum and dad liked him a lot. George and Iris were very young: she twelve and he fourteen. George was also very impressed by Al and his skiffle group and had asked to join but Al considered him to be too young and turned him down.

> **George:** *'My first girlfriend was Rory Storm's sister, Iris Caldwell… So I knew Rory before I knew the Beatles. I'd met Iris a couple of times and went round to her house and hung out. They (Rory) had a little basement that they were trying to turn into a coffee club. That seemed to be the craze in the Fifties."*
>
> *(The Beatles Anthology, p.29.)*

Little wonder then that Colin believes his first meeting with George in that *"little basement"* was not a coincidence.

"Thinking back it makes sense to me that if those two had been thinking of bringing George into The Quarry Men at some point they would have had to introduce him to me to seek my approval. Our meeting in the Morgue was clearly that moment in time. At no time that evening however, was there any mention of inviting George to join at the expense of kicking Eric out. But now I had met George I had heard all they needed me to know: young kid though he was (and he did look very young), as a guitarist he was in a different league to Eric. That evening at the Morgue emphasised just how much better George was.

Paul had certainly suggested to George he be at the Wilson Hall the time he played for John on the 'bus home. That had happened a few days earlier exactly as Paul tells it and George always said he first heard The Quarry Men at the Wilson Hall. So all that makes perfect sense.

With John suitably impressed, he and Paul now wanted George in and Eric out. I can't imagine John was looking forward to sacking Eric. He was his friend and a founding member of the group.

Eric was also my original friend in the band. So, John and Paul most probably feared if Eric was sacked I might leave with him in support. From a practical point of view drums were expensive, consequently drummers were hard to come by. So no doubt they had also agreed it would be best to keep me on board for a while longer. It also helps to explain why I was included in the decision to axe Eric. It was definitely a John and Paul decision but, for once, one they needed me to be a part of, simply I guess to keep me in the group a while longer.

From day one, I had known I wasn't indispensable. I still knew that was the case, but by this time I liked to think they liked me enough to want me to stay. Having said that, with every passing week I was becoming more and more aware of how pragmatic they could be."

40

MEETING AT THE GARDEN GATE

That something had been afoot during that strange encounter with the young guitar ace from Speke was soon disclosed.

"The weekend following our trip to the Morgue – mid-December time – I was just leaving my house on Heyscroft Road to go into town to meet Kevin and Charlie for some drinks when Nige Walley came racing 'round the corner on his pushbike. I was at the garden gate when he parked up against the wall and breathlessly asked me if I had a few minutes to spare, which I did. Without a moment's pause he asked what I thought of that lad, 'George', whom I'd met the other night at the new club venue. I didn't have to think for long because George had been very impressive so my immediate reply was that he was brilliant, really good, a bit young but really good on the guitar, which is exactly what John, Paul and I had already agreed on the 'bus home from the Morgue."

Colin's favourable assessment of George was Nige's cue to slip into managerial mode and deliver a speech about how much The Quarry Men had progressed from the start, moving away from skiffle – losing the washboard, tea-chest bass, banjo – towards being a rock 'n' roll band and so on and so on. He then noted that the introduction of Paul had made the group better 'musically': all of which was impossible to disagree with. As he listened Colin began to wonder why Nige had chosen this precise moment to stand on the street and present a review the group.

"All the time Nige was speaking I felt he was nervous which was unusual for him. Skirting around an issue was not his style, I could tell he was building up to something he was finding difficult to say and, of course, I now had a good idea what it was.

He continued by saying 'they' – by whom I knew he meant John and Paul – wanted the group to improve even more. Again I agreed. I was all for this; how could I not be, we'd started to earn some money and musically speaking were a much better unit. But by now I knew exactly where Nige's speech was taking him. George joining The Quarry Men left no room for Eric. He was out.

And so Nige finally got round to the point of his visit: 'John and Paul don't want four guitars, they want three guitars across the front with them singing and you at the back and so they want Eric out and George in'."

Ever the pragmatist, Colin knew immediately that any quibbles he may have had would not cut any ice. It was a done deal.

"Although Eric was the guy who actually got me into The Quarry Men I didn't imagine for one minute there was anything I could say that would make any difference. I felt bad about this, as Nigel obviously did, but by this point in time I was also feeling my own position was possibly not secure. (Paul had made one or two comments about my playing that I had taken to be criticisms. They were!) Nothing I could say would change things. To be frank, I was surprised my opinion had been sought. Consequently I simply said, 'Yes'. As far as I was concerned John and Paul were running the show and if that's what they wanted I had no problem with it.

I don't think Nigel was too surprised by my response. We both felt uncomfortable about it but this wasn't the old school chums band it had been just a few months ago; times had changed, The Quarry Men had moved on. So, he simply said, 'Right, I'll get back up to Mimi's and tell them that you're okay with it.' End of conversation. Before I knew it he was back on his bike, disappearing off down the road."

That *was* it.

Nige went off to John's house, from whence he had obviously been dispatched and where John and Paul were waiting to hear Colin's response. Once they did, it was on Nigel's shoulders that the responsibility of seeking out Eric and firing him fell. John and Paul had made the decision but didn't want to be the ones to wield the axe. Instead they insisted that was Nigel's job because he was the manager and that's what managers do: the messy bits.

According to Eric, Nigel did the deed by telephone, making it clear that unless he bought an electric bass guitar he had to leave. That was the stark choice Eric was offered, but buying a bass was never an option given how expensive they were. Eric was quoted as saying he couldn't see how he'd ever get such a sum back because he personally didn't believe the group would 'do any better' than what they were doing and wouldn't earn any more money. In light of this he wasn't prepared to fork out a lot of dosh on a bass. Nevertheless he felt very aggrieved at being dumped in this way.

Eric's dismissal set a precedent for what happened in 1962 when The Beatles' manager, Brian Epstein, was given the job of telling drummer Pete Best that John, Paul and George no longer wanted him, that he was out of the band and Ringo was in. As they moved into the next phase of The Beatles' journey, the other boys considered Ringo more suitable than Pete as their drummer and a better fit all round for the group. As in 1957 sentiment didn't come into it.

Eric was stunned by his dismissal. He hadn't seen it coming (just as Pete Best wouldn't). He was hurt and didn't let it drop.

'The following weekend, Saturday or Sunday, we were in Paul's house, just John, Paul and I, no George yet. We were rehearsing when the 'phone went and Paul answered. It was Eric, Paul just turned to John and, eyebrows raised, handed the 'phone to him saying, 'It's Eric, he wants a word with you.'

John became immediately embroiled in a conversation with a clearly unhappy Eric who was angry at being kicked out. John listened to Eric's tirade just answering his complaints directly, simply saying, 'Well that's the way it is, we want this new lad.' The longer the conversation went on I could see John was getting more and more agitated and impatient but Eric wouldn't let it drop.

I motioned to John and said, 'Let me have a word with him'. John passed the phone to me, at which point Eric started to become resigned to his fate. He'd realised John was resolute, he wasn't going to change his mind. I had a lot of sympathy for Eric. It's never pleasant to be rejected. It was hard to find the right words to say because I knew nothing I could say would change anything. So I just tried to offer some support and said, 'Look Eric, I am on borrowed time as well, you know, it's like football, someone takes the ball away you can't play however much you want to'.

He listened, quietly, and then asked what about the gigs we had lined up and mentioned that we would have some money coming in. I thought that maybe that was part of the problem for Eric; he was relying on this money so I said if the money's the problem you can have my share for whatever gigs we have already got in the diary for next year (even though I usually gave that to John and Paul). He thanked me but declined. I think the money angle was just a last ditch comment, you know, he'd been there through a lot of unpaid bookings and he was just making the point he would now miss out.

I did feel sorry for him, he was clearly upset. But that was basically it. In groups the personnel changes for a variety of reasons: personal, musical… survival! John and Paul knew what they were doing.

As a group we heard no more from Eric and even though he only lived just around the corner from me I didn't see him again for many, many years. Just as when Rod and Len left and I never saw or spoke to either of them again for 40 years, so it was with Eric. That was it, he put his receiver down, he was gone. I handed the 'phone back to Paul and John looked at me and said words to the effect of thanks for sorting that out, Colin. He never asked what I meant by my comment about being 'on borrowed time'. Maybe it was too close to the bone. I'm not sure he was listening too closely anyway. He'd had enough. What mattered was that Eric was out, George was in. From now on John and I were the only original members of The Quarry Men left."

Angry and upset at first, Eric would soon rally. He was not one to hang around. Being dropped from the group was the excuse he needed to quit his loathsome apprenticeship at Napier's. And so he did exactly that. He had no dad at home to deal with, no arguments to fight. Sometime in January 1958 Eric successfully sat some tests and enrolled as an officer cadet in the Merchant Navy, joining his first ship on 11th February before setting sail on the 14th.

And so, by the time Eric set sail for new horizons, for George Harrison, age fourteen, from Speke, Liverpool, opportunity had knocked. He was a Quarry Man and there was to be no looking back.

As for Colin, he never set foot in 'the Morgue' again. He has no memory of ever performing as a Quarry Man at the club even though he believes on the opening night of 13th March 1958 John, Paul and George did so as a guitar trio under the Quarry Men name. Despite other people's claims that he did perform with them at least once at the club, Colin has always denied he ever did. It was a short-lived venture anyway: by 23rd April 1958 neighbours led by a Mr. Douglas Brown had objected one too many times and the police closed 'the Morgue' for not having the appropriate licence.

41

COWBOYS AT THE SCHOOL DANCE

Colin's first memory of George playing with the group on stage was at a school dance.

"Our new boy wonder guitarist made his Quarry Men debut at a school dance in Speke of all places – a home town debut."

The school was Speke Secondary School on Central Avenue.

"It was huge with a massive hall and a stage so big that as a group we were so spread out we needed binoculars to see each other."

At this crucial point The Quarry Men's poor memory for the exact date of a show strikes again.

"It was in early January 1958 – possibly Friday 3rd, sometime at the start of the new term. We had not yet had time to rehearse with George. Well, I hadn't, that doesn't mean he, John and Paul hadn't done so."

While the exact date eludes him, Colin's memory for other details about this particular show are razor-sharp because it was a night he'd rather forget. In fact he got upset early in the evening and stayed that way all night. So much so he's still quite bitter about it, irked is the word.

"As I have mentioned by now I tended to be a little insecure of my place in the band. Pete had made his comment, Nige had snatched my drumsticks and Paul had also made comments, so by then it wasn't difficult to upset me. The way Eric had been 'sacked' quietly wrankled with me. As a result I could pull a sulk with the best of them."

In those days all that was needed to tip Colin into one of his famous blue funks was to be made to feel left out. On this occasion he felt even worse: he felt like a complete afterthought.

"What got me going was now we had this new kid in the band for whom my mate had been given the elbow. I hadn't liked that too much but had said nothing and bowed to the inevitable and accepted it. Now, almost immediately after all the fuss to get me to agree to Eric's removal, I was being made to feel like the forgotten man."

There had been no full group rehearsal prior to The Quarry Men's performance that night, which meant Colin had not practised with George at all before they stepped on stage in Speke. So he hadn't heard about the booking at an earlier rehearsal. Nigel had simply informed him of the booking by 'phone.

"I turned up with my drums and almost immediately I walked in the room my mood darkened."

The cause of his upset were standing right in front of him: three south Liverpool cowpokes.

"There they were – John, Paul and George resplendent in identical cowboy shirts. I was instantly miffed. I recognised these shirts because I had one in my wardrobe at home. Nigel had bought them a while back just before John and Paul decided instead to wear those famous 'white' jackets with the rest of us wearing white shirts and bow ties. We had all agreed Nigel should buy these for us and we would pay him back in instalments. Then they'd been shelved. I

guess George's arrival had given the shirts a new lease of life, the idea being: new member, new image."

Nigel says only Colin did pay him back. John, Paul, Eric and Len never did complete their payments because they were superseded by 'the jackets and bow ties' so, until this evening, The Quarry Men hadn't worn them; they'd been in cold storage. Nigel says he'd acquired them from 'Eric Levy'*, a credit draper/'a Teddy Boy shop' near the Odeon opposite Rushworth & Dreaper's. Eric Levy, the owner of the shop, was a member of Lee Park Golf Club. Nigel collected and distributed the shirts but never did pay all the money owed to Levy because the group, except for Colin, never paid up, which must have made it very tricky for Nigel whenever he bumped into Mr. Levy at the golf club.

(*This information has been provided by Mark Lewisohn based on his interviews with Nigel for the first part of his trilogy, 'All These Years, Volume 1: Tune In'.)

So Colin had rushed home from work, changed, grabbed his drums, made the gig in seconds flat but no one had bothered to tell him in advance to wear the cowboy shirt that he had actually paid for but no one else had.

"What really bugged me was that they had made sure 'new' boy George had a shirt but had forgotten to say anything to me about mine. I was further miffed by the fact that this meant I now stood out from the others, which I didn't like, not one bit. Visually I didn't fit in. In an instant I felt like I was on the edge of the group, an afterthought, not part of things: a passenger."

Battling his desire to just walk off and let them get on with it, Colin's interest was diverted by George and what he was doing with his guitar.

"I remember George had with him not only his hollow-bodied Hofner President guitar but since I'd first seen him at the Morgue he'd attached a small pick-up

to it. As I watched, somewhat agog, he was plugging a lead from his guitar into a small amp (that I later learned he'd borrowed from a friend). What struck me as I gazed on was, that in that very instant, The Quarry Men were going electric. We had become a rock 'n' roll band. Nobody had told me about that either."

This was real innovation. This was the first time The Quarry Men featured an 'electric' guitar on stage. George explained to Colin that he needed to 'amp-up' his Hofner for his solos to be heard. After all they were the reason he had been drafted into the group. So, for his debut, George had persuaded a friend and fellow guitarist from Speke called Kenny Johnson to lend him his amp. (Kenny played skiffle and country and in 1958 formed Sonny Webb and the Country Four. Country was Kenny's passion and in 1960 he moved to form the Cascades; later he fronted the Hillsiders and then Northwind. In the process he became a legend on Merseyside as the 'King of Country'. Later he would also host an immensely popular Country show on Radio Merseyside.) Kenny had taken some persuading. The amp was brand new and George was just 'a kid' but lend it he did and so, the first time George played with The Quarry Men he did so as an 'electric' guitarist. Years later Colin met Kenny, who confirmed this story.

"As gigs go it was poor. I hadn't rehearsed with George, the stage was too big, we were too spread out, adrift from one another, it was hard to hear each other and all night I was a sulking non-cowboy."

Sometimes it's not just your day or night. That night in the school hall it certainly wasn't Colin's. To this day it remains an 'if only' moment for him.

"At the end of what we all felt was an unsuccessful gig I was packing my kit away when I noticed two girls come on stage and ask if they could take

our photographs. Immediately John, Paul and George lined up in the middle of the stage resplendent in their fancy cowboy shirts. I was still sulking and pretended I hadn't heard."

John however noticed Colin was missing and called him to join them.

"I didn't. I'm afraid to say I just carried on packing away, muttering words to the effect I didn't have my uniform. Basically I ignored them and carried on sulking. I'd got the sulk up to a Force 9 by now and wasn't going to let it go. I heard John tell the girls I didn't have my shirt and so they took their photograph of John, Paul, George without me but with Arthur Kelly!"

The photograph of John, Paul, George and, just behind George's right shoulder, his good friend Arthur Kelly (another guitarist) in their cowboy shirts is possibly the very one Colin describes. (The ownership of the photo as this book was being written is unknown.) Seeing it you can understand how Colin might feel miffed being the only member of the band dressed completely differently from the others. Arthur stands out because he isn't wearing a matching cowboy shirt. No wonder Colin felt he stood out on stage. He would not have looked like a regular member of the group; your eye would be drawn to him because he looked the odd one out, possibly just a stand-in.

By his own admission this was not one of Colin's finest moments with The Quarry Men. In his defence however it has to be remembered he was still a young man, just nineteen, just weeks after the sacking of Eric. Some adverse comments about his drumming meant he was already feeling a tad insecure within the group. From his perspective, arriving in the school hall that evening to see George resplendent in his cowboy shirt, his own shirt in a drawer at home, Colin felt the newcomer was already more a part of things than himself. In a word he was 'hurt'!

Paul, Arthur, George and John and cowboy shirts

"I could be mardy in those days when things upset me. I do regret it now because I missed out on being photographed with George on his Quarry Men debut. It didn't come around again, the photo opportunity I mean. If only I had been a bit more mature I'd now have a photograph of myself as a Quarry Man alongside John, Paul and George. I wish I'd behaved better but I didn't. What happened happened."

Briefly putting his sulk to one side Colin agreed with the others that they needed to arrange some practices.

"The evening highlighted that although George was undoubtedly a better guitarist than Eric we hadn't automatically 'gelled' as a group. Playing with an electric guitar had altered the shape and sound of The Quarry Men. It was a big change that we needed to accomodate more carefully. Despite his greater talent George's mere presence in the group had not automatically made us better; we needed to rehearse."

The result was that The Quarry Men started to practise more frequently at Paul's house.

"We had a gig scheduled for Friday 10th January 1958 at the New Clubmoor Hall, which turned out to be a far more successful performance than the one at the school as far as we were concerned. Nevertheless, by the end of that show at the school in Speke The Quarry Men Mark III were up and running: John, Paul, George and Colin."

Before George even played a note at the New Clubmoor his presence in the group and the absence of Eric caused Charlie McBain concern.

"George did look very young and Charlie had liked Eric. Charlie's instinct on just seeing George was that he was way too young. John immediately clocked the look of anxiety on Charlie's face as he was introduced to our new 'lead' guitarist and was quick to reassure him by saying something humorous to

the effect, 'Mr. McBain, Eric's run off to join the circus. This is George Harrison who's come to help us out!'"

Colin says Charlie McBain cast a sceptical eye in John's direction; he knew Lennon's sense of humour and wasn't so easily taken in. Realising McBain remained unconvinced, Paul chipped in with some more believable detail.

"It's true, Mr. McBain, Eric's left the group. We wanted him to play bass but he wasn't interested."

It was only when Nige confirmed this to be the case that McBain relaxed.

"It's true. Eric left before Christmas."

Taking their cue from Nigel, Colin remembers Charlie McBain became beseiged as all The Quarry Men now chipped in to say how good George was on guitar, John especially, urging him to hear George actually play.

"Ask him to play that new record that's on the radio, Mr. McBain. He plays it as good as the record. Go on, George, play 'Raunchy' for Mr. McBain."

And so George did. Like everyone before him Charlie was immediately convinced.

ENDNOTES

George Harrison's guitar was a Hofner President. He'd bought this prior to joining the group. It was a German guitar imported into the UK by Selmer, one of several acoustic archtop models they had commissioned and which was made to their specifications especially for sale in the UK.

> **George described his guitar as** *"a cello-style, f-hole, single cutaway… which is like the German version of a Gibson. I got a pickup and stuck it on."*

Around the same time Paul bought a pick up and an amp. Electric guitars remained too expensive for British players, including Paul. As an alternative and like a lot of other budding cash-strapped guitarists he bought a pickup and stuck it on his Zenith and purchased an amp from Curry's.

> **Paul**: *"I got this green amp called an Elpico, which was great. It was really built for some bygone era, where there were mics and gramophones. It was probably the cheapest I could find, you know? Not being a cheapskate, but I didn't have that much money, and our family wasn't rolling in it, so I couldn't hit my Dad for it. I've still got it, and it's brilliant."* *

Once Paul purchased his Elpico, on stage George was able to 'go electric' as well by plugging into a second input on the amp.**
Paul also still has his Zenith.

(Sources: *Beatles Gear, Babiuk, p. 20. **Tune In, Lewisohn, p. 172.)

42

GEORGE PLAYS THE CAVERN

"Our rehearsals at 20 Forthlin tightened us up as a unit and expanded our repertoire to include more rock 'n' roll. 'Be Bop a Lula', 'Blue Suede Shoes', 'All Shook Up', 'Long Tall Sally' and 'Twenty Flight Rock' were already in the set but now came some Buddy Holly tunes like 'Peggy Sue', 'Oh Boy' and 'That'll Be The Day'. Remember in those days we would only be on stage for approximately half an hour or forty-five minutes maximum so we didn't do a very big set. Despite Paul and John agreeing we needed to play songs other groups didn't, we stuck with the tunes we liked best and which drew the best audience response. We weren't playing any of their original tunes. However, as 1958 dawned in terms of our repertoire The Quarry Men could no longer be described as 'skiffle'."

Thanks to Nigel bookings-wise things were also moving fast.

"The next time we played in public it was another Friday night, January 24. But this time not in Garston or Speke but rather at a club in the heart of downtown Liverpool – just three gigs in and young George Harrison was making his Cavern debut!"

The moment George stepped on stage alongside John, Paul and Colin at The Cavern things started to change yet again for The Quarry Men. His impact was immediate.

"It's a show etched into my memory because I remember I did something very strange which to this day I can't really explain. Instead of setting my drums

up in the Green Room as I always did wherever we played, I straightaway set them up on stage with my drumsticks resting on the bass drum and then even more bizarrely I left them there as I went over the road into The Grapes for a pint, leaving John, Paul, George, Nigel and Pete together in The Cavern."

On his return from The Grapes the moment he appeared at the foot of the steps leading down into the club Colin found an anxious John Lennon waiting to meet him.

"I immediately knew there was something wrong. I could see it in John's face. He was agitated about the band on stage. They were a skiffle group and John had watched in dismay as their washboard player had abandoned his instrument and started thrashing away on my precious drum kit. John knew me well enough to know I would not be happy, that sparks could fly. He didn't want me kicking off.

"Immediately I went to the Green Room to the side of the stage and the moment they finished their number I got the lad's attention and in no uncertain terms told him they were MY drums and to get off them. He eyed me up and for a moment there was a stand-off. It was very touch and go between us but I must have out-glared him for he just stood up, threw down the sticks and snarled in my direction, 'Stuff your drums' before grabbing his washboard to carry on regardless."

A case of feathers ruffled but no blood spilled; the best was yet to come.

"Soon after that little fraças we were on stage and had launched into a couple of skiffle numbers, 'Rock Island Line', maybe 'Railroad Bill'. But that was just the warm up: once we'd played ourselves in we changed gear, came out of the blocks ready to shake the joint as we started to rock: 'Be Bop a Lula', 'All Shook Up', 'Twenty Flight Rock' and 'Whole Lot of Shaking Going On'. In our minds these were some of our best numbers, guaranteed floor-fillers."

The Quarry Men were flying but to their gobsmacked dismay, particularly John's, the audience began to disappear.

The Cavern had/has a low barrelled ceiling. Situated at the end of a central arch, a low stage faced rows of seats. Either side of the central arch, obscured from the acts on the stage (because they were not illuminated) were two smaller arches.

John turned to Colin in dismay shouting, *'They're all leaving, walking out!'* He was clearly upset. What made it worse was that the more the Quarry Men put into their performance the more the audience shrank.

"We gave it everything but the sight of the audience leaving was really troubling. By the end we couldn't wait to get off. Back in the Green Room John was flabbergasted, despondent: he couldn't believe everyone had just got up and walked out. None of us could."

As The Quarry Men sat commiserating, wondering what had gone wrong, the door to the Green Room flew open and in burst a highly exuberant, highly animated Shotton and Walley. Clearly energised, with Nige nodding in absolute agreement, Pete exclaimed, *"God, that was great: the best show I've ever seen you do!"*

The boys were startled, Colin, John, Paul and George recoiled in disbelief.

"We looked at them as if they were crazy. Surely they were having us on: we'd seen those people leave. Why would they say this to us? Was it some kind of stupid joke?"

In utter disbelief John shook his head and cried out: *"What do you mean, best show we've ever done? The fucking audience walked out!"*

John's outburst drew Nige and Pete up sharp, momentarily silenced as the penny dropped and they realised that from the stage The Quarry Men could not have seen what was really happening on the club floor.

"Pete and Nige quickly set about reassuring us: yes – the audience had left their seats, no arguments about that, but not to walk out on us but because our performance had really got them going. Instead they were up on their feet dancing. The central arch was full of seats, which meant there was no room to dance in that space, consequently the audience had moved to the sides, where there were no obstructions. That's where'd they'd gone. Those spaces at the side were rammed with kids dancing."

As this registered with The Quarry Men, Pete shook his head and repeated his acclaim, *"No, no – you're wrong – they loved it. They were rockin'. Best show ever!"*

43

GEORGE PLAYS 'RAUNCHY'

Early in February (6th) the new-look Quarry Men played the Wilson Hall, after which they pursued their penchant for talent contests by taking the train out of Liverpool on a rare excursion 'over the water' to the Wirral peninsula.

Their destination was Meols and a Conservative Club within walking distance of the station where they were one of five other groups invited to play just four songs each. As talent contests went it was very much like all the others they had entered. At the end of the evening came the reckoning when the audience was asked to clap as loud as they could for their favourite group.

"We'd been here before on so many occasions. The audience clapped and once again we tied for first place with one of the other groups. In time-honoured fashion to reach a decision as to who was the ultimate winner between us, and to generate one last round of excitement, the compere asked both groups to each play one more song and for the audience to clap one last time for their favourite. The group who received the loudest clap won. We knew the drill."

Backstage tension ran high. At last, The Quarry Men were on the cusp of their first win in a talent contest. However, before they stepped back on stage there was a big decision to be made: just what song to play to blow the other group out of the water?

The debate was intense. Colin had observed that all through

the night the audience had been up and dancing, responding most strongly to the groups who played the best dance tunes. In his mind all The Quarry Men needed to do to win was to play a rocker. It seemed so logical but his heart sank when George suggested he could play 'Raunchy'. To George's way of thinking, such instrumental virtuosity would 'wow' the audience more than anything. Colin could not have disagreed more. George's choice, he felt, was as good as shooting themselves in the foot, a direct route to defeat.

"I told the other lads, 'No, no – these kids just want to jive. We should be playing something like 'Twenty Flight Rock', they like that sort of tune, something they can really dance to; they can't dance to 'Raunchy'."

Paul however was having none of it; he immediately sided with George, saying something along the lines of: *"No, we'll do 'Raunchy'. It's more impressive. George is right."*

John Lennon took a moment longer to decide but as he did so he caught the look from Paul and George and sided with them. Colin said not another word but knew instictively The Quarry Men would not be tasting victory that night.

"As soon as we got back on stage George just took off, one hundred miles an hour into 'Raunchy'. He totally ignored the beat I was trying to set up. He just got faster and faster, leaving me for dust and the others as well. We lost the plot completely. What we played ended up as just a big noise, a pile of crap: I stopped playing altogether, I couldn't keep up."

Impressive they weren't.

"Standing at the front Nige Walley saw that I'd lost the beat and helpfully shouted out at the top of his voice, 'Col's lost the beat! Col's lost the beat!' He was right, I had, but the thing was we were all over the place, a runaway train about to derail."

The Quarry Men had turned triumph into disaster.

On the walk back to the station the boys were quite glum. It was obvious that Colin had been right. However fast or however well George could play it, this time 'Raunchy' had been the wrong song in the wrong place at the wrong time. Grudgingly John and Paul acknowledged this fact. Inside his head however the events of the night had confirmed to Colin just where he and his ideas stood in the pecking order of the group.

"At least the Quarry Men had been consistent. Winning talent contests was not our forte."

44

MEANWHILE, BACK AT PAUL'S

"My memories of George coming down to Paul's house to rehearse are vague. At 20 Forthlin it was usually just myself, John and Paul. We would go up to George's house to rehearse but when we did I rarely took my drums. I'd go to his place more to sit in, hang out, maybe beat on the arm of a chair with my sticks, which I always took with me. I didn't connect with George so well, mainly because he seemed so much younger, in fact he was so much younger.

Each time we met by now the more obvious the musical bond between John and Paul became. One of the early things I noted was that John's guitar playing really improved thanks to Paul, who had taught him 'proper' chords. Harmonies became a feature of our performances thanks to Paul. The more time they spent together outside of group rehearsals more often than not they'd come to practices with new songs for us to add to our repetoire, which would be covers, not Lennon and McCartney originals."

As a social unit The Quarry Men were moving in different directions, an inevitable consequence of growing up. Colin's life as an apprentice was far removed from that of John's as a student or Paul and George's as schoolboys. He spent more time in the company of adults. Being older and effectively 'a working man', Colin's priorities were changing. A serious girlfriend to be with, money in his pocket and people to spend it on or with, be it girlfriend Joan or his drinking buddies. By now Joan and Colin had realised going to the cinema was not about the films; it was about being together. They were falling in love and had ditched their respective girl and boy friends to become a couple in their own right. At work Colin was surrounded by older men and he and his friends were being presented with different life goals within that working community.

John, Paul and George had fewer responsibilities; they were still far removed from the 'reality' of the 'adult' world in which Colin was living his life, although it was soon to be knocking on their doors very loudly and very clearly. They were united in their efforts to not let it in for as long as was possible.

Physically they were also closer, heading to the exact same place every day for school and college. They were also on a different musical and artistic journey to Colin. Obsessed with new songs they heard on the radio or on record or at dances, they spent hours studying guitars, dreaming about guitars, wanting to be Elvis… or Buddy Holly; they wanted to live their lives just making music, learning songs, experimenting with writing their own tunes. They were musicicans now; they took their craft/talent very seriously. This was in effect their apprenticeship but it was not like any studying they'd done before because it was being generated/imposed from within, not without. It didn't feel like being at school: rock 'n' roll did not have the adult 'seal of approval'. They weren't being directed or being given lessons to learn. Neither boy liked being told what to do. Indeed John and Paul rejected formal instrument teaching – John on the guitar and Paul on piano. They both did so because their instrument tutors wanted them to do things 'by the book', to abide by the rules, something which did not sit right with either of them. In John's – and Eric's – case when they attended classes together in the very early days they could see the type of classical guitar and music their tutor was playing and it wasn't the type of guitar the boys wanted to play and crucially it was going to take way, way too long. John liked things to be of the moment/to be available to him 'now!'. Similarly Paul didn't want his creativity constrained by doing things the 'right' or accepted way.

Inevitably Colin and the boys had reached a fork in the road; from now on they would be traveling along different routes.

"As we headed into 1958 I socialised less with The Quarry Men than I had at the beginning because I had my drinking buddies, Charlie and Kevin. Paul wasn't into drinking in those days, George was way too young to have been served in a pub and, of course, John was at Art College and if he wasn't with Paul or George, he and his student friends would be socialising in town. At the same time, John, Paul and George saw a lot of each other during the week because school and college were right next door to each other. Getting together to rehearse and hang out was so convenient, so spontaneous for them. So as 1958 progressed I really only met with them to rehearse and perform. Rehearsals would eventually begin to fall off, I guess because they didn't feel the need, seeing each other so regularly. Only occasionally, if we'd played a party together would we hang out afterwards – but that was rare. I suspected they were also playing together without me when the occasion allowed."

Before these fractures set in and not long after George joined The Quarry Men – sometime in early March '58 – Paul's house became the group's most regular rendezvous for rehearsals.

"This was Paul's idea because his dad had a piano in the front living room that he allowed us to use. Jim played his piano a lot. It was not just there for show; it was very much a part of McCartney family life. They were a very musical family. Around the same time George came on board, Sunday became our regular rehearsal day rather than Saturday."

Change was in the air. Nothing could be taken for granted any more.

"Not long after this change of rehearsal day was initiated, drum kit in hand I arrived at number 20 to find a boy I'd never met before sitting at Jim's piano, his back to the living room. As the stranger turned to look at me, Paul piped

up to announce, 'This is Duff from school. We've asked him to join the group to play piano.'"

Significantly this was the first Colin had heard of this new addition to the line-up. Whereas he'd been asked to approve the sacking of Eric and the arrival of George into the group, his opinion on the presence of a pianist in their line-up had not been sought. It was another reminder of his own place in the scheme of things. The new Quarry Man's full name was John Duff Lowe. He was in the same year as Paul at the 'Inny', where he was simply known as 'Duff'. So, 'Duff' it would be in the Quarry Men.

It was clear to Colin that Duff's presence in the group had been sanctioned by John, further evidence of Paul's growing say in all things Quarry Men.

He was right: each boy had found their musical soulmate. John was now attending Art College, situated right next door to the Liverpool Institute, and they would see each other at lunch times when Paul would slip into the Art College canteen to meet with John. George was also a pupil at the Institute and so would often accompany Paul. Little-known to either Colin or to Jim McCartney, John and Paul would also rendezvous at Forthlin during the week when Jim was out at work and they should have been studying. From the outset Jim had not taken to John; he considered him to be a Teddy Boy and feared he could be 'a bad influence' on Paul, to whom he delivered the warning, 'He'll get you into trouble, son'. John did not defer to parents like most youngsters do and so most parents usually did not 'warm' to him, referring to him dismissively as 'that Lennon'. Hence Paul had been told John could only come to number 20 when Jim was present, consequently he had no idea Paul was now 'sagging off' school behind his back to spend time at home with Lennon writing songs, playing records, goofing around, smoking Typhoo tea, learning new chords and practising.

As for Duff, Paul and he had actually encountered each

other several months before they became pupils at the Liverpool Institute. In February 1953, aged ten (going on eleven), they'd both auditioned for the Liverpool Anglican cathedral choir. They hadn't met before the audition and didn't get to know each other on the day. They both failed their auditions but by pure chance happened to be photographed standing next to one other at the event.

Duff went on to pass the audition second time around, joining the choir in October '53, but Paul never tried again. Not long after their shared choral experience both boys passed their Eleven Plus to become pupils at the Liverpool Institute from September 1953.

Colin was immediately impressed with Duff.

"The thing was Duff was a demon piano player: he could play the piano parts note perfectly on 'Mean Woman Blues' (the B-side of Jerry Lee Lewis's December 1957 UK number one, 'Great Balls Of Fire'), which we all loved, especially that arpeggio at the beginning and the same with Little Richard's 'Tutti Frutti'. He was good: I knew instantly why Paul had recruited him."

The presence of Duff in the group so soon after George's arrival was a further sign that John and Paul were getting very serious about their musical ambitions. As a band each new recruit was moving The Quarry Men up a notch: almost by the day they were becoming more accomplished. Of the five original Quarry Men only John and Colin remained. True, Nigel Walley still held onto his position of manager but his tenure was to end during the spring of 1958 when he was diagnosed with traces of TB and entered a sanatorium, and consequently his work for the group ceased. This had an almost immediate impact on bookings and the structure of the group. Without Nigel at the helm they began to dry up and communications within the group became fractured, and Colin was always the last to know and sometimes didn't get to know at all.

Pete Shotton remained close to John, turning up regularly to gigs but in all other respects The Quarry Men were a different band musically and socially. Very much a vehicle for the shared ambitions of John and Paul, theirs was the relationship that mattered and not long after Duff's arrival the most significant element of that burgeoning musical partnership revealed itself.

45

IN SPITE OF ALL THE DANGER

"It was during a rehearsal with John Duff Lowe that Paul introduced a song he said he'd written himself. From comments they'd made I already knew John and Paul were dabbling in writing their own tunes individually and helping each other out but this was the first time Paul actually introduced a tune he'd written with the intention that the group would learn and perform it. It was called 'In Spite of All the Danger'."

Colin remembers Paul later introducing 'I Lost My Little Girl' to The Quarry Men with a view to the group also performing that.

"Although we worked on it, it never became part of our set. Paul just never felt happy with it."

From the moment Paul introduced 'In Spite of All the Danger' Colin knew John was cool with this development otherwise Paul would not have been allowed to do so. And, although it was Paul's song, it was John who sang lead. He was still top dog.

"Paul introduced it to us just like he would a song by Buddy Holly or Elvis: no fanfare, no fuss, just down to earth, exactly as he would any other new tune we were going to work up to play on stage. He guided the changes, and from the start John sang lead."

Colin's growing feeling of having become the outsider in the group was further reinforced by this development.

'That afternoon in Paul's front room Paul, John and George were already familiar with the song. The three of them had obviously previously worked out its arrangement. Within just a few weeks George had become very close to that central partnership of John and Paul although not an equal. So when they played it through for Duff and I to learn, it was John on vocals, Paul on rhythm guitar (and harmonies) while George played a solo. They knew their parts already. As we started work on it Paul was quite particular with Duff, stopping the performance occasionally to interrupt him and show him exactly what he wanted him to play on the piano. Duff listened carefully and did precisely as Paul directed. I was left to my own devices: two on the cymbal, one on the snare, one on the bass. For me it was straightforward. Within two or three run-throughs we pretty much had it down to Paul and John's satisfaction."

For all Colin's outward cool, this event registered as a real musical departure. In those early, early days of rock 'n' roll the norm was for groups to always play other people's songs – usually the hits of the day. Groups didn't even think to write their own. The reasoning was that the kids on the dance floor wanted to hear something already familiar and popular, favourite tunes they knew well or which were played on the radio and were riding high in the charts, especially songs they could dance to – 'hits'! Audiences did not want to hear a band's own tunes that they'd never heard before. Also, few other bands possessed the ability or imagination or application to write their own material.

The introduction of a self-penned tune was groundbreaking. Colin was not aware of any other group in Liverpool who were writing and performing their own material. 'Covers' was the name of the game, so original material was real innovation.

"I was impressed. Not only was it written by Paul; even more to the point it was actually good. I liked it. It sounded like a song Elvis might sing. I didn't

say anything at the time but inwardly I was in awe. It was proof of Paul's talent and the burgeoning ambition of himself and John."

Paul's song was loosely based on Elvis's 'Trying to Get to You' and Colin would be further impressed when Paul insisted on including George as a co-writer of the tune because he had come up with the guitar solo in the middle. (Paul didn't need to be so generous, but he was taking his writing seriously, behaving professionally and being right with everyone.)

By now Paul's dad had started to take a more active interest in what the boys were doing. He would hover around during rehearsals and sometimes comment on what the boys were playing.

"At some point in the afternoon (usually around 4 p.m.) Jim would always go and put the kettle on and make everyone a cup of tea. ('Two sugars for me please, Mr.McCartney.') He would also pick us up on points of grammar in lyrics and urge us to sing with clear diction."

Jim was indeed very particular about people speaking correctly and clearly and obeying the rules of grammar. He did not like what he called 'Americanisms', especially the foreshortening of words. As Colin recalls: *"He'd grumble when John and Paul sang something like 'That'll be the day' and suggest 'That will be the day' as more appropriate."*

Jim's dislike of 'Americanisms' would later provide Paul with an anecdote he still occasionally likes to tell. On Wednesday 26th June 1963 The Beatles performed at the Majestic Ballroom in Newcastle-upon-Tyne. After the show in their shared room at the city's Turk's Hotel, John and Paul composed a song they thought could be a possibe follow-up to their number one hit 'From Me to You'. This new song they'd composed was called 'She Loves You'. Either the very next day, Thursday 27th or possibly Saturday 29th, both rare days off for the Beatles at that time, the two convened at 20 Forthlin Road to put the finishing touches to the tune, working on it in the dining room while Jim sat watching TV in the front room.

Once they were satisfied they had it nailed, the boys proudly shared it with Jim, whose opinions as a former band leader they valued. Jim certainly shared their enthusiasm for the song – it was undeniably catchy – a perfect follow-up he agreed – but he drew the line at the repeated 'Yeah! Yeah! Yeahs!' suggesting that instead they drop this 'Americanism' to sing, 'She loves you, Yes! Yes! Yes!' His advice, of course, fell on deaf ears… leaving Paul to comment, *"He just didn't get it."*

46

EATING GLASS

Meanwhile, back in 1958… Duff Lowe's presence at rehearsals became quite regular. Colin felt he really added to the group sound and his contribution to 'In Spite of All the Danger' greatly enhanced it. However, he was not a regular presence at gigs.

"First, he could only play a show if he knew in advance that the venue had a piano. The Wilson Hall and the New Clubmoor had pianos but not all the others did. Secondly, Duff had a real problem with his parents. They didn't know he was part of a rock 'n' roll group. At home they didn't like him playing Jerry Lee Lewis songs or anything that wasn't classical. They'd say, 'If you can't play properly, John, don't play it all.'

From what I know they would never have countenanced him being in a rock group. Also, he didn't live near the rest of us, he lived over north Liverpool way so most times he'd have to catch at least two 'buses to make our shows. He had to tell his parents he was going somewhere else other than to meet up with reprobates like us. Then he'd sneak out with his cowboy shirt on underneath a regular shirt and coat, a pair of old drainpipe jeans John had given him hidden under his coat which he'd change into in the gents toilets on the roundabout at the top of Penny Lane. Real cloak and dagger stuff."

Such were the rigours and risks for a young grammar school boy engaging with that demon rock 'n' roll. Not only were the Teddy Boys out to get you should you ever dare to look in their direction but your parents could be an even more serious adversary if they disapproved of the music – and in many, many cases they did. Duff's parents were not unusual in this respect.

"The two 'buses thing was a real problem for Duff because he had to get home on time to avoid incurring the wrath of his parents. Consequently he would leave shows early to ensure he was on that last 'bus. I remember one time at the Wilson Hall we were close to finishing a set, had just finished a song but when we looked to the piano at the start of the next number Duff had gone, no word of goodbye."

One gig Duff Lowe *did* make was a Sunday afternoon talent show at a Labour Club in Toxteth. (Duff remembers it as being held at the Stevedores and Dockers Union in Anfield, near the football ground.) Wherever it was, it was definitely not where Duff's parents would have wanted him to be: they would have thrown a fit had they known exactly where and for what purpose he was headed on that particular day.

As has been apparent throughout *Pre:Fab* Colin and The Quarry Men were suckers for talent shows but how they must have regretted their decision to participate in this particular one.

"The most memorable thing about that show was a young man whose act consisted entirely of eating glass. It sounds incredible as I say it now; at the time it was mind-blowing. I remember laid out in front of him on the stage were a selection of glass items: tumblers and light bulbs. His entire act consisted of him carefully putting each item onto a piece of cloth, folding this over then hitting the item through the cloth with a hammer to break it. He'd then unfold the cloth, individually pick up the larger pieces, pop them into his mouth and start crunching away. As might be expected, in between gorging on each item he said very little."

Colin remembers the audience – like The Quarry Men – sat agog in a state of utter disbelief. It says everything about this particular act that it could silence either a bevvied lunchtime audience in

Toxteth or the inebriated members of the judging committee at the Stevedores and Dockers Union.

"When we went back stage to grab our gear we were amazed to see this lad stuffing handkerchiefs into his mouth to stem the bleeding. He'd cut all his gums. We didn't see any evidence of the glass itself so goodness knows what had happened to that or how long it took before he dropped dead. I'll never forget him standing in front of us his mouth rammed with bloodied cloth. We all looked at each other in disbelief. It was so unnerving even John Lennon was lost for words."

Following the glass-eater on stage The Quarry Men found themselves traumatised. Little is remembered of their performance by anyone who was there.

"We certainly didn't win and I don't think that chap did either. On the way home all we could talk about was the glass eater. He'd literally stopped us in his tracks. To this day if I close my eyes I can see him standing there in front of me, a look of disbelief on his face, his mouth full of blood-soaked handkerchiefs. What a twit!"

47

SETTING RECORDS STRAIGHT

Another Sunday, another rehearsal at Paul's: frustratingly the actual date is not recalled but Colin thinks it was early July. On this particular occasion Paul's main concern was that The Quarry Men rehearsed, 'In Spite of All the Danger'.

"I soon understood why he was so focused on us getting that song right because during our tea break Paul informed us all that he had discovered there was a recording studio in Kensington where people could go to make a record. He thought it would be a good idea for us to do this."

How Paul had discovered the whereabouts of this particular recording studio was most probably through George Harrison. George had been dating Iris Caldwell, younger sister of Alan, leader of the Texan Skiffle Group. George had become a regular visitor to the Caldwell family home. He would dearly have liked to play in Al's group and would have known Johnny 'Guitar' Byrne, Al's partner in the group, who doubtless would have told him about the disc he had cut in a studio in Liverpool. There is every possibility Johnny or Al would have played this to George. Johnny had recorded it with a chap called Paul Murphy. It was a two-sided single: 'Butterfly' and 'She's Got It' (a Little Richard song). One copy only. Cut at Percy Phillips studio in Kensington, Liverpool, on 22nd June 1957, it is one of the earliest known recordings by anyone associated with 'Merseybeat'.

It seems highly likely George had mentioned the disc and the studio to Paul whose ambition and imagination would have been immediately engaged.

"However Paul had got to know about the studio didn't really matter but his news immediately caused excitement among us because Buddy Holly was making records, Elvis was making records but we weren't. In fact we hadn't even thought about the possibility of The Quarry Men cutting a disc, so the realisation that we could was a very exciting prospect."

Records were very special in those days, the holy grail for singers and groups. Anyone could play in a band (especially a skiffle group) but to cut a record meant you'd gone up a notch. You'd made it – you were a star!

Once the initial banter stalled, reality then set in for The Quarry Men.

"It wasn't long before one of us raised the crucial question of how much it would cost. Paul had really done his homework because right away he said he'd inquired and to cut one disc would cost us 17s and 6d."

This news put things into perspective for The Quarry Men. 17s/6d was less than a pound (£) but in 1958 it would have seemed steep for boys who were not earning. (By today's values it was approximately £13) Only one of the group, Colin, was in employment, although John earned five shillings a week pocket money if he cut the lawns at Mendips for his Aunt Mimi. Paul was not averse to doing a part-time job like a paper round to raise some much-needed extra cash for things he wanted.

"While I sat mulling this over Duff piped up to say that as there were five of us it would work out at 3s/6d each. For myself that was much less of a problem but for the other lads it was still something to consider. Don't forget in those days 3s/6d would have got you into the cinema four

times over. After some discussion it was agreed that among us we would raise the money, such was our determination to make a record. I never did discover how they all acquired their share of the price. Most probably from their parents. I wondered what Duff had told his parents the money was for."

The source of their funds was of far less importance to the boys than to actually arrange a date to record.

"Paul was especially keen to set a date. Our enthusiam was high and he knew this was the time to strike. The first thing to decide was on which day of the week we could all convene to go into the studio. As a student John was flexible but I didn't want to take a day off work and Duff, Paul and George had school and so it was agreed we'd do this on a Saturday. Paul said he'd inquire when the next Saturday was available for us to record: the sooner the better was our consensus."

Energised the boys now wanted to perfect the songs they had chosen to record.

"The first we'd chosen was a particular favourite of ours: Buddy Holly's 'That'll Be the Day'. A highlight of our 'live' set we loved that song and in our heads that immediately became the 'A-side'. Looking back I now recognise it had greater significance than any of us consciously realised at the time. It was a Buddy Holly tune and, of course, his influence on all of us, especially John and Paul, was immense. Buddy was the one who'd drawn the blueprint, set the example for John and Paul to follow of writing their own songs. To record that number was almost a tribute to Buddy while, 'In Spite of All the Danger' signified a kind of passing of the baton."

Eager to get that very new 'original' song right, more practises were necessary.

"We wanted to be able to play it as well as we could play 'That'll Be the Day'. John, Paul and myself agreed we'd meet one evening during the week at John's Aunt Mimi's to do some extra rehearsing. Duff didn't come because Mimi didn't have a piano. He was so good anyway I doubt he needed to rehearse. Accordingly we convened at Mendips and during that mini-rehearsal Paul said he'd been over to Phillips studio during his Monday lunch break from school and booked the studio for the following Saturday and so it was agreed John, Paul, George and myself would meet at Penny Lane to catch a 'bus to the Hippodrome on West Derby Road where we would link up with John Duff Lowe: Paul had also found out that there was a piano at the studios that Duff could use."

This was a very big deal for The Quarry Men, so just like that very first Carroll Levis audition at the Empire the boys were a mixture of excitement and nerves, laughing and joking together as they sat on a 'bus en route to Kensington. This felt special.

"Once we linked up with Duff at The Hippodrome we walked along West Derby Road to Kensington Road and on to the studio at number 38. Actually it didn't say 'studio' on the door because the front of the premises was a shop called 'Phillips Battery Charging Depot'. In those days there were still many radios in circulation that were battery powered and people would take their radio batteries to such shops to have them charged."

Colin's correct but by the mid Fifties there was a decline in battery-generated radios and so by the time they visited Phillips' shop it was also selling electrical goods, televisions – even records – and in 1955 as a second source of income Percy Phillips set up his recording and record pressing studio, which he named 'Phillips Sound Recording Services'. Percy was happy to record virtually anyone who walked through the door, provided they had the right money in their hand. And so on any given day entering his shop door could have been a howling dog (no wolves in the UK) to howl along to piano accompaniment or Ron Wycherly (aka Billy Fury) or local singer Betty Roy or comedian Ken Dodd or ventriloquist Ray Alan or even The Quarry Men.

Whatever enthusiasm The Quarry Men had felt as they set out on this great adventure it would have been sorely challenged by the appearance of Percy F. Phillips studio. Seen from the outside it was a very ordinary Victorian terrace house converted into a shop of which there were thousands across the city (despite the Blitz). 'Dead ordinary' was the expression – dead ordinary and small to boot. What a come-down. Their vision of what a recording studio would look like had been established by what they'd seen in 'The Girl Can't Help It'. In no way did number 38 Kensington come close. There was certainly neither glamour nor even the tiniest hint of glitz.

However, for Colin Hanton, George Harrison, John Lennon, John 'Duff' Lowe and Paul McCartney there was to be no turning back.

"We were a few minutes early so when we entered the shop we were politely shown into a smaller back room where we were asked to wait 'quietly'. Duff remembers that somewhere in the near distance we could hear a lady recording an aria. So we did as we were told and sat very quietly, each one of us contemplating our situation for this was our much anticipated 'Elvis' moment. In our heads we were sitting in Liverpool's equivalent of Sun Studios, Memphis, Tennessee, with our own Mr. Phillips at the controls. I personally was wondering if, like us, Elvis could hear buses and trucks running up and down the street outside or a woman singing opera as he sat waiting to cut 'That's All Right'."

Not long after the lady opera singer emerged from the studio Mr. Percy F. Phillips himself appeared in the doorway to beckon the boys into his recording studio.

Mr. Percy Phillips in his recording studio

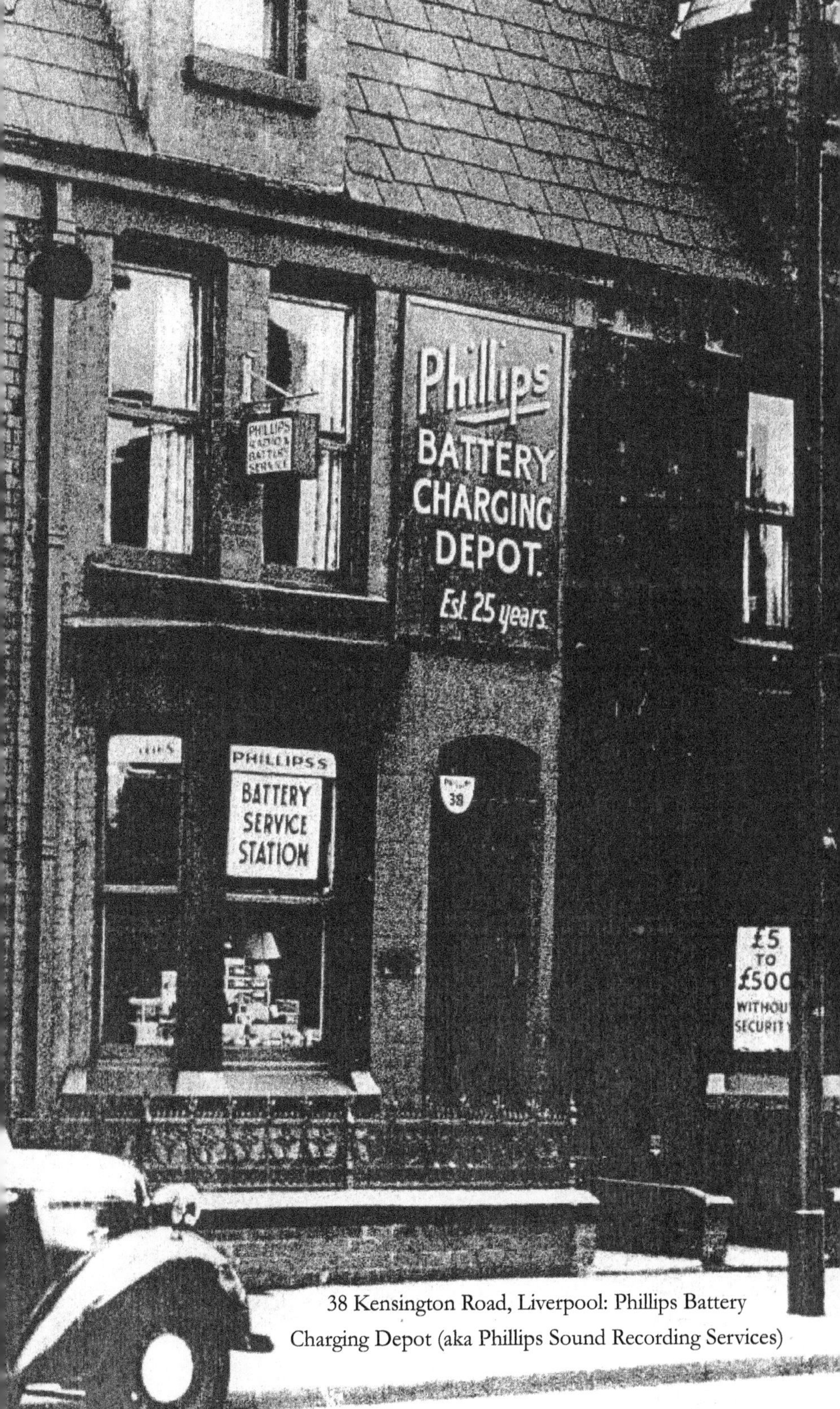

38 Kensington Road, Liverpool: Phillips Battery Charging Depot (aka Phillips Sound Recording Services)

"Mr. Phillips looked just like anybody's dad, which is not a criticism but just further emphasises the very ordinariness of the situation in which we found ourselves. He invited us to join him in his studio where we stood briefly taking it all in. There were were no windows visible to us (they were covered with heavy curtains). The room itself was about the size of a dining room in a typical Victorian terraced house (which it most probably had been originally). It was about four metres by three. I remember there was just one lonely light bulb hanging from the ceiling illuminating this very small space.

Once we were inside the room Percy covered the door with a thick quilted cover (somewhat like an eiderdown) to further soundproof it. Percy's recording equipment was at the back of the room next to where a window had no doubt once overlooked the back garden but which was now covered by heavy blankets. On the wall above the recording equipment were photographs of stars of the day who had cut a disc in this very room. On seeing these photos, a tape recorder, disc cutting machine and four-track mixer (although I didn't know what they were at the time, they just looked impressive) our spirits began to revive. I also spotted a piano, three mics and several sets of headphones. I guess it was all fairly rudimentary but back in those days for us it looked professional enough. This was more like it! Now the adrenalin began to kick in."

Phillips wasn't one to hang about so he quickly started to position the boys and prepare for the recording.

"I was the first one he sound checked to see how loud I would be so he told me to set my drums up in the corner furthest away from the recording deck. He listened to me on earphones and told me I was too loud. I remember I moved a little further back, as far as I could go, but he still said I was too loud. Despite it being summer it wasn't a particularly warm day and so I was wearing a thin scarf and that inspired me – I removed it and spread it across my snare drum to muffle the sound. That seemed to please him."

As he moved to position the other boys Percy Phillips paused.

"It was as if he'd just remembered something he'd forgotten, which indeed he had. He stopped and turned to look at the lads near him at the mixing desk and asked which one of us was going to pay him? Percy Phillips could see we were just young lads and so I think he had most probably begun to wonder if we actually did have enough on us to pay for the session before taking things any further. Although Paul had told us it would cost 17s/6d, before we coughed up John must have decided to double check that was the right amount because he asked how much Mr. Phillips wanted. Percy confirmed that it was 17s/6d for the recording but added that it would be much better if he recorded us on reel to reel tape rather than straight onto disc because that would give him the opportunity to edit before transferring our recordings to disc. This sounded like a good idea until he told us that doing it that way would cost an additional 2/6 making our total bill just £1.00."

Percy had dropped a bombshell that immediately threw the session into jeopardy.

"John and Paul exchanged questioning glances as if to say was this extra really worth it or was it just a con to extricate more dosh from us? To our knowledge it hadn't been mentioned before. For us this was unknown territory. It sounded plausible but we just did not know.

I knew that John, Paul, George and Duff had struggled to come up with their 3s/6d's so there was no way we could now just pull an extra two shillings six pence from our pockets. On the other hand, none of us wanted to end the session because of a lack of cash. We desperately wanted to walk out of that studio with a record in our hands so, as ever in our moments of need, we turned towards our leader, who in turn turned towards Percy Phillips and very emphatically exclaimed, 'There's no way we are paying a £1'.

Nonplussed Percy just nodded, accepted the decision, collected the cash we did have and carried on.

Once we were all set up and Paul and George plugged into Paul's Elpico amp he asked to us to run through the songs we wanted to record because he wanted to time each tune to ensure there would be enough space on each side of the disc for our chosen numbers. Percy had positioned the three guitarists

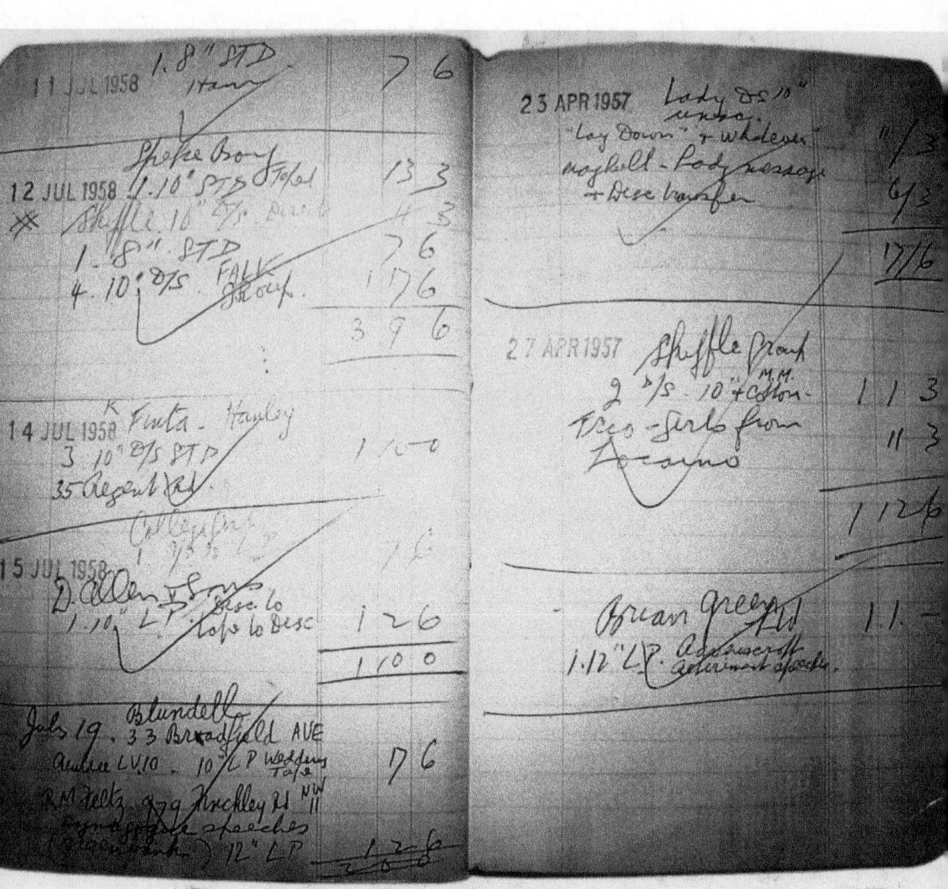

Percy Phillips studio log book, 12th July 1958

around a single microphone in the centre of the room while Duff took his seat at the piano, as ever, his back to the rest of us. This was it, no stopping us now. All went quiet and as soon as we got the nod from Percy The Quarry Men rattled through 'That'll Be the Day' in fine style, Percy timing us as we did so. He was happy because we came in under time; he could see no problem recording that song."

Confidence was high: one run-through, no hiccups. Next up was the much rehearsed but still very new 'In Spite of All the Danger'.

"We'd spent so much time practising this song but it wasn't second nature, we were still becoming 'familiar' with it. And as we knew Percy was timing us, it definitely felt like there was more pressure on us. No surprise then when our first attempt didn't go according to plan. Paul stopped us mid-song. I seem to remember he spoke to George about his guitar solo and once that issue was resolved we tried again and ran through the whole song without a hitch, although towards the end I could see Percy getting agitated; there was clearly something up. He was pointing at his watch and signalling for us to cut the song. Immediately the time check for 'In Spite of All the Danger' ended Percy told us it was too long and would take up too much room on the disc – it had to be shorter. He wanted us to cut a verse but John refused, saying, 'No, we're going to do it the way it is, we're paying, we'll do it our way'. By now I could see Percy was becoming a tad frustrated so he did not argue; he just shrugged and urged us to 'Get on with it.' I guess he thought he'd let us find out the hard way. Clearly he wanted us to crack on with the actual recording straight onto vinyl. He hadn't got all day. After all he needed us out of the studio ready for his next client (who most probably was going to cough up the full £1).

We got the signal and launched into the actual recording. One take only for each song, no second attempts. We went straight into 'That'll Be the Day', completing it without a hitch. Having cut the song to vinyl, Percy took the disc off the machine, wiped it with a cloth and flipped it over ready for us to record on the other side. On the signal from Percy we began 'In Spite of All the Danger' knowing that the clock was against us. Once again, as we neared the end, Percy began to wave at us frantically, making the 'cut' sign with his hand across his throat. There wasn't much we could do to go any faster. I wasn't sure just what Percy expected us to do. We just kept on with our performance and just as we struck the last note so the arm lifted up off the disc. We'd made it but with no space whatsoever to spare.

I remember that for a brief moment right at the end we all stayed silent, holding our breath, looking at each other as we did so just letting it sink in what we had just done. We'd cut a record! As this reality did register we began to relax and chatter excitedly as Percy carefully took the newly minted 78rpm disc from the deck, wiped it gently with his cloth and put it into one of several paper sleeves he had to hand. Prophetically it was one for Parlophone Records."

At the end there was no playback. Already paid for and now bagged up it was time to leave the building. Percy had previously pointed out that the disc had a limited lifespan: the more it was played the less good it would sound.

Before The Quarry Men knew it they were back on the street clutching that oh-so-precious item: a 78rpm double-sided shellac single of themselves singing and performing. This was the real deal.

"Oh boy were we excited: The Quarry Men were now recording artists. Look out, Elvis, here we come! As we walked towards the 'bus stop we passed the disc around among ourselves, each one of us gazing at it in wonder, cherishing the feel and weight of that magical item we now so proudly held in our own hands.

Among us it was agreed we would each take a turn in taking the record home to play to our families and, without a word being said, it was taken for granted John would be the first one to do so. I think Paul was going to be the next. Then George: the new world order was in place."

Colin split from the boys to go home at this point. He wasn't joining them to hear the disc; he needed to catch a different 'bus to them because he wanted to drop his drum kit off at his house before returning immediately to town to meet with Joan.

"The others went off together, I'm not sure where. I can only imagine they went either to Julia's or Paul's to listen to the record; both parents had a record player and Julia and Jim would have been eager to hear it. Most likely I think they would have gone first to Paul's to play it to his father and then John would have taken it round to his mum's."

For Beatles fans and historians the accepted date on which this historic recording took place has become 14th July 1958. If that was the case it would make it a Monday, just one day before the death of Julia. It's certainly the date that appears on the commemorative plaque now affixed above the door of Percy Phillips' former studio.

Colin has never agreed with this being the date – and still doesn't. He doesn't like the plaque much either.

"It's got the date wrong and more to the point it's not my picture on it. Its designer told me he was unable to locate me or find a photograph of myself, so he used a picture of a young Ringo instead, so it actually depicts John, Paul, George, Duff… and Ringo."

No wonder why Colin is not very happy.

"When they were planning and designing the plaque no-one bothered to find me and ask for a photograph. Had anyone taken the time and trouble to do so I would also have told them the day The Quarry Men cut the record was a Saturday and so the exact date was the 12th July 1958 at approximately 11am."

Neither Colin nor Duff was given sight of the plaque before the day of the unveiling (26th August 2005).

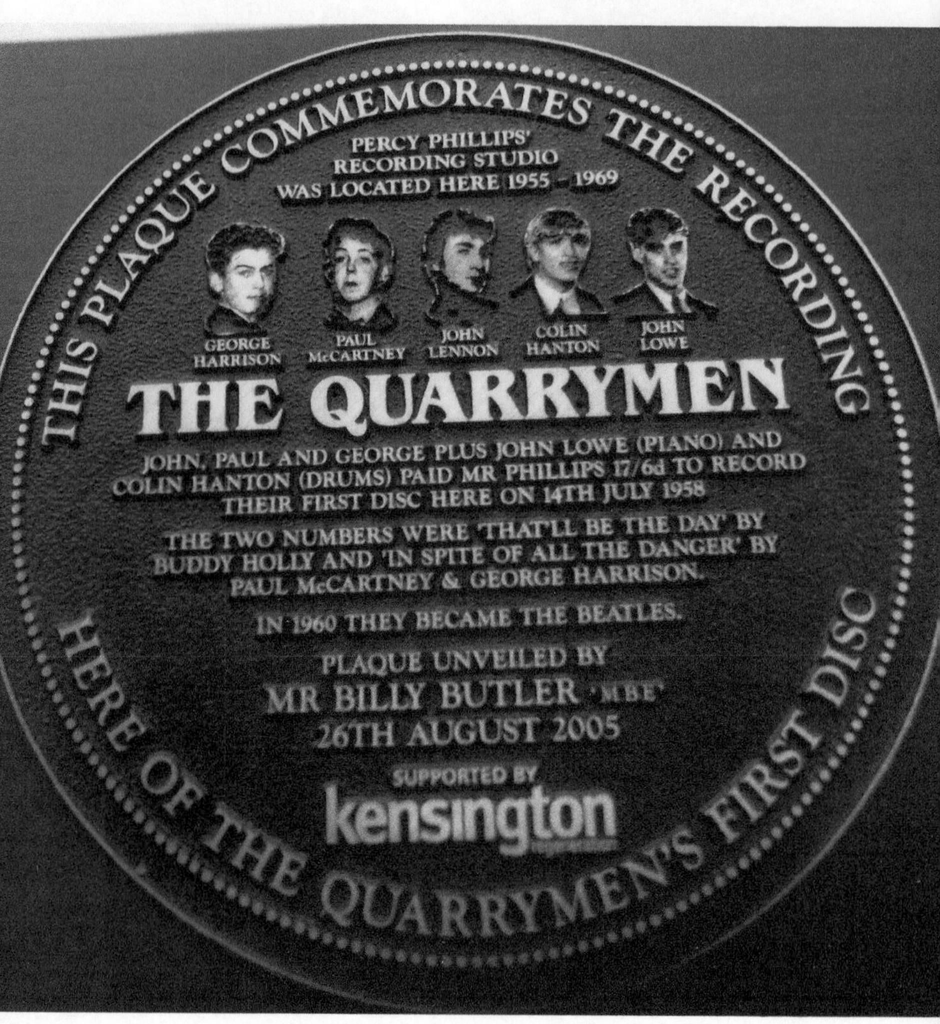

Commemorative plaque outside 38 Kensington

"I was shocked and very angry at what I saw. When I was introduced to the designer I asked why he had not contacted or consulted me. He told me he had been unable to trace me, which really rankled because my name and number was one of eight Hantons (all related) in the telephone directory at the time. The chap had simply not made the effort and used an image of Ringo instead."

Duff and Colin were the only Quarry Men present at the unveiling and were both handed small commemorative replicas of the plaque with Ringo's image on them. To appease Colin the designer made a second small commemorative replica of the plaque – this time with Colin's image on it (as provided by Colin). It remains one of only two in existence – a second was made for display at The Beatles Story museum in Liverpool. Sadly, to this day the offending 'Ringoised' version remains in situ on the building in Kensington.

"The reason I clearly remember the date and the time of that famous session is because I had arranged to meet my girlfriend Joan at 2 p.m. in the city centre that same Saturday, very soon after the session. The plaque on the wall outside the site of Percy Philips studio may say we cut the disc on the 14th of July but that was definitely not the case. The 14th. was a Monday, a working day, a day when I had to be at work. I'm not sure if schools would have broken up by then but if they hadn't George would possibly have been there although knowing him that would not have been much of a deterrent. Paul and Duff most probably would have already left after taking their O-Levels. The point is, there is no way I could or would have taken a day off work for this, it would have been frowned upon by my employers, and the ultimatum I'd received from my boss when I'd asked to take a day off to attend the audition in Manchester was still fresh in my mind. I wasn't going to put my job at risk. Plus, importantly, I would have lost a day's pay, which I wasn't going to do given I was about to lay out money to make the record. And don't forget whatever I earned from Quarry Men bookings I was already giving to John and Paul so I would have been well out of pocket.

Colin's personal replica copy of the offending plaque, showing his picture

The whole subterfuge Duff had constructed to keep his father from knowing he was playing in a rock 'n' roll group was better maintained by the recording being on a Saturday morning. For all his father knew, Duff would have been just going into town.

However all that is irrelevant because what seals the date as Saturday the 12th is my meeting with Joan. It was a special day. I was a Catholic boy but Joan was Church of England and the 12th July is a major day in the Protestant calendar. It's the date of the Battle of the Boyne, when the Protestant Orange Order march to celebrate the defeat of the Catholic James II. In Liverpool in those days they marched from Sefton Park to St. George's Hall (and back). This was a big event in the city in those days. They could be lively affairs. Fights between Protestants and Catholics went hand in hand with the event. Despite the difference in our religions Joan and I were very close. This is how I remember the day and date so clearly.

Joan had agreed to go into Liverpool that morning to watch her friends, who were members of the Lodge and who were participating in the march. She was going to view the march as it arrived at St. George's Hall and then walk around the corner to view it again as it and her friends proceeded up London Road on the way back to Sefton Park. And that was where we'd arranged she would be waiting for me when I came back into town after returning my drums to Woolton. I remember it clearly. From London Road we went into town on a date. Don't forget we were a serious courting couple by now."

So that's what Colin did: raced home to Woolton, deposited his drums, raced out of the house, jumped on the next 'bus back into town for his rendezvous with Joan.

"I caught up with her on London Road as the march was walking back to Sefton Park. No one paid any attention to us. All eyes were on the marchers, the cheers and the singing, the banners and the marching bands. We were just a courting couple standing together on the side of the road taking in the spectacle. We were a case of love overcoming religious barriers and it's been that way for Joan and I ever since!"

Such is the marker Colin carries inside his head, which firmly nails the date The Quarry Men recorded at Percy Phillips as July 12th not the 14th.

48

JULIA

'Life is what happens to you when you are busy making other plans.'

Prophetic words. John's words, written for his second son, Sean, in his song 'Beautiful Boy'. Words of wisdom gained from bitter experience.

"At the very moment of our collective excitement for having made a record, tragedy struck. On the evening of Tuesday 15th July 1958, John's mother, Julia, was knocked down and killed in a road accident as she crossed Menlove Avenue just yards from her sister Mimi's house, John's home. She had been visiting Mimi. John was still living there, although at the time he was actually down at Julia's, waiting for his mum to return."

More often than not Mimi would have accompanied Julia to the 'bus stop but on this evening she did not. According to Michael, the student lodger who was in the house with the sisters, when the 'bus was due Mimi was still in her slippers and so there was no time for her to put on her shoes to walk with Julia across the road and, besides, they could see Nigel Walley at the garden gate about to come in. Julia said goodbye to Mimi, told Nigel that John was down at her house and together they walked to the corner of Menlove Avenue and Vale Road, where they parted company. Nigel turned to walk home along Vale and Julia to cross Menlove to her 'bus stop on the other side.

Just a few steps after bidding each other goodnight Nigel heard a terrible squeal of brakes and a loud bang. Startled he turned to see Julia literally flying through the air. She had been struck by a motor car. Immediately he raced to Julia's side but as he made to kneel beside her where she lay in the road, Nigel saw a strand of her beautiful auburn hair blow across her face, and in that moment he knew she was gone.

Although Nigel knows he could not possibly have foreseen what was about to occur, to this very day he is haunted by his memories of this tragic accident, regretting not having spoken to Julia for just a few more moments so delaying her walk to the 'bus stop.

Colin cannot recall how he learned of Julia's passing but it would have been very soon afterwards: Woolton was a small village and so the news quickly spread.

"As I left the boys that Saturday lunch-time we were buzzing with the excitement of making a record. It felt like there would be no stopping us now. I know John was so looking forward to playing it to his mum. I can only hope he did, that Julia got to hear John singing on disc.

Of all the people in his life at that time whom John would have wanted to hear our record it would have been his mum. She would have loved it. I know she would have been so proud of what he had achieved. I can imagine her singing along, playing it to her daughters, Jackie and Julia, and to her partner, Bobby. I hope this is what happened. It was Julia's reaction and positivity he would have sought above anyone else's.

In my experience Julia was so supportive of John and his musical ambitions. More than anyone in his life at that time she understood what music gave him. Julia had been encouraging him from the very start (even in the face of Aunt Mimi's disapproval). She helped him to acquire that cheap Gallotone Champion acoustic guitar so that he could fulfil his dream of forming a group, she taught him banjo chords to get him started, she played him Elvis and Gene Vincent records, records that she herself loved and bought. We didn't know any other parent who bought rock 'n' roll records.

She was the exception. This was something they shared. Mimi could never have understood what they found to value in rock 'n' roll music. None of our parents except Jim McCartney and George's mother enjoyed or understood what playing music and being in a group meant to us. Certainly none of our parents understood or liked rock 'n' roll like Julia did.

She would have appreciated Aunt Mimi's concerns over John's studies but what mattered more to Julia was that John gave his dreams a run for their money, that he had fun and fulfilled himself. Julia was also such a lovely person to be around; vivacious, funny, warm, kind and loving. She was so different from our Mums in the way she behaved, more like an older sister who was tuned into us as youngsters in ways our own parents weren't. She dressed so much more stylishly. She sang along with us and danced with us. She was outrageously funny and lit up the space and people around her wherever she was, whoever she was with. For all of us in the group it was inconceivable that she had gone. God knows what it was like for John and his sisters."

Both Paul and Colin had lost their mothers and they understood the pain John would now be experiencing.

"I had lost my own mother and knew his sense of loss would be overwhelming. They had told me my mum would come home but the reality was that, even as they told me this, the people around me knew she would not do so. They never prepared me for what they knew was inevitable. No one took the responsibility. Instead it was easier, less painful to say nothing. I was left believing that one day she would return. I have never forgiven them for that lie. Like John, for me there were no good-byes. For John the violence and unexpected suddenness of his mum's death would have been totally devastating and cruel, his heart broken in an instant, no prior illness to sound an alert, nothing. It was a tragedy he and his two younger sisters, Julia and Jacqueline, would carry forever inside. So much would be left unresolved. Julia's passing surely marked them all for life."

49

THE LONG AND WINDING STORY OF THE QUARRY MEN'S 78RPM DISC

Julia's funeral took place on Monday 21st July. Colin did not attend the church service nor the family wake.

"I felt it was private, very much a family affair: more so than usual because of the violent and sudden way in which Julia had died. Rod, Len, Duff and Nigel also did not attend. Possibly Paul and Pete would have been there, maybe George, maybe Ivan. Eric was probably away at sea."

As would be expected, all things Quarry Men faded into a distant background for all the boys. The euphoria of making their record instantly paled into insignificance. John would 'disappear' within himself for awhile, consumed by grief, desperately trying to come to terms with his mother's passing.

And yet that record survived. It was not cast to one side or ever completely forgotten. It got played, much more than was realised it would be or was possibly intended to, or good for it. And somehow it did not get broken or warped and along the way it didn't wear out. This was a minor miracle to say the least for those old shellac 78s were incredibly fragile. Knock them ever so slightly against something and they would shatter. Leave them in the sunshine a moment too long and they would warp never to be flattened or playable again.

One by one the disc moved between the boys. First from John to Paul, then from Paul to George and then from George to Colin before finally ending up in John Duff Lowe's hands, where it would stay for many years safe and secure in the bottom of a drawer.

"I took it home and proudly played it to Joan, Mum and Dad, my sister Lynne, older brother Brian, and younger brother John D, the next-door neighbours – sisters Geraldine and Colette – my drinking buddies Kevin Hanson and Charlie Roberts. They were all mightily impressed because in those days to have made a record was a bit special. At some point Charlie asked if he could borrow it to play at his work place. He worked at Littlewoods, the huge football pools company situated in a magnificent art-deco complex on Edge Lane. They also sold clothes by mail order and produced a massive illustrated catalogue featuring pictures of all they sold. Hundreds of women worked there – some of them would check the coupons to see if anyone had won the 'jackpot'. They would listen to music being played over the tannoy in the canteen. They were encouraged to take in their own records to be played. Charlie wanted to take our record in to work for the ladies to hear, so I let him borrow it. He told me it got played several times and received a 'mixed' reaction. Some had liked it, some were not impressed. For some reason I never asked for it back, but this meant it maybe got played more than we realised."

In Colin's mind the record was associated with the death of Julia and so maybe this is why he never chased it up. As 1958 progressed 78rpm records became redundant as the new 45rpm discs replaced them as the favoured format for singles.

"It stayed in Charlie's possession for several years, languishing in the pile of old 78s he rarely – if ever – played. During this time Charlie married Sandra and not long after, during the Sixties a short-lived craze for melting old unwanted 78 records to reshape them into plant pot holders, ashtrays and bowls swept the nation.

Sandra decided to try this for herself. And so it was while fashioning some of Charlie's old 78s into plant pot holders she picked up that old Quarry Men's single to dip it into a pan of boiling water to soften it ready for moulding, at which point she paused. Thankfully something about the label in the centre caught her attention. It did not look like the others – it was different, it was hand written. Fortuitously Sandra read it, saw the names 'McCartney, Harrison' written underneath the title of one of the songs, 'In Spite of All the Danger', and immediately pulled it back from the brink oblivion. Realising this record was a bit special and possibly neither hers nor Charlie's to dispose of she determined to ask Charlie about it. When he told her its back story they decided it should be returned to its rightful owner. Well done, Sandra. Hero!"

Fortunately for history and Beatles fans everywhere, Sandra's quick thinking and Charlie's subsequent course of action ensured that that single-copy Quarry Men 78 was saved for posterity. Charlie recognised it immediately and it was returned ending up in the posession of John Duff Lowe.

For the next twenty years it would be Duff's wife Linda who ensured this precious and unique artefact was kept safe. It was laid flat in the bottom of Duff's sock drawer. Unknown to Duff, fearing for its safety whenever they went on holiday Linda wrapped it securely and took it with them. Thus she ensured that if ever their home was broken into while they were away this ultra-precious record would not be taken. Good thinking, Linda.

In 1981 Paul McCartney discovered that Duff still had the record. Paul said that he, John and George had often wondered where it had ended up or whether it even still existed. He was therefore delighted to discover it had survived, unwarped, unbroken, in relatively good condition and still playable. He went on to purchase it from Duff.

Paul had the original record 'restored' as much as was possible and had 50 copies made that he gave as presents to family and friends (along with an accompanying seven-inch 45rpm copy just in case its recipients in 1981 did not have equipment that still played 78s). Sometimes described as 'the World's rarest or most valuable record', it eventually enjoyed a worldwide release in 1995 when both sides appeared on 'The Beatles Anthology Volume 1', thus giving Colin and Duff the very special thrill of hearing themselves perform on a Beatles record alongside John, Paul and George. (For purposes of the 'Anthology' Paul had had the original 1958 version edited down from three minutes twenty-five seconds to two minutes forty-five seconds. No doubt a decision of which Percy Phillips would have wholeheartedly approved.)

Since The Quarry Men reformed in 1997, both songs have become mainstays of their set.

50

END GAME

For Colin the recording at Percy Phillips and the tragic death of Julia marked the end of an era. From then on things were never quite the same for him within the group.

He'd continue as a Quarry Man for a while longer but could sense that those winds of change he'd felt with the sacking of Eric were now clearly blowing in his direction.

Nigel's ill health and subsequent relinquishing of his managerial role meant that bookings became infrequent and the lines of communication between the members of the group fractured. As a result Colin seemed to miss out on rehearsals, some talent contests and some gigs such as the opening night at 'the Morgue'.

John and Paul had become tuned right into each other. The death of Julia formed an unspoken bond between the two. George was not party to that but musically he was tuned in, growing closer all the time.

As has already been mentioned, physically they inhabited the same territory: college and school. Lunchtimes would find John, Paul and George ensconced in the Art School basement canteen gorging on chips and playing their guitars, lost in their own private world of rock 'n' roll dreams.

Equally their various homes were just a 'bus ride away, where they could also gather, regularly, happily skipping school and college to do so. Paul's home was a favourite for John and Paul especially. Jim would be out at work and so the two 'sagged school' to rendezvous in 20 Forthlin Road's tiny front room, immersing themselves in music.

Dreaming out loud they would be talking rock 'n' roll, playing guitars, listening to songs and records, embracing all things Elvis, Buddy and Little Richard. So inspired, an old Insitute exercise book was slowly filling with the words and chords to 'Lennon and McCartney originals', the rule of thumb being that if after writing a song the next day they could not recall the tune they did not return to it. Why waste time on it? If its authors could not remember, what hope their audience?

Colin was aware of most of that. Maybe not the details of their writing collaborations but the rest. He also suspected that as either a duo or a trio they were frequently getting together, even performing together at parties and weddings. He, of course, was at work and courting so did not have the opportunity to participate in most of these activities. And maybe that is how they liked it. Colin was several years older, a working man, an apprentice, had money (not a fortune but more than them) in his pocket; his social habits and friends were drawn from work, his outlook was different, he was not focused in the same way they were. Dating Joan, going out dancing or to the cinema and meeting up for a drink was the focus of his down time. In the course of a day, week or month their paths would, in normal circumstances, have been very unlikely to cross... when they did now it was infrequent, at their convenience – not Colin's – and almost exclusively to perform.

Colin believes that the major factor was Nigel's illness. During the spring of 1958 Nigel fell ill and spent time in a sanatorium, consequently his role as manager lapsed. He had been the glue keeping the group rolling along and in touch with each other, informing them of bookings he'd secured. John, Paul and George were indeed playing occasional gigs without feeling the need to include Colin although they would still do so when they felt they needed a drummer. Consequently he would play with them in larger spaces like dance halls – venues where the drums were fairly essential to pump up the volume and secure the beat.

Beatles expert Mark Lewisohn confirms this fact. In his mighty 2013 tome 'Tune In' he states that as a trio John, Paul and George were playing smaller, often private events – albeit under different names. As 1958 drew to a close they performed at a party as 'The Rainbows'. During the last week of November as Johnny and the Moondogs they played an audition at a second Carroll Levis discoveries show held in Manchester. It was at this event that John apparently acquired a guitar from a rival performer that he took home to Liverpool. Although they got through to the second round, the likelihood of their missing the last train home meant they didn't stay for the crucial grand finale.

Adopting the handle of 'The Japage 3', under which guise they would be very briefly managed by John's art college friend Derek Hodkin, on Friday 19th December they played a Harrison family wedding (although Hodkin did not actually arrange this). On this occasion, according to George, all three lads got drunk. John and Paul played at Hodkin's student party but in reality Hodkin did very little for the boys and his enthusiasm for management very quickly waned. He did however secure them an audition at La Scala Ballroom on 2nd March 1959 which in turn led to the offer of a second date for May 8th. Soon after that initial audition Hodkin was gone, tired of the whole exercise, tired of George in particular. Later that spring as Quarry Men gigs dried up George also performed with the Les Stewart Quartet.

Duff had also faded from the scene not long after playing on the record.

Colin has always felt that John had a greater loyalty to him than either Paul or George. He was an original member of the group. Paul's ability on the drums meant he could sometimes be critical, no doubt thinking he could do it better. Colin understood that if a wedding reception was held in someone's house then a drummer might well have been too noisy and so he might not have been invited/included. He's very philosophical about these apparent exclusions:

"I was known for playing loud. I played the way I did and did not like to be told how I should be playing."

Even so as 1958 trundled on Colin did play the occasional booking with the boys, still billed as The Quarry Men. Colin's modesty sometimes means he declines from mentioning he was actually asked to join another group.

"Early in December 1958 someone handed me a note in the village (Woolton) with a phone number on it and the name of a boy and girl duo (possibly brother and sister) that we'd met a number of times at different venues. They were from Speke. When I called the number I spoke to the girl, who asked if I would play drums for them at a forthcoming booking. Initially I was both flattered and nervous. Flattered that someone else would consider me as a worthwhile enough drummer but nervous that I might not be up to the job they wanted me to do. I also had loyalty to The Quarry Men. For all that had gone on with Eric and my feeling of being dispensable, I still did consider myself to be a Quarry Man and at that point I did not want to abandon them. When the girl started to talk dates and mentioned December 12 I felt a sense of relief. This was my birthday: I could use it as a way out. So I simply said I had a prior engagement and politely declined the offer."

Although he knows the precise date for some of these final shows with The Quarry Men, for others Colin's memory is not so sure. What follows are his memories of appearances beyond July 1958 and into early 1959 for which he cannot recall the exact dates.

"We played a club in Window Lane, Garston, called The Woodcutter's. We also played a 21st birthday party in Reynolds Hall at the bottom of Quarry Street in Woolton, just down from the Swimming Baths and now the site of

the Woolton Village Medical Centre. I particularly remember that booking because in those days the hall itself belonged to St. Mary's Church, which was used as an overspill for my junior school and was where I had attended class. I remember telling John, Paul, George that it had been my classroom for a year and it amused us to think that we were about to play wild rock 'n' roll music in a space where not so long ago it would have not have been allowed through the door. The father of the lad whose birthday it was kindly gave us some bottles of beer as we sat to listen to his speech, which I enjoyed. Indeed, when he finished I was one of the first to start clapping, rather vigourously. John was somewhat taken aback by my enthusiasm. I remember him looking at me somewhat askance and asking, 'Did you really enjoy that speech, Colin?' 'More than I can tell you, John' (or words to that affect) I replied. Fortunately we weren't given more than one beer and so we all stayed sober and behaved ourselves.

Another show I remember from earlier times – possibly from the spring time when Nigel was still managing us – maybe one of the last he arranged for us – was at the Pavillion Theatre, better known to the locals as 'The Pivvy', at the top of Smithdown Road on the junction with Lodge Lane. Can you believe, it was another talent contest?

It started at 2 p.m. on a Sunday afternoon. I remember that as we waited for our turn to perform there was a young eighteen/nineteen year old solo singer on stage performing a popular song of the day, the opening lines of which were spoken. It could have been 'Tom Dooley' that the Kingston Trio had had a hit with. As he tried to deliver these spoken words the compere/judge interrupted him to complain he was talking and should be singing. 'Don't talk the words: sing them!' he demanded.

I knew the song and understood what the singer was trying to do and so had sympathy for him but when he tried for a second time the compere again angrily shouted him down. It so upset the lad he fled the stage in tears. It was an unpleasant and uncomfortable scene to witness. John and I commented to each other that the compere had been unecessarily harsh. It turned us against him. However, we did not have time to reflect further for within minutes we were on stage performing. Most probably we would have played, 'That'll Be the Day', one of our favourites that we thought we did really well and was always a good choice for an audition. The compere thanked us for performing but that was it. He never spoke to us again. Once again we had failed to impress and slunk away from the Pivvy grumbling that he was a nasty piece of work whom we didn't like anyway and who wouldn't recognise talent if it bit him on the bum."

Possibly the final date The Quarry Men would play at the Wilson Hall, certainly with Colin on drums, was on Thursday 1st December 1st 1958. Colin remembers the show but says although they played a good set his main memories are of the times either side of the set rather than of being on stage itself. On arrival they set their gear up on stage, which now not only included Colin's drums but also Paul's tiny amp. John was still playing his acoustic Gallotone Champion that Julia had helped him purchase. After setting up Colin went out for a pint. This was a habit he'd slipped into at bookings, which he admits had begun to cause the other boys, John in particular, some concern.

"I remember telling John, Paul and George I was nipping next door to 'The Alexander' to meet up with Kevin and Charlie. I can still see the look of concern on John's face as I left the Green Room. He'd already told me we were due on stage at eight and as I left I reassured him I'd be back in time to play. John's fears were a bit exaggerated but not without some justification. I'm not sure exactly why he worried quite so much because I had only failed once not to return and that was way back at that wedding when John broke the washboard over Pete's head. I'd never done so since."

John Lennon was worried Colin might linger a while too long at the bar and miss the show because by this time within The Quarry Men Colin's reputation had begun to precede him. After a beer or two he could become boisterous, the life and soul of the party, less aware of more pressing commitments. So maybe John was remembering that wedding but more likely he was anxious because Colin was now in the habit of disappearing for a drink before they were due on stage and may return in a lively mood.

"On this occasion I was saved in the nick of time by one of the locals standing at the bar. Charlie, Kevin and I had downed a couple of pints and were chatting to this old chap who asked what had brought us to The Alexander. I told him I was a drummer with a group who were playing at the Wilson Hall next door. When he asked what time I was on stage and I replied 'eight' he just nodded at me, looked at his watch and told me it was ten to. Before I knew it I had downed the rest of my beer and was hurtling through the doors of the Wilson Hall. The relief on John's face when I walked into the Green Room with minutes to spare was something to see."

By now George had really begun to add an extra dimension to The Quarry Men's performances and although Colin can't remember too much about their actual performance that night at the Wilson Hall he does recall they played a good session.

"Why it stands out in my memory is that there were quite a few jivers in the club and the more we played so more of them began taking the floor to dance, which was always a sure fire sign for us that we were going down well. As we left the stage there was a palpable buzz in the hall and I remember we felt pleased with ourselves because we could sense the evening had got off to a good start for the punters. Mr. McBain would be pleased, which was always useful in ensuring we got asked back. But of course I don't know if they did because I can't remember playing with them there after that evening."

As 1958 turned into 1959, on 24th January, The Quarry Men were part of the entertainment at a late Christmas Party held at the Woolton Village Club on Allerton Road in the centre of the village, just across from what is now a sunken car park.

"A local firm, I forget whom, held a belated Christmas party for its staff because they had not been able to book a venue prior to Christmas. It was held

in the upstairs room where there was, and still is, a stage, a bar and small dance floor. I was keen to get into this club because when we first moved into Woolton my dad had joined it and was a member of the billiards team.

When he knew I was going to be playing there he'd told me that after he'd remarried and left the club he'd left his cue in the billiards room (in its special metal case with his name on). He fully expected the cue to still be there and asked me to locate it and retrieve it. Dutifully I spoke to a member of the club who took me into the billiard room but a search of the racks of cues and cases did not unearth one with John Hanton's name on it."

As for The Quarry Men's performance Colin says it was brief, unmemorable.

"I cannot say much more than it was a John, Paul, George and Colin booking. Apart from the date on which we played the only memory of the event any of us seem to have retained was mine of that missing billiard cue. It's said we played 'a ten-minute selection of skiffle numbers' but I don't think we'd all turn up there just for a ten minute slot. I can't see any one paying us to play for just ten minutes. It wouldn't have been worth our while or theirs, plus we weren't playing much, if any, skiffle by then. Paul and George were plugging in. We considered ourselves a rock 'n' roll band. I reckon we would have played our usual half-hour set."

However a key fact about this show that marks it out from all other Quarry Men bookings is its location.

"Woolton Village Club is the only booking The Quarry Men ever played in an upstairs room. This is an important detail because it has somehow found its way into Paul McCartney's memory of playing the New Clubmoor Hall, where he says, 'We played upstairs at the Conservative Club.' There was no upstairs room at the New Clubmoor Hall. The Woolton Village Club is also next to a bank, which The New Clubmoor wasn't. I think Paul simply confused the two bookings. As the years slip by I know myself just how easily that's done."

51

ALL GOOD THINGS...

"No more than a fortnight after that booking at the Woolton Village Club we played the Finch Lane Busman's Sports and Social Club, Dovecot, Huyton. I have never forgotten it because it was the very last time I ever played with The Quarry Men."

The exact date may be hazy but fortunately everything else about the evening is seared into Colin's mind

"George's dad, Harry, had organised the booking for us because he was a 'bus driver and as far as I remember he was a member of the Club's committee as well. He had certainly recommended us. Whatever his position, he was instrumental in us getting the booking. It was a prestigious venue for us, famous in its day for being where some of Liverpool's best comedians performed.

I arrived at the club with John and Paul. Pete was with us that night as well. George was already there with his mum and dad and so we went over say hello. Almost as soon as we had done so, the MC for the night joined us, introduced himself and showed us into the Green Room. It was quite luxurious, by far the nicest, plushest Green Room in which we'd ever been, especially when you consider that more often than not in the venues we frequented, a 'Green Room' was usually little more than a backstage toilet. This was definitely more than a cut above. Proudly displayed on the walls were framed photographs of local celebrities who had performed there: Ken Dodd, Ted Ray, Arthur Askey – stars past and present. Either already legends in Liverpool, or in the case of Ken Dodd fast becoming so. We were well impressed.

Next the MC took us backstage so I could take my drums and set them up. At this time the curtains were closed. A stage with curtains was also very impressive. Places like the Wilson Hall or New Clubmoor did not have curtains. As I sorted my drums John and Paul positioned the club's mic stands. Looking out to front of stage from my vantage point behind the drums, John was to my right, Paul in the middle and George (without a microphone) to my left. Paul and George were using a very small amplifier that Paul had purchased, a tiny Elpico into which both boys now plugged. John was still acoustic. The MC asked us to play five songs. He told us that he'd announce us from the front of house and that he wanted us to start singing the moment the curtains parted. When the time came for us to perform this is exactly what we did. It all felt very professional."

As John came to the end of their fifth song there was a glitch: the expected closure of the curtains did not happen.

"We all looked to the sides of the stage in expectation and anticipation but the curtains did not budge, well one of them wouldn't. It was the curtain on the right; despite the best efforts of a chap in the wings it refused to move. So instead of us standing on stage twiddling our thumbs John announced to the audience that we would do another number while the curtain was fixed. And so we did; this time as we completed our extra song, to everyone's relief the curtain moved and we disappeared from the audience's view.

As we left the stage the chap working the curtains congratulated us for covering the situation so professionally. The MC also approached and congratulated us, telling us we'd performed really well and that if we wanted to go to the bar there was a pint each waiting for us. At that very moment the evening began to unravel for The Quarry Men."

It has to be remembered these boys were very young and three of them unused to drinking. Alcohol was not as readily available as it is today and the modern drink culture simply did not exist.

One pint would have been more than enough for these boys; beyond that and they would become rapidly worse for wear. Even Colin, who was older and more used to imbibing, was still only 'a beginner'. It didn't take too much or too long for him to become obviously tipsy.

"Unfortunately we didn't stop at one pint. We had several. George Harrison recalls we were drinking 'black velvets' – a lethal mix of Guinness and cider, a challenge for any beer drinker, certainly not for the faint hearted or the novice drinker who couldn't hold their drink. We even took drinks with us back to the Green Room, where we continued to have quite a party. As far as I can recall George abstained after that first beer and remained relatively sober but in no way did he hold back from some noisy partying."

George would undoubtedly have been aware that his mum and dad were out there and he would not wish to embarrass them, especially as he was below the legal age for drinking, but there was little to stop these older boys from doing what they wanted although Paul was also below the legal age to drink. On this evening however he did not hold back.

"At one stage I remember standing on a chair in the Green Room singing away at the top of my voice. We were really into it, no holds barred. It was at this very point that the MC returned to inform us: 'Okay boys you're on again in five minutes.' The change in our behaviour since we'd come off stage must have taken him by surprise, although I don't recall him saying anything specific at that precise moment. I doubt I'd have taken any notice if he had. I was in party mode now – but what had got through to me quite clearly and was alarming me quite considerably was his statement that we were expected back on stage. It was news to me, a complete bolt from the blue. In the arrangements leading up to the night no one had told me we had been booked to play two slots instead of our usual half-hour opening session.

George was certainly aware we were expected to do so, I can't be certain

John and Paul knew, although it seems more than probable they did. Whatever any of us knew or didn't know somehow, quite drunk and not really capable of playing, we teetered and tumbled back on stage. As we did so, to me in my inebriated state only George appeared to be in command of himself. Unfortunately, my mood was darkening by the moment. From happy drunk to angry drunk. I felt annoyed with them for not telling me we were booked to perform a second set. The MC had not mentioned it when we arrived; he'd obviously assumed we all knew.

Fumbling and fooling around we managed to find our places on stage. The curtains opened and, as before, we attempted to start performing the moment they did, but we were ragged and by the end of the first song John and Paul were finding it hard to focus on performing at all. They were mostly laughing and joking together, lost in their own private world. As a group we were almost oblivious of the audience, completely focused on our in-own jokes and stupidity. George had become quiet and acutely embarrassed.

It was a complete debacle. Instead of going seamlessly from one song to another the pauses between became longer and filled with inane babble. During one very long pause I became acutely aware of the audience looking at us. I knew exactly where we were and what we were meant to be doing and so I called to John, 'John what number are we doing next?' Instead of this bringing him up sharp he collapsed further into fits of laughter and commented to Paul, 'Look even Colin doesn't know what he's meant to be doing'. which they both found hilarious. In front of an audience we had wowed with our first set we had now literally fallen apart. To prevent further embarrassment the MC ordered the curtains to be drawn."

Now entombed and alone in the curtained-off back stage area reality began to penetrate The Quarry Men's inebriated haze. Realising their evening was over, they unceremoniously slunk off stage back to the Green Room.

"This time the chap on the curtains was not so complimentary, wasting no time at all in telling us, 'You have really let yourselves down lads, that was

a disaster.' He didn't need to tell me, even with the world spinning rapidly around me and my mind truly addled I was acutely aware we had cocked up big-time."

As The Quarry Men entered the Green Room, Colin recalls John collapsed into his normal position when sat in a chair – left leg over the arm, the other stretched out in front of him. Moments later a series of visitors arrived to tell the boys they had really made a disaster of their 'opportunity'. The MC in particular laid it on the line with words to the effect, 'You really made a mess of that', but, of course, more colourfully expressed!

"As his words resounded in our ears he went back into the hall only to return a few minutes later to inform us that he'd had a word with the manager of The Pivvy, who had told him after what he'd seen he was definitely not going to be booking The Quarry Men. I remember trying to process what the MC was saying. I was totally mystified. I had no idea whatsoever what he was talking about. The Pivvy? The manager? We were definitely not going to be booked? What was going on – why was he here? I was completely in the dark as to what he meant.

Then the MC turned on his heels to leave the room and concluded his tirade with the words 'All I can do is to ask him to come and have a talk to you', which had had no effect on John and Paul, who simply continued to laugh and giggle. Those black velvets were lethal. George, embarrassed, just stood listening to all that was being said.

For me the MC's appearance in the Green Room had the effect of sobering me up sufficiently to the extent that I was aware something was happening that wasn't good: something I didn't know a thing about. Everyone seemed to understand (even if they appeared not to care a jot) what the MC was talking about, except me. Again I'd been left out of the loop. Whatever it was, either before or on the night itself, it had gone out of the other three's heads to say anything to me about the manager of The Pivvy being here. It was just so frustrating to be left out of the picture, always the last one to know."

Pete Shotton had been in the audience and witnessed The Quarry Men's spectacular fall from grace. Whereas Colin was in the dark as to the further opportunity this evening had apparently promised, Pete was fully in the know and now proceeded to inform Colin. Apparently the manager of The Pivvy had been specifically invited to hear The Quarry Men with the possibilty of offering them a series of bookings. John, Paul and George knew this and had told Pete what was at stake but had not told their drummer. Now, as Pete brought Colin up to speed, to say the least Colin was irked, and having had a drink or two was not in the mood to be mollified.

"I was angry. What was really getting to me most of all was that, even though by then he wasn't in the group, Pete knew exactly what was going on but I didn't. It really struck home that once again no-one had let me know what was happening; they did not seem to care, they just contacted me when they needed me. I felt like the dogsbody, a spare part. It had become the theme of the times.

Now Pete had filled me in. I knew what a big opportunity was on offer that night – a residency at The Pivvy. Once I did understand it just wound me up even more. The manager at The Pivvy had turned it into a bingo hall and wanted a group to play during the interval. For us it could have meant playing up to five nights a week and providing us with a steady income (especially useful for John, Paul and George, who were forever penniless) and a great opportunity to practise in front of an audience. It was the playing every night that I thought was the big thing we'd have gained – it would have tightened us up, turned us into a much better group. For me that was a big deal but I now understand maybe playing in a bingo hall was not what the others were about. In reality I can see clearly how that may not work for students and schoolboys hellbent on a career playing music, but in a drunken haze, as I was then, I wasn't seeing things that logically or clearly."

As he'd promised or threatened – depending on your point of view – the MC returned a third time to confront the inebriated Quarry Men, this time accompanied by the manager of The Pivvy.

The group, who had been on such a high during the interval, were now coming down fast. Especially Colin, but sobriety was not making him any calmer. Spirits were sinking low; the atmosphere in the room was turning sour, if not mean.

"The chap from the Pivvy began addressing us by congratulating us on the our first half performance. I can hear his words as clearly as if he was standing in front of me now, he said, 'You were bloody good.' Back in 1959 that was a pretty strong statement for a man of his experience to make; to me it was an independent adult appraisal. He was in the business, so it meant something, it wasn't just a friend saying it. His words were direct, to the point and left me in no doubt as to how impressed he'd been. However, he then moved to critique our second performance. Again he did not mince his words. 'It was the worst performance I've ever seen. Had I only arrived for the second half and not seen your first performance I would have wondered why I had been invited down here tonight to see you in the first place.'"

From then on it only got worse as the manager of The Pivvy began to lecture The Quarry Men telling them what they already knew – that they had to have more respect for their audiences, that they were a shambles and so on and so on. He didn't let them off the hook. Heads should have hung and maybe in Colin and George's case they did, but not in John and Paul's. They didn't stop laughing and joking, not paying attention, making silly, sly comments about the manager himself.

"The problem was the man from The Pivvy had clearly come straight from his bingo hall where he had been on stage MC-ing. Consequently he was dressed in his stage attire, a smart dark suit and his face still caked in stage make-up. He had oversized bright red lips, big red rosy cheeks. On stage, under spotlights they may have looked okay; unfortunately close up under the electric lights of the Green Room as he stood lecturing a bunch of half-cut teenagers he looked absurd, like a clown. And, unfortunately this was not lost on John Lennon. Of all the people he could be standing in front of, trying to appear

serious and strict but wearing heavy stage make-up, John Lennon was not the one to choose. I doubt John heard a word he said. As his lecture ramped up so did John's ridicule. John's focus was not on the advice being imparted but on the absolute comicality of the chap's appearance. Even sober it would have been hard for any of us to ignore, John especially. It was a major distraction that John could not resist."

John's running commentary on the manager's absurd appearance had not been lost on the poor chap, who was fully aware and increasingly irritated by John's sarcasm but had valiantly tried to ignore him. The final straw came when, Colin says, John bluntly described him as, *'Looking like a fairy'*.

"John's words were the final straw; he gave up his attempt to put us right, ceased his diatribe and accompanied by his fellow MC bowed out gracefully while also managing to wish us well in the future. At the time I thought this was very gracious of him. Despite John and Paul's buffoonery and ridicule he'd kept his dignity, which we hadn't."

Left alone together Colin says the four Quarry Men and Pete didn't exactly fall silent. John and Paul were still merry and noisy; George however had gone quiet, maybe contemplating what words might be said by his dad when he got home.

"From his dad's perspective we had let him down badly. Harry had trusted us to do our best. He had been instrumental in getting us this booking and the club itself had gone out of their way to ask the chap from The Pivvy to come and hear us. They'd set up an audition that they had no need to. They were being helpful. George's dad was being helpful. It was also something to which John, Paul and George had apparently agreed. And the man from The Pivvy had clearly been very busy, jumping into a taxi to ensure he got to see us in time he'd left his club still wearing his stage make-up. People we didn't know had gone out of their way and been very generous. I felt we'd thrown it back in their faces."

Once the dust had settled and they'd sobered up, no doubt all of them would feel the same way too. At the time, however, it was an increasingly sober Colin who felt the most obvious remorse.

"I know it's easy with hindsight to say but I think I was right. It was a big opportunity missed. Someone had done us a favour and we were being impolite. Who knows what might have happened, what further regular bookings it may have led to? Folk like these MCs all knew each other; they recommended acts to each other. On the other hand it may have not been right for us. Five nights a week may have been too much of a commitment for any of us especially as John, Paul and George were students of one kind or another. But in my mind it would have been better to have found out by giving it a try, of being offered it and having the opportunity to turn it down.

Ultimately I suppose it wasn't a dance hall or a dance hall audience we would have been entertaining and maybe that's why John and Paul may not have considered it important but it was an opportunity to be paid to rehearse and hone our stage presentation. Maybe it was too early in their career for those boys and most probably not right for me (in the evenings I liked seeing Joan or my friends for a drink. I loved the cinema and true romance was blossoming). But on that night, standing in the Green Room looking at those other lads who lived so much for their music, it seemed to me like a big deal. It felt like we had blown a big opportunity. Significantly for me it underlined how they were now so into doing their own thing and that I was on the outer edge of all that. I think that was what the whole debacle brought into absolute focus for me and was winding me up so much.

The age difference was beginning to tell. They had developed a bond that excluded me. It was just the way it was. Our worlds had drifted apart. I truly believe there was no plan or conspiracy to leave me out, it was just circumstance. With Nigel gone the glue that held us together, kept us in communication with one another was no longer there. Our shenaningans that night became the focus for my growing resentment with the way I perceived they were dealing with me."

Tiring of the whole shebang, Colin and the others just wanted to get out of the club and go back home.

"Pete and I went backstage to pack my drums away and our thoughts turned to the 'bus ride home. By now I was feeling very glum, little was said, I'd slipped into one of my well-known sulks."

Drums in hand, Colin and Pete returned to the Green Room to collect John and Paul. George had decided to accompany them rather than face his parents. George knew he was in trouble.

> **George***: "By the time we had to go on again, we were totally out of it. We embarrassed ourselves and everybody else, and my father was very pissed off: 'You've made a show of me… and all that."*
>
> *(The Beatles Anthology, p.31.)*

No wonder. Likewise, Colin was pissed off with everyone, including himself.

"With me hungover and John and Paul still inebriated and joking between themselves we said a few hang-dog goodbyes to whoever was around and skulked off to catch the 'bus on Prescott Road (on the corner with Finch Lane). Our plan was to all go into town from where John, Pete and I would catch the number 4 back to Woolton, while George and Paul would have caught the number 86 to Allerton and Speke."

As the boys wandered towards the 'bus stop, an uneasy silence descended and the mood among them darkened.

"I wasn't finding the continued half-drunken banter between John and Paul funny anymore. It had become irritating and I was less and less inclined to ignore it. The straw that broke this particular camel's back was when

Paul began to speak in a ridiculous voice that he and John clearly found very humorous, very Goon-ish.

To me the voice he adopted sounded similar to the way a couple of my friends at work spoke who were deaf. I knew Paul didn't know them and I also knew very well he wasn't poking fun at them or deaf people in general but for some reason I allowed it to really wind me up. I wasn't amused and I wasn't in the mood to indulge him. It became the focus for my resentment, call it what you will. Standing there in the dark I was able to bottle my growing irritation with him and just stay silent; inside however my fuse – which everyone knew could, on occasion, be short – was beginning to burn low."

The arrival of the 'bus did nothing to bring Colin out of the black hole into which he'd descended. If anything it just intensified the situation. John and Paul had not noticed that Colin had barely said a word to them now for nearly an hour. They were reaching the point when fatigue was kicking in and only they could appreciate their lame jokes.

"Once we settled into our seats on the top deck of the 'bus unfortunately Paul continued speaking in that silly voice and I continued to let it bother me. By now I was feeling outright anger about the way the evening had panned out and Paul's voice had become the focus for my bad temper. If I had a critic in the group it was Paul and so, subconsciously, I was probably feeling some anger towards him even before the evening had started. Everything that was irritating me and upsetting me about being in the Quarry Men was now buzzing around inside my head. That whole evening summed up how frustrated I'd become. I wasn't enjoying it any more. The drink I'd consumed only contributed to my dark mood. I did my best to stay cool but the more I suppressed it the worse I felt. In the end my temper just broke."

From past experience The Quarry Men knew that when roused Colin was not someone to be trifled with. At this precise moment he'd become well and truly trifled.

"I snapped. My temper blew and Paul was the unfortunate target of the full fury of my anger. I remember screaming at him, 'Shut up speaking in that stupid bloody voice!' Such was the fury in my voice I frightened myself, so goodness knows how he must have felt. But from that moment I had his full attention. Shock and horror registered on his face, the voice silenced. John and George both looked absolutely startled. I'd stopped them in their tracks too."

The three future Beatles had seen the dark side of Colin Hanton and did not like it one bit. A stunned silence settled over the boys.

As ever it was Pete Shotton who was the first to react. Sensing danger, possibly violence, he jumped up out of his seat and shouted to the irate drummer, *"Col, quick, this is our stop!"*

Colin reacted immediately and without bothering to look exactly where they were he joined Pete in dashing down the stairs, grabbing his drums and exiting the 'bus. Before he knew it Pete, who'd grabbed his bass drum, and he were standing on the kerb while the 'bus carrying John, Paul and George disappeared into the night. It was a metaphor for the future.

"As the 'bus drew away with John, Paul and George still on board, it dawned on me as I looked around that Pete and I were nowhere near town or our intended stop. We were on Queens Drive. This meant I could grab the 81 to my home but as it wasn't where we had intended to change 'buses to allow Pete, John and I to travel home together to Woolton, Pete would now have a bit of a hike home once the 81 dropped us both in Woolton village."

Pete had acted quickly to diffuse a very volatile situation and Colin now began to regain his composure. He'd shocked himself.

"Pete was always good at reacting positively to tricky situations and taking the sting out of any trouble he could see brewing (or, as in this case, which had literally erupted in their faces). I'll never know what I'd have done or said next on that 'bus as I sat facing Paul. I was gripped by fury. Everything that had

been building up inside me simply exploded out of me in that single cry of rage. Thanks to Pete's quick thinking, trouble had been nipped in the bud."

As Pete and Colin travelled home together they analysed the evening. On the surface it had been a case of too much drink and boys too young to hold it. More significantly, underlying all that was Colin's growing disenchantment within the group.

"I remember complaining to Pete that the root of the problem was that neither before or even on the night when I arrived for the booking had anyone informed me what was afoot. No one had told me the booking was also an audition for another club or even that we were expected to play a second set. That's how it had been ever since the incident of the cowboy shirts. I must have made it extrememly clear to him how pissed off I was and that this sort of stuff had happened once too often. Pete said very little. He just listened, let me unload. He agreed that the first half had been great and after that it had been all downhill but mostly he just listened, took it all on board as I sounded off."

Stepping off the 'bus in Woolton village the two boys said their good-nights. Colin thanking Pete for helping him out. All that needed to be said had been said. No doubt Pete would let the others know how he felt.

"As I watched him disappear into the night I felt grateful for his intervention, he'd stopped things becoming really unpleasant. Even so as I picked up my suitcase and bass drum to walk home, inside I was still raw. Everything that had happened over the past few months was still going round inside my head. This was unusual for me. There had been other incidents and other things said that had bothered me but which I'd rationalised and let go. Or maybe not. Clearly I hadn't, instead I'd just been bottling everything up. This time it had been different. My outburst wasn't just a reaction to the missed opportunity at The Pivvy; it was about much more than that. It had been brewing in my subconscious for quite a while. It was about me being made to feel unimportant, left out, used, ignored.

I enjoyed being a Quarry Man. I liked being on stage, playing and entertaining folk. It gave me a buzz, especially if the audience got up and jived. I enjoyed the cameraderie of the group. But it wasn't my life. It was theirs.

This time, this evening, during this performance something had broken and I knew I couldn't fix it. More to the point I didn't want to fix it. It all felt inevitable. I'd been left out one time too many times.

I never heard directly from John, Paul or George again and I never attempted to contact them. My pride was such that I thought the ball was in their court and deep down inside I knew that I'd had enough. I wasn't going to go chasing them. More to the point I didn't expect them to come chasing after me. My days as a Quarry Man were over.

I went home still smarting and placed my drums on top of my wardrobe, where they would remain for the next thirty-eight years."

52

WHO'S THAT SITTING ON THE BACK SEAT?

"As the weeks passed I began to think less and less about the group. I accepted that the night at the Busman's Sports and Social Club had been the end. In all honesty I can't say I missed it. For over a year I'd not taken my cut of whatever fee we earned; I'd left that in the pot for the others to share. As 1958 had played out I had felt more and more marginalised. I had come to realise John and Paul in particular were growing extremely close and that George was already far closer to them than me. I didn't feature in their plans. Intuitively I knew my time was up.

I liked them all individually. I felt John was protective of me; if I was coming in for criticism he'd always defend me, tell the others to back off. He was sharp and funny but we all were. All of the Quarry Men, whatever the line-up, there was a Scouse cameraderie that being in a group sparked between us. Paul's ability as a singer and guitarist really impressed me. Looking back, obviously with the benefit of hindsight, it was clear even then they had something special. The music meant more to John and Paul than anyone else I've ever known. They were on track almost from the moment they met. George was still very young when I knew him but he had that same passion and obsession. We all were very young, but George was just younger than the rest. Five years younger than me. He was quite small and physically still looked more like a boy than a young adult. That matters when you are in your teens. I never really got to know him. From the moment he joined he always seemed integral but it was John and Paul's show; they told him what to do. What sticks in my mind is how good he was on the guitar and I know that is what John and Paul recognised and did not want to lose. He also did seem like a good person. I certainly feel extremely proud to have played in the same band as those three amazing musicians.

Words fail me to explain how special it is to look back and know it was me who was there on the day John met Paul, that it was me who drummed behind John, Paul and George when they cut their very first record and played The Cavern together for the very first time. That I was present when John and Paul played to us, as a group, some of the very first songs they ever wrote. That's some story. They enriched my life. I feel very proud and very happy to have shared those days with them. For the most part it was great fun."

Some weeks later, at 4 p.m. on a Friday afternoon, Colin walked out of work ready to begin the serious business of the weekend. He was with an older workmate, Joe Fagan, who coincidentally had attended The Quarry Men show at the Locarno in 1957 when the group had played as a trio because Eric Griffiths had been ill.

"Together Joe and I hopped on the 81 to Woolton, already deep in conversation as we went up the stairs to the top deck. As we did so a familiar voice piped up, 'Here's Col!' It was George. I looked around to see him and Paul sitting on the back seat with John on the seat immediately in front of them. No more was said. As I was still talking to Joe I just waved to acknowledge I'd seen them. A few seats further up I sat down and Joe and I continued our conversation. Two or three stops further on there was a lull in what we were saying so I took the opportunity to excuse myself and go back to talk to the boys. But as I turned to walk back down the aisle I saw immediately that their seats were empty; they had gone.

Where they had got off would have been nearer to Hunts Cross, which was nowhere near any of their homes nor Woolton village. I had not been aware of them leaving, I heard nothing so I can only assume they had taken the first opportunity to disembark as quietly as they could to avoid me noticing. They didn't want to talk to me. If I hadn't already realised it, I knew it then – our times together were definitely over. I never saw them as a threesome to speak to again.

53

CROSSING PATHS

He might never spend time with the three boys together again but with both John and Colin living in Woolton it was inevitable that they would occasionally bump into each other, if not in the village itself but on the 'buses in and out of town. And they did, on at least three memorable occasions.

One evening, sometime between Monday 20th July and Friday 28th August 1959, Colin encountered a weary John Lennon sitting on the top deck of a 'bus homeward bound for Woolton. The two had always got on well and between them there was no lingering resentment from the incident at the Busmen's Social Club. Quickly they settled into catching up.

"I was taken aback to hear John's news that he had a summer job working on a building site. For me this was almost like hearing that he'd joined the army rather than pursue his musical ambitions.

I could barely conceal my surprise. I was gobsmacked, especially when he told me it was in the wilds of Lancashire, somewhere in the countryside near Southport."

Colin's surprise was justified. John was renowned for being almost allergic to hard physical work and early mornings. Just to get to work on time John would have to have left Woolton sometime around 5 a.m. For a night owl like Lennon that really was dedication to a cause.

"John was at pains to tell me it was only temporary and that he hated every minute he was there. He told me it was hard physical work and he had to use a pick and shovel. He also said he had undertaken the job during the college summer vacation purely in order to earn enough money to buy an electric guitar. Just imagining John Lennon wielding a pick axe strained my imagination to the absolute limit."

John's comment about an electric guitar indicated that he was still at college and still pursuing his music. The Quarry Men were never mentioned but clearly John was still playing.

"John also said in part he was doing it to show Mimi he was serious about performing and wanting an electric guitar. He told me that if he came into Liverpool for the evening direct from the building site to play with his group or do any socialising he'd bring a change of clothes with him and get changed in the toilet cubicle on the train back into the city. Mostly though he complained of being 'knackered' all the time."

Thanks once more to amazing Beatles sleuth Mark Lewisohn, (see 'Tune In', p. 220–1, 222–3). we know John did indeed work on a building site in Scarisbrick, Lancashire, between the dates mentioned. He acquired the job through his Art School friend Tony Carricker, whose dad was the general foreman. During the long college summer vacation the two students had signed up as general labourers on the site of a new waterworks.

John stuck it for just over a month. He was dismissed for being 'unsuitable' and on the very day he got the push he left no time to make good on the point of his physical exertions. He and his Aunt Mimi journeyed to Hessy's where a deposit of £17 was paid for John's first ever electric guitar, a Hofner Club 40. Was this deposit John's hard-earned money or Mimi's equally hard earned cash?

A day later, on Saturday evening 29th August 1959 The Quarry Men performed at the opening night of The Casbah Coffee Club in West Derby. This time out the group comprised John, Paul, George and Ken Brown. Ken was a fellow-survivor of the ill-fated Les Stewart Quartet in which George had been playing until it imploded a week before the opening night at The Casbah at which they'd agreed to play. To help Mrs. Mona Best, the Casbah's owner, out of a tight spot, George recruited his redundant Quarry Men pals to fill the gap. Unfortunately, minus Colin. This was one of many nights when, for John, Paul and George, the rhythm was most definitely 'in the guitars'.

Not long after that meeting with John from the vantage point of the top deck of another Woolton-bound 'bus Colin caught sight of John standing at a 'bus stop kissing a girl he later learned was Cynthia, John's girlfriend at Art College.

The third time Colin recalls bumping into John was yet another 'bus ride home.

"John came and sat next to me and on our journey home we talked about his new band he'd called 'The Beatles'. During our chat he told me they had just got a new drummer called Pete. John sounded very excited about how things were going with his new group, although he pointed out the only thing 'new' about them was really their name and their drummer. Amazingly he never mentioned that within days they'd be leaving to go and play in Hamburg."

One way or another Liverpool City Transport had kept Colin in touch with the progress and fortunes of his old group. His final close encounter with the boys came on the afternoon of Friday 10th July 1964. A momentous date in Liverpool's history. It was one Colin shared not only with The Beatles but with almost the city's entire teenage population.

This time there was no meeting on the 'bus: John's days of using public transport were over and Colin was driving his own car. John, Paul and George were with Ringo in a sleek black chauffeur-driven limousine travelling from Speke through Allerton towards the city centre. They all proceeded down Mather Avenue past Forthlin Road where Paul, Mike and their father, Jim, had still been living until just a few months earlier. While Liverpool prepared to honour its boys, Colin was on his way to the dentist's on Smithdown Road.

"Momentarily as I drove along I was so focused on my impending ordeal at the dentist (in those days it could be akin to visiting the local torture chamber) I forgot just who was coming to town that day but from the moment I started driving down Mather I was resoundingly brought back to reality. All along the road there were crowds of people gathering, young people in particular, many of them holding banners with 'The Beatles' written on them, or placards with the individual names of the boys in the group. The Beatles were flying in to Liverpool for a civic reception in their honour at the Town Hall and later they were going to the Odeon for the northern premiere of 'A Hard Day's Night'. From the noise I could hear as I drove down Mather Avenue I could tell their entourage must not be too far behind.

In fact I was only some five or ten minutes ahead of The Beatles and their entourage. Anticipating the group would not be far behind me everyone on the side of the road was getting very excited and started to wave at myself and other folk driving along. I waved back. Everyone was waving at each other. It was a good-natured crowd and, being Liverpool, everyone was joining in. It was party time. Just the day to arrange a visit to the dentist!"

As he drove along, the irony of the occasion was not lost on Colin. For a short while it even felt like he was leading the procession, his old friends somewhere behind bringing up the rear. It reminded him of that Saturday some seven years earlier, 6th July 1957, when he and John Lennon sat next to each other on the back of a lorry during a procession around Woolton village immediately prior to the St. Peter's Church Garden Fete. Crowds had lined the streets of Woolton that day to wave at a band passing by.

There, at the start of their fabulous journey, Colin was here at the moment of their greatest home-town triumph, inadvertently escorting them home as heroes.

"As I pulled off the road to park up for my appointment, sure enough a few minutes later the boys drove by. Despite all the people in front of me on the pavement I still managed to catch a glimpse of John and Paul in their suits but not George or Ringo.

I stood and looked towards Liverpool, reflecting on what was happening to them, thinking how exciting it must be to be them. I didn't feel jealous or upset; I felt proud. Proud of The Beatles and all that they had achieved and were still achieving. For themselves, for music, for Liverpool. I also felt proud of myself.

I may not have become a wealthy rock star but I was very happy. I'd married Joan, whom I loved. We had a good home and I was doing well at work. I could walk the streets of Liverpool unrecognised and unbothered, without an escort, but if ever I was asked to tell my story I could raise an audience for there were few other folk who have a story quite like mine.

Ringo was not there the day John met Paul or when John, Paul and George played together for the very first time at The Cavern or stepped into a studio to cut a record. Those were my memories that I shared not just with the three Beatles but with Rod, Eric, Len, Pete, Nigel and Duff, special memories. To this day they still stop people in their tracks – me included."

COLIN HANTON: A CHRONOLOGY

12 December 1938 Colin Hanton born in Liverpool.

December 1953 Leaves school.

Jan. 1954 Starts work at Guy Rodgers.

Autumn? 1956 Buys a drum kit from Hessy's in Liverpool.

'Late' 1956 Joins John Lennon's Quarry Men skiffle group.

12 December 1956 Colin's 18th. birthday. At his party his new pals in The Quarry Men, including John, help him celebrate.

'Early' 1957 Plays Lea Park Golf Club, Childwall Valley Road, Gateacre, now regarded by The Quarry Men as their first 'public engagement'.

6 July 1957 With The Quarry Men plays the St. Peter's Annual Church Fete in Woolton. Encounters Paul McCartney for the first time.

December 1957 Is introduced to George Harrison at what what will become known as 'The Morgue Skiffle Club' in Oakhill Park, Liverpool.

24 January 1958 George Harrison makes his Quarry Men debut at The Cavern alongside John and Paul on guitars and Colin on drums.

12 July 1958 Records two songs with The Quarry Men in Percy Phillips studio in Kensington, Liverpool. The Quarry Men personnel on that occasion were Colin, John Lennon, Paul McCartney, George Harrison and John Duff Lowe.

January/February 1959 Plays his last ever gig with John, Paul and George at the Finch Lane Busman's Sports and Social Club.

12 December 1959 Colin, looking very cool, gets the keys to the door!

6 March 1965 Marries Joan.

17 April 1968 Allison, Colin and Joan's first daughter, is born.

27 August 1969 Christine, Colin and Joan's second daughter, is born.

January 1987 Colin's dad, John, dies.

1990 Family reunion for the Hanton siblings.

July 1997 The Quarry Men regrouped with original members Pete Shotton, Eric Griffiths, Rod Davis, Len Garry and Colin.

6 September 2001 Emily, daughter of Christine and Craig Watt, Colin and Joan's granddaughter, is born.

May 2017 Family reunion.

6 July 2017 Quarry Men Rod, Colin, Len and Duff along with former manager Nigel Walley (on washboard) celebrated the 60th anniversary of the day John met Paul by sitting on the back of the lorry as it paraded around Woolton to and from the church field (now a school field). The original driver from 6th July 1957, Doug Chadwick, was at the wheel.

They were joined on the lorry by Chas Newby, who, in December 1960, very briefly but very signicantly played bass in The Beatles alongside John, Paul, George and Pete Best when they returned from Hamburg without Stuart Sutcliffe. Chas memorably was in the band when they played their legendary gig at Litherland Town Hall on 27th December 1960. Chas now regularly performs with The Quarry Men.

In the afternoon there was a garden fete followed by a grand dance in the Church Hall. The Quarry Men (plus Nige and Chas) performed at both events. Among the many guests were John Lennon's sisters Julia and Jacqueline, John's cousin David, Beatles Fan Club Secretary Freda Kelly, Tony Bramwell, close friend of The Beatles – from childhood – and folk who attended the fete of 1957. A splendid time was had by all.

Colin at his 21st birthday party.

Colin and Joan cut their wedding cake

John and Peggy, 1973

John D, Colin, Lynn, Brian

'Reformed' Quarry Men: Rod, Eric, Pete, Colin and Len, Chicago

Emily playing Granddad's drums in St. Peter's Church Hall, Woolton, Liverpool

Family reunion, Penny Lane: Colin, Craig, Joan, Gary,
Emily, Christine and Allison, 2017

The Quarry Men post 2005:
Rod, John Duff Lowe, Colin and Len

Outtakes #1

BEING A SHORT DISCOURSE ON THE ORIGINS OF SCOUSE AND SCOUSER

The word 'Scouse' is a marker of Liverpool's history as an international, cosmopolitan port, its origins as colourful and open to interpretation as the people themselves.

The first known use of the term – according to Webster's dictionary – is dated in 1706. As it developed as a port after 1700 so Liverpool became a centre for international trade and industry, a veritable melting pot of migrants, languages and dialects as traders and sailors from parts of Northern Europe, Ireland and elsewhere in Britain settled in the area. The word 'Scouse' itself 'almost certainly' comes from 'lobscouse', which is Baltic and derives from the Latvian words 'labs kauss' and/or the Lithuanian phrase 'labas kausas', both of which mean 'good ladleful'. Lobscouse is a meal of 'stewed or baked meat with vegetables and hardtack (a simple type of cracker or biscuit)' commonly eaten by sailors throughout Northern Europe that also became popular in seaports like Liverpool.

However, long before the 1700s Britain and Liverpool had become home for visitors from abroad, especially from Scandinavia. During the 9th and 10th centuries Liverpool, Lancashire and the Wirral were all settled by the Vikings. West Derby ('Wild Deer Park') was to become their biggest settlement. Some researchers suggest 'Scouse' comes from Norway, where 'lapskaus' is a traditional dish and therefore the name is as old as the Vikings. Hence it is hugely likely 'lapskaus' or lobscouse may have been eaten in and around Merseyside long before the city's development as an international port.

No-one knows for certain but these ideas and origins sound as compelling as any on offer. One way or another it seems that the Liverpudlian predilection for a good, easy-to-make, nutritious, filling and cheap meal resulted in them becoming so closely associated with the dish it became their nickname. (For fans of Paul and Linda there is a veggie alternative known as 'blind scouse'.)

Nowadays 'Scouse', the accent, reaches out as far as Runcorn (Cheshire), Skelmersdale (Lancashire) and even as far as Flintshire in north Wales and is very distinct from the accents of Lancashire and Cheshire. Originally largely confined to the city itself it spread further afield during the Fifties as the city rebuilt itself after the destruction wrought on its people and their homes during the Second World War. Post-war many of its citizens 'migrated' into new and pre- and post-war developments in the area officially known since 1974 as 'Merseyside' and, of course, took their accent with them.

(**Sources**: Wikipedia, the free encyclopedia; www.meriam-webster.com/dictionary.)

Outtakes #2

THE BATTLE OF THE BOYNE 1690

Marches are held annually to celebrate the Battle of the Boyne, fought in 1690 when Protestant King Billy (William III of England, II of Scotland) defeated the Catholic King James II who had been King of England until he was overthrown in 1688 by Dutch Prince William of Orange and his wife Mary, who then became co-regents of England. William was dubbed 'King Billy' by his Protestant followers. The defeat of James was the death knell of James's attempt to regain the British crown. This was bad news for Irish Catholics. A hundred years later it led to the establishment of the Orange Order in County Armagh, members of which were sworn to maintain 'Protestant ascendancy' in Ireland. Even today it celebrates the battle by holding yearly marches on or around 12th July. As can only be expected these do little to heal wounds and bring people together.

Outtakes #3

GOING BACK TO THE FUTURE – THE FIFTIES

In writing Colin's memoirs I often found myself following leads that were fascinating but ultimately much of the information I gathered along the way has not made their way into the finished text. Here are some notes I thought readers may find interesting. Nothing comes from nowhere and I always like to know from where things originate and so these jottings sort of fit into that basket.

Some Background Notes

Colin Hanton's story, the story of The Quarry Men, took place in the 1950s. In so many, many ways the world was not as it is now. It was a time of momentous change. To fully appreciate the phenomenal impact The Beatles had on the world, not just Britain, some insight into the Fifties is required. I know the Sixties is the decade everyone hails as the decade when the doors came off their hinges but the Fifties was, in its own truly revolutionary way, the time when the roots of 'youth culture' took hold. For Britain in particular the iron grip of Victorian morals and class barriers was fractured and challenged never to be the same. Below are some notes on factors that formed the background to Colin's story and consequently the stories of John, Pete, Eric, Rod, Ivan, Nigel, Len, Paul, Duff and George.

Place and Time

Suddenly, after the end of the Second World War, moving into the 1950s to the nation's teenagers it seemed that just being young was all that mattered. As the world settled back on its axis youth was the adrenalin fix on which considerable social change fed. Teens were the future. A line had been crossed, a fresh start made, a new world had begun. It was almost as if no-one else had ever been teenagers before. And in a sense they hadn't. The raising of the school leaving age in Britain activated by the Education Act of 1944 gave young people a period of 'extended adolescence' unknown to previous generations and by doing so helped create the phenomenon of the 'teenager'. Pass or fail that bloody Eleven Plus everyone got an extra year at school during which to kick their heels and test the waters.

Colin Hanton was in every sense of the words 'an ordinary young man'. There was nothing in his first seventeen years to suggest he was destined to become an integral participant in one of the 20th Century's most enduring stories. It was his good fortune to be a 'teenager' at the very moment this word was being coined. And like all upon whom fate smiles Colin happened to be in the right place at the right time doing something for which he had a passion: drumming.

The place was Liverpool and the time was the Fifties.

First: the Place

Liverpool was healing after the devastation of war. A city in ruins, two thirds of its houses destroyed or left uninhabitable by 'the Blitz'. Bombsites proliferated, vast swathes of the city had been reduced to rubble. Prefabricated houses were erected, those so-called 'temporary' homes thousands who had lost their homes during the bombing raids as Hitler tried to pulverise the city into oblivion. Liverpool was rebuilding itself physically, socially, economically and emotionally its people, their sense of humour well in tact, bravely stepping into a new world in which nothing could ever be quite the same.

Next: the Time

War had ended but it remained the ever-present threat. The Cold War had begun. East versus West, communism versus democracy. Life was lived with awareness of the proliferation of mutually destructive nuclear weapons. Everyone knew that from now on the world could be destroyed in an instant. Subliminally it was the gun to the head that could be fired at any time. Potentially it didn't get much hotter than that.

The Birth of the 'Teenager'

As the Fifties dawned the British hovered between a new beginning, which produced a state of anticipation, and potential sudden extinction, which tapped into the still raw memories of the war.

The physical scars were all around them in bombed-out buildings and broken places. None more so than London and Liverpool. The terrible personal losses inflicted on families the length and breadth of the land by both World Wars remained open wounds, the healing barely begun. The shocking and unbelievable cruelty of the Holocaust and the nightmarish hell of imminent nuclear devastation were realities impossible to fully comprehend.

Balanced against this was the promise of a better life engendered by the establishment of the welfare state, which included the creation of the NHS in 1948 and prior to this the provision of free schooling for all pupils and the raising of the school leaving age for all pupils to fifteen courtesy of the Education Act of 1944. Also known as the 'Butler Act', it made it a duty for local education authorities to provide school meals and milk and also introduced the dreaded Eleven Plus examination.

Despite the promise of better things to come, reality for most was still a mundane job, the daily grind on low pay looking to make ends meet, a council house and marriage by age twenty-one. Men remained better paid than women, who were still viewed as 'housewives' first and foremost. If you were extra lucky/bordering on middle class then life offered more because you'd live in a semi-detached house with a mortgage and a car thrown in. Life was better, but by no means was everyone living on easy street.

However, compared to their parents' generation, in many ways Colin Hanton's and succeeding generations would be deemed lucky: very lucky indeed. For a start they weren't going off to war. Over time they would have more of everything than their pre-war parents ever did, especially time: time to be young and to think about what being young meant and what life actually held in store.

For a start, by making them spend longer at school the Butler Education Act gave post-war generations more time to avoid having to get a job. Success in the Eleven Plus provided the chance of receiving that golden ticket of opportunity previously denied to most 'ordinary' working folk, i.e. access to a grammar school education, which in turn could lead to the possibility of attending university and entry into professional careers of which their parents could only have dreamt. For the generation who fought the war, 'education' was perceived as the way out of poverty and onto the gravy train, a reward for their sacrifices in the name of king and country. A better future beckoned.

The Butler Education Act introduced a tripartite system of secondary education. In theory it promised all children a brighter future. For most, however, it translated into spending more time at school with more time on their hands and little prospect of social or economic advancement. Unfortunately, not everyone was going to pass that Eleven Plus exam and go to grammar school (depending where you lived it could be just 9% who did); the vast majority were destined to fail, indeed failure was built into the new system. Thus the exam was immediately divisive. Those who secured a grammar school place were perceived as 'brainy' (the elite) while the vast majority who failed were thought of as average – or below – intelligence ('thick' in everyday parlance), potential 'factory fodder' (as opposed to 'cannon fodder' before the war). They would attend either a 'technical' or 'secondary modern'. No wonder middle-class parents in particular put so much emphasis on their children passing the Eleven Plus. Children who had been friends at Primary school would often shun each other after the exam because those who'd passed had 'crossed the line' and were no longer 'one of them'.

In other respects as the Fifties began everything remained in place as it had done since Victorian times to maintain a class-driven status quo designed to persuade people not to step out of line or challenge the system but to 'know your place'. But something had broken. Both wars had made the ordinary working man and woman examine the concept of 'equality', the social order, old values would begin to be questioned and to crumble: cracks had appeared in the wall.

The war *had* changed how the sexes perceived their lot in life. It had been a leveller. Women had realised they could do 'men's work' – and were actually good at it. For that is exactly what they had been doing when the men were away fighting the enemy: they were working in the factories and farming the land. Two World Wars and the sacrifices that had been made had brought about the belief that class should not be a barrier to progress. There should be a level playing field with greater opportunities for those not born into privilege.

More powerfully than ever before, ordinary folk began to demand a different future, one that didn't rely on privilege or exam success but on opportunity, personal ability, personal skills and hard work. The established order could – and should! – be challenged.

Thus the Butler Education Act was welcomed as an agent of change, one that would give the nation's young people greater opportunities in life. In theory it opened the doors of educational opportunity for all. Before the war the majority of young people left school without qualifications to go immediately into employment. For most there would be no place at college or university, no welfare system, only the urgent need to earn money to pay your way and help support your family. Literally at age fourteen school could end on a Friday and work begin the following Monday. The school uniform would be discarded and overnight youngsters became junior versions of their parents, dressing like them, doing similar jobs, sharing their responsibilities as earners, contributing to the family income.

By extending the time young people spent at school the Butler Education Act initiated what Bruce Springsteen calls that 'extended period of adolescence'. 'Teenagers' had been created.

Going to the 'Flicks'

Television in the UK was in its infancy. Very few people owned a TV set at the start of the Fifties. Watching 'the telly' was not a national pastime; it was a rarity. Beyond reading literature, reading the newspaper, playing cards, knitting and doing jigsaw puzzles were popular pastimes at home. The main source of home entertainment however was listening to the radio. Every home had at least one radio, many operated by batteries that could be taken to a shop to be recharged. Everyone loved the radio. Whole families would gather round to listen to the news and their favourite shows. The music that was played was mainly 'live', very middle of the road and adult-orientated. (Uncle Mac's Favourites was a Saturday morning radio show dedicated entirely to a young audience.) Records got very few spins because of 'needle time' restrictions. 'rock 'n' roll did not exist, swing and jazz were popular, dance bands proliferated. For most Brits radio provided their window into the world.

Outside of the home the cinema and variety theatre remained the predominant and hugely popular means of entertainment. An estimated ten million Brits visited the cinema at least once a week. Individual cinemas would have up to three changes of programme per week. The importance of cinema in the UK and its influence on its vast audience cannot be underestimated. Many people would go twice or even more times a week. A ticket to the cinema was relatively cheap and you got a lot for your money: advertisements, trailers for forthcoming attractions, a Pathe news bulletin, usually a low-budget B-film and, of course, the main feature. You could also buy yourself some sweets, a soft drink (usually Kia Ora Orange Squash) or an ice cream. Consequently going to the cinema (or the 'flicks' as it was often called) was a hugely popular, much-favoured form of escape from dull reality.

Many cinemas were very luxurious; stepping inside, you entered a different and glamorous world that made you feel privileged, hence they got the name 'picture palaces'. Lots of deep-pile carpet, velvet and ornate decorations, paintings and portraits of famous stars adorned the wall. Those cinemas that had seen better days however were often quite seedy, smoke-filled and referred to as 'flea pits'.

For a couple of hours in the smoke-filled darkness of those packed picture palaces and flea pits people could feast on sweets and fire their imaginations. And for the denizens of the back row – who more often than not were courting couples, if the stars were aligned, which they very rarely were, it was a dark, public but almost private place in which to enjoy a moment of passion where more than the film might reach a climax.

The Influence of American Culture

The majority of feature films screened in the UK came out of Hollywood, California, USA, and told stories of the pleasures and pitfalls of the American way of life. (Significantly, when TV did start to take off in the UK many of its most popular programmes/series also came from the USA.) Consequently the British public and those new-fangled teenagers were exposed to a lot of 'Americana' and 'The American Dream'.

The British view of what America was like, what Americans were like as people and how life was lived over there, was arrived at by frequent visits to the pictures and later through a glass screen at home. This celluloid larger-than-life vision of the USA was particularly persuasive in changing attitudes towards the way the Brits lived their own lives. The USA seemed so much more modern and advanced. Americans were better off, their homes brighter, bigger and filled with all sorts of amazing gadgets. The adage was that what Americans have today, the British would get in ten years time. Teenagers were particularly impressed.

What they saw was, of course, not real life but it was very persuasive. They believed it to be true. Consequently most British teenagers could be forgiven for believing most Americans lived in fast-paced, vast cities dominated by skyscrapers, light and noise which were populated by gangs, gangsters and cops who all chewed gum and drove fast noisy cars. And if they didn't live in New York, Los Angeles or Chicago it appeared Americans lived near to the beach in pleasant detached sunlit homes surrounded by neat gardens and white picket fences. They all had money in their pockets as well as guns; they drove big flash cars, smoked better cigarettes, drank Coca-Cola and dated pretty girls/cool-looking men, they surfed all day and partied all night. In the not-so-distant past they rode horses, were handsome and handy with a six-gun, killed Indians, outlaws and punched cattle. Heroes wore white stetson hats and the villains black. Oh, and yes – it was always sunny and warm, not cold and grey like the UK; apparently the 'Wild West' or California lifestyle was reality for all Americans – or so we thought.

No doubt about it, America was where it was at. It's to where British teens looked for something different and exciting. It was a vision of the future, a better life. Britain, by comparison, was war-torn, grey, smoggy and cold, down at heel and parochial. It was Victorian, boring, hogtied by tradition, firmly stuck in the past.

Significant Teen Movies

Somewhere over the rainbow in the USA the lot of the emergent teenage generation which began with Marlon Brando in 1953's 'The Wild One' was further personified in the films of James Dean – especially 'Rebel Without a Cause' (1955) – and, most significantly for British teens, 'Blackboard Jungle' (1955) featuring Sidney Poitier, closely followed by the first rock 'n' roll exploitation movie, 'Rock Around the Clock' (1956). It was clear from these movies 'teenagers' had become a force to be reckoned with. Why else would they be making films about them?

A significant and dark British contribution to this US-led genre of films depicting teenage deliquency was the 1958 Basil Dearden-directed 'Violent Playground'. It starred Stanley Baker, Anne Heywood, Peter Cushing and David McCallum. Significantly it was set in Liverpool, where the city's inner-city estates are depicted as breeding grounds for juvenile crime/delinquency. McCallum's character, Johnnie Murphy, the leader of a teenage street gang, owed a lot to the roles played by Brando in 'The Wild One', Dean in 'Rebel Without a Cause' and Vic Morrow in 'Blackboard Jungle'. The film portrays rock 'n' roll as a negative influence on teenagers. In one scene the music drives them into a trance during which they become scarily violent. (N.B. Freddie Starr, aka Fred Fowell, appears in the film as Tommy, a member of Murphy's gang.)

For the future Beatles, seeing 'The Girl Can't Help It' in the summer of 1957 would prove seminal. Not only does the moment when Jayne Mansfield sashays onto the screen make every young boy sit bolt upright in his seat (in more ways than one), it is the moment British teens see their American rock idols in 'glorious' Technicolor for the very first time. In Liverpool alone, at least a thousand dreams of becoming a music star will be launched. When Eddie Cochran performs 'Twenty Flight Rock' he will not only impress sixteen-year-old John Lennon but also fifteen-year-old Paul McCartney. Paul will learn and later perform the song for John and The Quarry Men when he is first introduced to them in July of that year. Lennon was impressed enough by Paul's rendition to invite him to join his group. Paul recalls, *"Knowing all the words to 'Twenty Flight Rock' was part of the currency that got me into The Quarry Men."*

Marlon Brando's 'The Wild One' (1953) was very influential in the USA but had much less of an impact in Britain, where it was described as 'a spectacle of unbridled hooliganism' and considered so threatening to society's well-being it was denied a cinema rating. This effectively meant it was banned. Only a few local authorities permitted some limited screenings. Ten or so years later in 1964 the British Board of Film Censors cited that year's riots by Mods and Rockers as further evidence why the film should continue to be denied a certificate and so the ban remained in place until 1967, by which time its moment had really gone.

However, in the Beatles' Anthology series George Harrison suggests it as a source for the band's name because the motorcycle gang in the film is called 'The Beetles'. He says the idea came from John Lennon's Art College friend, Stuart Sutcliffe. Even if Liverpool had been one of those authorities which had allowed some screenings it's highly unlikely that any of the Beatles saw it at a mainstream cinema when it was first released. Harrison would have been only ten in 1953, Lennon and Sutcliffe thirteen and McCartney eleven: too young to be admitted to any respectable cinema on their own. By the time he was at Art College with John, Stuart had become a massive fan of Brando's and attended college screenings of his films and, according to Neil Aspinall, knew the scripts off by heart, including 'The Wild One'. As a result it could have been the source of the name. Stu's suggestion then, but, significantly, with his fascination for words that carried more than one meaning, John would tweak the double 'e' to 'ea' to place The Beatles in the same ballpark as The Crickets, Buddy Holly's band. Holly was John's hero. For British fans 'cricket' could be either a chirruping insect or one of our national sports. The 'Beatles' sounds like an insect but its spelling suggests something to do with rhythm. (John of course had his own say on the matter and claimed the name came to him 'on a flaming pie'.)

Despite its limited release in the UK, 'The Wild One' did have a significant impact on rock 'n' roll chic when its adherents locked into its sense of style. Brando's character, Johnny Strabler, is swathed in a black leather motor cycle jacket, making such a garment ever after a *de rigueur* item of any self-respecting rock star's/teenage rebel's wardrobe. Elvis would use Strabler as a model for his role in 'Jailhouse Rock' and both he and James Dean grew sideburns in homage to Brando's character.

On visits to local picture palaces British teens would watch open-mouthed as Dean's colourful and romantic but troubled character in 'Rebel Without a Cause' kicked over the traces and came into conflict with his parents. The rowdy and violent high school kids in 'Blackboard Jungle' also struck a chord. When first shown in Britain 'Rock Around the Clock' was banned in some UK towns because a teenage audience in London went nuts during a screening and the film had to be stopped until they ceased dancing in the aisles.

Whatever the gripe such celluloid teenagers had against the world, the agents of oppression seemed always to be parents, teachers, politicians and unscrupulous businessmen, i.e. adults in general. (Just one listen to Eddie Cochran's 'Summertime Blues' and you'll get the picture). And although Brits may have been the poor cousins languishing in the fog and gloom on the other side of 'the pond', intuitively British teenagers sensed that they had much in common with the lot of their American cousins. The simmering restlessness and suppression felt by many British teens was given a telling outlet when 'Blackboard Jungle' was released in the UK. It was a rich mix of inter-racial, inner-city teenage tensions, anti-social behaviour, violence and a flick knife which significantly featured rock 'n' roll in its soundtrack: 'Rock Around the Clock' by Bill Haley and his Comets. It remains a potent – and for its time – realistic movie.

When first shown in London in 1956 its teenage, predominantly Teddy Boy/hooligans audience began to riot. Seats were torn up and they danced in the aisles. Thereafter wherever it was shown riots were likely to break out. Juvenile delinquency had arrived big time in the UK.

But not everywhere. For some the film was not the cathartic experience they were expecting. John Lennon went to see it full of expectation: *"I was very surprised. Nobody was screaming and nobody was dancing in the aisles like I'd read. I was all set to tear up the seats too but nobody joined in."*

Such films and their vision of a different way 'to be' worked away at the teenage psyche. Teenagers began to express themselves as a different/'new' generation in the way they dressed, spoke, behaved, the music they liked… and played. Importantly these films suggested that for all their extra cash and material wealth many American teenagers shared a similar angst to their British counterparts. They also were restless and dissatisfied with their lot; they too were oppressed by the stultifying power of adults who just didn't 'get it', who didn't understand them. Adults were all about keeping the kids tied down, keeping things the same; they were boring and wanted to make their children boring too. What a typical teenage boy or girl wanted was for their parents to stop bugging them, to cut them some slack and give them their freedom.

Hence a bond was created. Teenagers were in this together. Here or in the USA, it was them against the adult world.

No wonder J.D. Salinger's novel 'The Catcher In The Rye' struck such an immediate chord with young people. Written for adults and published in 1951, its themes of teenage angst and alienation were perfectly in tune with the zeitgeist of its time. The novel's anti-hero, Holden Caulfield, who had serious issues with 'phoney' adults and the adult world, could well have grown up to be troubled teenager Jim Stark as played by James Dean in 'Rebel Without a Cause' (1955).

The big question was, how could British teens break out? A strict Victorian moral code prevailed to keep British society buttoned up and nailed down. Sex and swearing didn't happen. Well, of course they did, but folk just did not swear as openly or as frequently as they do today and family planning was down to accepting the barber's offer of "something for the weekend, sir?" For most teenage boys on the verge of puberty such an offer was one they were usually all-too self-conscious and embarrassed to accept, especially when sitting in a barber's chair with their backs to a room full of older men whom they could see facing them in the mirror (and who most probably all knew their dad).

Consequently, with sex off limits (or a very risky business to say the very least) and the death penalty keeping everyone further under control, the promise of this new extended adolescence people were calling 'teenagehood' seemed destined to prove a damp squib here in the buttoned-down, strait-laced, know-your-place Great Britain.

Also it rained a lot in the UK. It got icy, smoggy and foggy too. Summer lasted about as long as a weekend. Few adults, never mind teenagers, could afford cars. This impacted on how the British lived their lives.

Rock 'n' Roll

And that's where music, the sounds of rock 'n' roll records, came in. They filled a void in that extended adolescence. If films told the bigger picture, records articulated the everyday concerns of being young. Not everyone could be a film star but they could make music or maybe be in a band. You didn't have to visit a cinema to enjoy rock music. Teens lucky enough to have access to a record player could listen to it at home on their own or with friends, fellow teenagers. It was an exclusive teen experience they could share and appreciate. They owned it; their parents simply did not 'get it'. Records rang out like aural postcards from the USA to speak of the new reality, a world utterly focused on teenage concerns. These discs were the call to arms that British teens had been waiting for, the sound that would give them their voice and eventually separate their generation from their parents' generation in a way that generations had never been separated before.

Not only was this new music blatantly about sex and style but it created a brand new exclusively teenage world of 'cool'. The songs encouraged rebellion – and narcissism. They spoke of new pre-occupations in which only teens could indulge in and/or get hung up about: girls, boys, broken hearts and broken promises, cars, motorbikes, garish clothes, shoes, crazy hairstyles, gangs, fights, coffee bars and jukeboxes, record players, records and record charts. It was a pre-occupation that focused on being 'cool', of being 'hip', looking sharp – and a way of talking that was all their own 'daddy-o'! Records helped establish and cement a teenage identity.

At best for parents the advent of the teenager was threatening, at worst alienating. It was the gathering domestic storm of the Fifties. Fifties parents, the generation that fought the war, hadn't had any of this stuff to deal with when they were growing up. No wonder they struggled to comprehend it when it sat itself down next to them at the kitchen table or on the living room sofa.

As former young men and women when they were in their teens they'd had to suppress any thoughts of rebellion. They simply hadn't got the time or the money. What had pre-occupied pre-war young people was finding a job, contributing towards their keep and on top of all this they were the generation who took on the Nazis and saved the world. Their youth had been spent doing something of real gravity and importance. They had been raised in a society in which Victorian morals and social regimens prevailed. Sex was a dirty word or a duty ('lie down and think of England') to further procreation, not enjoyment for enjoyment's sake: an act performed in the dark and only after marriage. They respected their parents and adhered to the dictum 'children should be seen and not heard'. No wonder that to them their children's pre-occupations with themselves, each other, sex, pop idols, clothes and this outrageous music appeared frivolous, self-indulgent, hugely annoying and, ultimately, an utter waste of time.

If this wasn't enough along with all this baggage their children were becoming increasingly moody, remote and ungrateful. As the Fifties wore on and parents attempted to communicate with their children, to put their foot down, to suggest that it was time 'to grow up' and – most inflammatory of all – remind their children that they had 'fought the war for you!' such interventions could induce meltdown. 'You don't understand!'

Almost at a stroke parents became the enemy – interfering, out of touch. Spoilers intent on spoiling the fun. They didn't understand and it was a waste of time trying to explain. Times were tough, the generation gap had burst wide open. This was true social revolution. It was the emergence of 'youth culture'.

On 20th July 1957 Prime Minister Harold Macmillan proclaimed that we Brits had 'never had it so good'. While some members of society might not agree with him, in a sense 'teenagers' certainly hadn't. Angst and nuisance parents aside, never before had being young promised more. They were beginning to feel important and have fun in a way preceding generations never had. If the Russians or Americans could destroy the entire planet with just one of those atom bombs then all the more reason for them to cast off the shackles of convention and tradition and live for today.

Conscription

Even so, for all the good times teenage boys were experiencing throughout the Fifties a metaphorical noose hung above their heads. They knew that their newfound freedoms were destined to be snatched away from them for up around the bend awaiting on them all was 'conscription'.

A hang-over from the war, conscription came courtesy of the National Service Act 1948, which set the exact date on which teenage kicks would end. As from 1 January 1949 that date would be between ages seventeen and twenty-one (provided they were healthy). On that date young men could be called-up to dedicate eighteen months of their life in the service of king/queen and country. In 1950 in response to the British involvement in the Korean War the length of conscription was increased to two years. 'Call-up' day was the day you got a haircut, ditched the fancy clothes (especially those fluorescent socks!), cut the crap, donned a uniform and toed the line. It was the time 'to grow up': you were in the army now.

While there is no doubt that for some young men conscription offered a way out of grinding poverty, an opportunity for adventure, a chance to see the world and learn a trade that could set them up for a better life, for many more it was dreaded. The killjoy of all killjoys.

Luckily for John, Paul, George and Ringo, they avoided 'the call-up' when the British government decided in April 1957 that conscription would end with the '1939 Class'. In other words, those born on or after 1 October 1939 would not be called up. Paul would later acknowledge the ending of conscription as a key factor in ensuring The Beatles ever happened.

Bill, Elvis and Lonnie

Rock 'n' roll erupted big-time in Britain in 1956 courtesy of Bill Haley and his Comets and their massive hit record 'Rock Around The Clock'.

While Haley certainly opened the door he and his music could not hold a candle to the exotic and sexual splendour of the genre's most sensational singing star, an unbelievably handsome boy from Tupelo, Mississippi, called Elvis.

Elvis's first hit record in the UK was 'Heartbreak Hotel', which became a top five hit in June 1956.

Even before Elvis sang a note, with just a curl of his lips, a glance from those dark, half closed bedroom eyes, a shy but knowing smile and the provocative sexual motion of his hips, teenage audiences became uncontrollable. The sheer blatant sexuality, addictive loudness and fierce outrageousness of it all fired up the kids (especially the girls) to fever pitch.

Elvis Presley and rock 'n' roll came from the USA. The music spoke of sex, style, having a good time and reckless abandon. Its inherent promise: to deliver the kids from the days of old. The rocking beat seemed to cause teenagers to lose control and in extreme cases could apparently induce delinquency. Like the characters portrayed by Brando in 'The Wild One', Dean in 'Rebel Without a Cause', Sidney Poitier in 'Blackboard Jungle' and Elvis himself in 'Jailhouse Rock', rock 'n' roll was perceived by adults to be volatile and dangerous. In Britain, gangs of outrageously attired youths called Teddy Boys armed with chains, flick knives and a penchant for rock 'n' roll music became the scourge of decent society. Rock 'n' roll and all that it stood for threatened to overturn the very conventions that tied our parents to the yoke. It raged against the foundations of decent society. The rule book was being ripped up. Or so we thought.

The problem was that, while American kids usually had cash

in their pockets, most British kids didn't. For Brits, economic reality was ever on hand to stall dreams. No two ways about it, British teens were perpetually strapped for cash.

Desperate though they were to plug in and rock, British teens simply couldn't. Those new-fangled beautiful, shiny electric guitars; the essential, defining instrument necessary to play rock 'n' roll, crucially were not manufactured in the UK. (Well, alright, the British-made Grimshaw S.S. Deluxe debuted in 1957 and a certain Tony Sheridan would play one, but in general terms they were as rare as hen's teeth.) Like skyscrapers, Cadillacs and blue jeans, electric guitars – especially the Fender Stratocaster (Buddy Holly's signature instrument) came from the USA and not a single shop here stocked them and, much more to the point, they were prohibitively expensive to import. They were a vision of a seemingly distant future way beyond the means of British youth. Electric guitars were being made in Germany but in 1956 we weren't speaking to them. And so, while a ticket to the flicks and records were just about affordable (although those early shellac 78s were a risky investment because they broke oh-so-easily), actually plugging in and playing that rock 'n' roll music remained the stuff of dreams.

Thank goodness then for a young (twenty-four years old in January 1956), Glasgow-born guitarist and singer with the Chris Barber Jazz Band called Lonnie Donegan. His recording of 'Rock Island Line' played in a style called 'skiffle' would reach number eight in the UK charts in January 1956. Lonnie preceded Elvis. What is crucial about Lonnie is how his records and 'skiffle' music opened the door for British kids to make a noise all of their own. Lonnie's music could be played on acoustic and home-made instruments. Home made. No cost involved. For cash-strapped British youth here is the key element that allows them in, enables anyone to form or be in a band at no expense and with no musical training. And skiffle had a nifty rhythm, fast-flowing lyrics (American words and place names) and you could move to it. Thousands of skiffle groups would be formed in the wake of Lonnie's success and popularity. He really was the man.

British teenagers had discovered a way to make themselves heard. And, as Colin's story tells us most clearly – they certainly did – and how!

Outtakes #4

NOTES TOWARDS A TALE OF TWO RECORDS: 'RAUNCHY' & 'GUITAR BOOGIE'

The electric guitar galvanised a generation in the Fifties in the UK. Teenage boys in particular were irresistibly drawn to it. As 'the' instrument of rock 'n' roll it became the instrument to die for. Beautiful to look at and incredibly exciting to play, it was almost sexual in its appeal. For budding teenage British rock 'n' rollers like John Lennon, George Harrison and Paul McCartney the electric guitar became an obsession. The Fender Stratocaster was the subject of many a youngster's dreams. George was typical of teenage boys up and down the land for whom learning to play the hits of the day note-perfect came between him and his sleep.

Many hit records of the early rock era were instrumentals featuring the irresistible twang of an electric guitar. Of these, Bill Justis's 'Raunchy' has the distinction of being the first. Along with 'Guitar Boogie', which was not strictly rock 'n' roll it, would play a prominent part in the story of The Quarry Men.

Even in 1957 'Guitar Boogie' had been around a while in several different versions by several different artists. It was not a current release and its original style was not rock 'n' roll. During Paul's attempt to perform it on stage on his Zenith acoustic guitar to secure his place as The Quarry Men's lead guitarist he fluffed the moment. However, he was savvy enough to know that, regardless of this, the group needed a lead guitarist if they were to move beyond 'skiffle' into rock 'n' roll, the music to which he and John were in thrall. Paul knew such a transition required a dedicated lead guitarist who could play solos at the drop of a hat. And so his thoughts turned to his school friend, George Harrison. Barely out of short trousers, George was an aficionado who lived for his guitar. When introduced to the boys, as an audition piece George did not reel off 'Guitar Boogie' or an already over-familiar rock 'n' roll riff from a song such as 'Be Bop a Lula' but instead he weighed straight in with an absolutely brand new (in the UK) only-just-released-not-even-in-the-charts instrumental featuring a very catchy repeated electric guitar hook. This was mightily impressive for John Lennon.

'Raunchy' was not yet in the UK charts but since its release in November 1957 had been getting more and more air time and was steadily climbing the charts. It would sneak in at number twenty-five between 10th and 16th January 1958, climb one place to number twenty-four the following week, disappear the next week to re-enter at number twenty-three on 31st January, peaking at number eleven a month later. John and Paul knew of it, could play bits of it but that George could already play all of it 'note perfect' revealed his dedication to the cause. While most young guitarists were struggling to master the riff, there, in front of them, George Harrison was playing it like he'd been doing so all his life. Maybe he didn't yet need to shave but he could surely play his guitar like he was ringing a bell.

'Raunchy' was not going to be a tune George forgot in a hurry. He would also stay tuned to Justis's other releases on the Phillips International label.

Single label of 'Raunchy', Bill Justis

The singular adventures of 'Raunchy'

USA Release: 23 September 1957
UK Release: November 1957
A-Side: 'Raunchy'
Performed by Bill Justis and his Orchestra.
Written by Bill Justis and Sid Manker
Produced by Sam Phillips
Time: 2.20 minutes
B-Side: 'The Midnight Man'
Written by Bill Justis
Record Label. USA: Phillips International
UK: London Records HL S8517

Chart Placings:

USA: 'Raunchy' reached number two and sold over one million copies and earned Justis a Gold Disc. In the same year it was also a hit in the USA for Ernie Freeman (Imperial) and Billy Vaughn (Dot).

UK: It climbed to number eleven in the Singles Chart (21–27/ February '58). Justis's version spent approximately two and a half months on the UK chart. It would most probably have climbed higher had it not been for UK artist Ken Mackintosh and his orchestra, who cut a version of the tune for the HMV label (POP 426) which reached number nineteen on 7th February.

Bill Justis was a trumpet and alto saxophone player and while his saxophone features strongly on the record, what actually blew everyone away, especially lads like George, was the distinctive guitar riff played over and over by co-composer Sid Manker. Duane Eddy would hear Manker's deep, bass string, echo-laden guitar sound and build his early career around it.

But 'Raunchy' holds the distinction of being the first, ground breaking, big rock instrumental hit and with it the sound that became known as the 'twang' had arrived.

Bill Justis, a brief biography

Born on 14th October 1926, in Birmingham, Alabama, Justis grew up in Memphis, Tennessee. He attended Tulane University in New Orleans where he performed with local jazz and dance bands on trumpet and saxophone.

On return to Memphis in 1951 he worked for Sam Phillips at Sun Records. At Sun he'd record his own tunes and arrange music for Phillips' artists such as Roy Orbison, Jerry Lee Lewis, Johnny Cash and Charlie Rich (whom he apparently 'discovered').

'Raunchy' was released in the USA among the first batch of singles on the Phillips International label on 23rd September 1957. Justis and Manker based their tune on the melody of an old Southern tune called 'Backwoods'.

Significantly, based on the success of 'Raunchy', Sam Phillips released an album by Justis entitled 'Cloud 9', the first to be issued on his Phillips International label (LP 1950). Credited to the Bill Justis Orchestra on the cover, the music inside was described as 'Far Out Tunes' with 'that Raunchy Sound'. Clearly George Harrison was aware of this record; his album by the same name was released on his own Dark Horse label on 2nd November 1987. It was the last studio album George released during his lifetime.

Although Justis was the chief instrumental man at Sun, his relationship with Phillips did not endure. In the spring of 1959 he and Jack Clement were fired for 'insubordination'. Just what they had done to upset Sam was never made clear.

As a solo artist, 'Raunchy' was Bill's biggest hit. The closest he came to chart action again in the States was with 'College Man', which climbed to number forty-two in the singles charts in March

Album cover for 'Cloud 9'

1958. However, in 1963 he scored a number one in Australia with 'Tamoure'.

He went on to play sax on the soundtrack to Elvis's 1964 movie *Kissin' Cousins* and produced successful instrumental albums for the Smash label. According to Ray Stevens it was Justis who gave him the word 'gitarzan', from which Stevens fashioned a million-selling hit. Justis also wrote several film scores, most notably *Smokey And The Bandit* (1977), *Hooper* (1978) and *The Villain* (1979).

Aged just fifty-five he died from cancer in Nashville in 1982.

Guitar Boogie

Arthur Smith was a textile mill worker born in Clinton, South Carolina, in 1921. He became a celebrated Country music instrumentalist and composer who played guitar, fiddle and banjo. In 1945 he wrote the instrumental tune 'Guitar Boogie', which he played in the style known as 'guitar hillbilly boogie'. This was a massive hit for Smith, selling in excess of three million copies. It gave him the name of Arthur "Guitar Boogie" Smith and earned him a gold record. Smith also wrote the tune 'Feudin' Banjos' in 1955, which later became famous as 'Dueling Banjos' for the 1972 movie *Deliverance.*

Although sometimes cited as one, if not the first, rock 'n' roll record, Smith's 'Gutar Boogie' is not rock 'n' roll. It is played in an 'uptempo twelve-bar boogie' style. Smith was a fan of Tommy Dorsey and picked up his boogie-woogie style from listening to him and his big band.

A regional hit in North Carolina, when Smith first released it on the Super Disc Records Label as by 'The Rambler Trio featuring Arthur Smith' it was re-released in 1948 by MGM Records (who had bought Super Disc and Smith's contract). This time it went out under the name of 'Arthur (Guitar Boogie) Smith and His Cracker-Jacks'. By 1949 it was all over the American Country and

Single label for 'Guitar Boogie' / Arthur Smith

Pop Charts – this is when it sold the vast majority of those three million records mentioned earlier.

Wikipedia describes it as 'an early popular example of hillbilly boogie… a link between 1940s Western swing and honky-tonk and 1950s rockabilly'.

In 1953 two rock and roll versions of the tune entitled 'Guitar Boogie' or 'Guitar Boogie Shuffle' were released in the USA but neither became a major American rock 'n' roll hit. That did not happen until it was renamed 'Guitar Boogie Shuffle' and was recorded by Philadelphia band Frank Virtue and the Virtues in 1958. It was their version that became a number five hit in the Billboard Hot 100 pop chart in 1959.

As it was in the autumn of 1957 when Paul played 'Guitar Boogie' on stage at the New Clubmoor, Virtue's version could not possibly have been the version he had heard/learned. More likely it was either Arthur Smith's original version or there's an outside chance it was one of those two earlier 1953 'rock 'n' roll' versions: the Super-Sonics' 'Guitar Boogie Shuffle' (Rainbow Records R-4097) or the Esquire Boys with Danny Cedrone on guitar's 'Guitar Boogie' (Nickleodeon 102-A).

Odds are it was Arthur Smith's classic version and that it was a disc the McCartneys already possibly had at home. Jim McCartney would bring home records from the market and so maybe, just maybe, one time snuck amongst these was a copy of Smith's original version with his Cracker-Jacks for it had received a UK release in 1950 on the MGM label.

Colin Hall

October 2016

THANK YOU VERY MUCH

'Pre:Fab!' has been very much a two-hander. Colin and Colin ('Colin here' and 'Colin there') have spent much longer on this project than we first envisaged when it was first mooted back in 2015. We've had much fun along the way and by taking our time Colin Hanton has been able to explore and reflect upon his memories in much greater detail than he has previously ever done. This time out he's not had to share the platform with someone else or several others. This time he's gone beyond answering just the 'usual' questions and so some stories and insights have not been shared before.

No man is an island and so as our journey progressed we were joined along the way with fellow travellers whose kind interventions, support, encouragement, advice, knowledge, memories, insights, memorabilia and photographs have ensured we reached our final destination. So may we take a moment to thank those good souls without whom this book would not have been possible.

Colin Hanton in particular wishes to thank: Joan for her love and support down all the years. Colin and Sylvia Hall for all their efforts and support. Nigel Walley and Charlie Roberts for their memories, support and photographs. Geoff Rhind for his permission to use his iconic photographic of The Quarry Men that he took at the Woolton Church Fete on Saturday 6th July 1957. Unsung hero Jean Catharall for her support, friendship and bright idea of bringing the Quarry Men back together in

1997 to help save the Church Hall from demolition! Cousin Roger Meadowcroft, friends Peter Phillips, Colin Robinson and Christine Westcott for their support and photographs. Relda Griffiths for friendship and memories of Eric. Dave Ravenscroft for his help, insight and enthusiasm. Julie Gornell at the Penny Lane Development Trust for her support and encouragement. Jo Piggott (also at the PLDT) for her patience in compiling all Colin's photographs. Tom McConnell for his artistic input.

And of course Colin says a mighty thank you to his fellow Quarry Men, Rod Davis, Len Garry and John Duff Lowe for their support not only on this project but down all the years together. Also Eric and Pete, much missed.

But most of all Colin Hanton wishes to thank John Lennon, Paul McCartney and George Harrison, without whom this book would not have been written.

Colin Hall says big thanks also to all of the above (especially Sylvia – my rock, my love and my inspiration).

Colin Hall also wishes mighty thanks to: Bob and Trudie Harris for their unwavering faith, friendship, inspiration and support. Mark Lewisohn and Spencer Leigh for their professional generosity, encylopaedic knowledge, wisdom and friendship. Freida Kelly for her kindness and friendship. Jan Vaughan for her generosity and support. Gary Watson, whose enthusiasm for guitars and rock music has inspired me ever since we were teenagers back in the early 1960s. Good guys and great friends, Bob Owen, Chris Chadwick and Chris Stanley for constantly diverting my attention away from my studies in the late sixties to check out who was on at the Mountford Hall and O'Connors. Danny Scott for inviting me to write music reviews for 'What's On in London'. Sean McGhee, R2's amazing editor. Sam Genders and Liam Bailey for their sublime music and the opportunity to manage their early careers. Dave Upton for the friendship and Ritz crackers. And last but not least: Colin Hanton for asking me to write his story. It's been a privilege, an honour and great fun. Thanks, Colin.

Colin Hanton and Colin Hall

Photo Credits: *Every effort has been made to trace/acknowledge the copyright holders of the photographs used in this book. In order for any errors or omissions to be corrected in future editions, please contact The Book Guild Publishing.*

BIBLIOGRAPHY

Scouse – Wikipedia, the free encyclopaedia

Wikipedia, the free encyclopaedia, Scouse (food)

www.merriam-webster.com./ dictionary

Teddy Boys, Teddy Girls – Wikipedia, the free encyclopedia

A Trip Through Liverpool's Rich Irish History, Declan McSweeney, Liverpool, The Northerner, The Guardian, 15 October, 2012 www.theguardian.com

History & Policy, What Does It Mean to Be British? Belfast and Liverpool's Experiences of Adaptation and Reaction, 1880 – 1921, Gareth Jenkins, 4th March, 2011, www.historyandpolicy.org

Never Had It So Good: A History of Britain from Suez to the Beatles, Dominic Sandbrook (Abacus, 2006)

Lonnie Donegan and the Birth of British Rock & Roll, Patrick Humphries (The Robson Press, 2012)

Title deeds for 'Vega', Vale Road, Liverpool, courtesy of Dave Upton

The Complete Beatles Chronicle, Mark Lewisohn (Chancellor Press, 1996)

The Cavern: The Most Famous Club in the World, Spencer Leigh (SAF Publishing, 2008)

The Beatles In Liverpool, Spencer Leigh (Omnibus Press, 2012)

All These Years Volume 1: Tune In, Extended Special Edition, Mark Lewisohn (Little, Brown, 2013)

John, Paul & Me Before The Beatles: The True Story of the Very Early Days, Len Garry (Fast Print Publishing, 2014)

John Lennon: The Boy Who Became a Legend, Michael Hill (Penin Inc Publishing, 2013)

John Lennon In My Life, Pete Shotton and Nicholas Schaffner (Stein And Day, 1983)

The Making of the World's Rarest Record, John Duff Lowe, Limited edition audio CD.

Paul McCartney Many Years From Now, Barry Miles (Vintage, 1998)

The Paul McCartney Encyclopedia, Bill Harry (Virgin Books, 2002)

The Perfect Storm (The anotated diaries of Johnny 'Guitar' Byrne), Spencer Leigh, Features section of his website www.spencerleigh.co.uk

The Quarrymen, Hunter Davies (Omnibus Press, 2001)

The Beatles: The Authorised Biography, Hunter Davies (Heineman, 1968)

Beatles Gear, Andy Babiuk (Backbeat Books, 2001)

The McCartneys: In the Town where They Born, Kevin Roach (Trinity Mirror, 2014)

The Beatles Anthology by The Beatles, (Cassell & Co, 2000)

Thank U Very Much Mike McCartney's Family Album, Mike McCartney, (Panther, 1982)

Beatles In Their Own Words, Barry Miles (Omnibus Press, 1978)

John Lennon In His Own Words, Miles (Omnibus Press, 1980)

John Lennon The Life, Philip Norman (Harper Collins 2008)

The Fab One Hundred And Four, David Bedford (Dalton Watson Fine Books Ltd., 2013)

Lennon: The Man, the Myth, the Music – The Definitive Life, Tim Riley (Virgin Books, 2011)

John Lennon, Ray Coleman (Futurama, 1985)

The Guinnness Book Of British Hit Singles, 1952-1977, Jo & Tim Rice with Paul Gambaccini & Mike Read (Guinness Superlatives Ltd., 1977)

20 Years Of British Record Charts 1955–75 with commentary by Peter Jones & Tony Casper (Queen Anne Press Limited, 1975)

Beatles Beginnings CD Series – Nick Duckett's anotated booklets from these: Quarrymen One: Skiffle – Country – Western; Quarrymen Two: Rock 'n' Roll; Volume 8: The Quarrymen Repertoire (Rhythm and Blues Records)

Roots, Radicals And Rockers, Billy Bragg (Faber & Faber, 2017)

DISCOGRAPHY (SELECTIVE)

All records are UK 'singles' (45s & 78s) releases unless otherwise stated. The highlighted songs either feature in the narrative of PRE:FAB! or were tunes performed by The Quarry Men.

The details of each record are listed as follows: Date disc entered the UK chart (or released if it did not chart), A-side, B-side, artist, Record label and catalogue number, highest chart position. Chart positions are as stated in 'The Guinness Book of British Hit Singles' (various editions) unless otherwise stated.

September 1939 *USA release*: **In The Mood**/I Want To Be Happy, **Glenn Miller and his Orchestra** (Bluebird Records B – 10416 – A). This song became extremely popular in the USA in 1940 just before Billboard began publishing its weekly 'National List Of Best Selling Retail Records' on 27th July. In that first chart Miller had three songs in the top ten but not the number one, which was occupied by 'I'll Never Smile Again' By Tommy Dorsey and his Orchestra with Frank Sinatra and the Pied Pipers. Many years later a snatch of 'In the Mood' is played by the orchestra at the end of The Beatles' 1967 anthemic summer number one, 'All You Need Is Love'.

1949 *USA release*: Chicken Shack Shuffle/**Skiffle Blues, Dan Burley & his Skiffle Boys** (Exclusive – 77x). Did not chart.

November 1950: **Guitar Boogie**/Be Bop Rag, **Arthur (Guitar Boogie) Smith and his Cracker-Jacks** (M-G-M 48-S-39) This was the UK release for Smith's well travelled hit.

1954: **Back to the Delta LP** (Decca – LF 1196), Ken Colyer's Jazzmen/**Ken Colyer's Skiffle Group.** Did not chart (side one featured Ken's Jazzmen, side two his skiffle group), track one, side two was **Midnight Special.** (See below, February 1956 Backstairs Session EP by Lonnie Donegan.)

19 July 1954 USA release only: **That's All Right**/Blue Moon of Kentucky, **Elvis Presley** (Sun 209). Did not chart nationally in the USA but reached #4 on the Memphis chart.

7 January 1955: **Rock Around the Clock**/Thirteen Women (And Only One Man In Town), **Bill Haley and his Comets**, (Brunswick 05317). #17 (Charts for just two weeks before re-entering the UK chart on 14 October 1955, when it climbs to #1 in November and stays on the charts for seventeen weeks. It will re-enter the chart again on 21st September 1956, climb to #5 and remain on the chart for another eleven weeks. It will keep on returning – again on 14th December 1956, 4th January 1957, 25th January 1957 accumulating a further six weeks on the chart. It hits the UK top twenty twice more in 1968 and 1974, reaching #20 and #12 respectively, and remain on the charts for eleven and twelve weeks respectively.

6 January 1956: **Rock Island Line**/John Henry, **The Lonnie Donegan Skiffle Group** (Released in November 1955 as a 78rpm on Decca Jazz F 10647), #8 (Charts for thirteen weeks, re-enters the chart at #16 on 13 April 1956 for three weeks.)

February 1956: **Backstairs Session EP**, **Lonnie Donegan's Skiffle Group** (Pye Nixa – NJE 1014), (No chart position, four tracks: **Midnight Special**, New Burying Ground, **It Takes a Worried Man (To Sing a Worried Song) aka Worried Man Blues**, When The Sun Goes Down.)

27 April 1956: **Lost John**/Stewball, **The Lonnie Donegan Skiffle Group** (Pye Nixa N 15036) The Lonnie Donegan Skiffle Group, #2 (Charts for seventeen weeks.)

11 May 1956: **Heartbreak Hotel**/I Was The One, **Elvis Presley** (HMV POP 182), #2 (Charts for twenty-one weeks.)

June 1956: Down Bound Train/**Mule Skinner, Ken Colyer's Skiffle Group** (Decca Jazz F-J.10751 (No chart position.)

6 July 1956: **Skiffle Session EP (Railroad Bill**/Stackalee/The Ballad of Jesse James/Ol' Riley), **Lonnie Donegan Skiffle Group**, (Pye Nixa NJE 1017), #20 (two weeks on the chart.)

13 July 1956: **Be Bop a Lula**/Woman Love, **Gene Vincent**, (Capitol CL 14599), #30 (Charts for two weeks, re-enters the chart at #16 on 24 August 1956 for three weeks and makes a second re-entry on 28 September 1956 at #23, remaining on the charts for an further two weeks.)

13 July 1956: **Bad Penny Blues**/Close Your Eyes, **Humphrey Lyttelton**, (Parlophone R4184), #19 (Charts for six weeks.)

July 1956: **Oranges and Lemons**/Truckin', **Eric Delaney and his Band** (Pye N15054). (Did not chart.)

24 August 1956: **Lay Down Your Arms**/Daydream, **Anne Shelton** (Philips PB 616), #1 (Charts for fourteen weeks.)

9 November 1956: Rip It Up/**Teenager's Mother (Are You Right?), Bill Haley and his Comets** (Brunswick 05615), #4 (Charts for eighteen weeks.)

8 February 1957: **Long Tall Sally**/Slippin' and Slidin', **Little Richard** (London HLO 8366), #3 (Charts for sixteen weeks.)

March 1957: **Come Go With Me**/Whispering Bells, **The Del-Vikings** (London HLD8405) (Did not chart in the UK but reached #4 in the USA Billboard chart. NB it was released on Dot records in the USA where the group's name was spelt with two 'l's', The Dell-Vikings.)

8 March 1957: Rip It Up/**Baby Let's Play House, Elvis Presley** (HMV POP 305), #27 (one week only on the chart.)

22 March 1957: The Cumberland Gap/**Maggie May, The Vipers Skiffle Group**, (Parlophone R 4289), #3 (six weeks)

April 1957: **Twenty Flight Rock**/Dark Lonely Street, **Eddie Cochran** (London HLU 8386), (These are the details for its UK release – it did not chart in the UK.)

7 June 1957: Gamblin' Man/**Putting on the Style**, **Lonnie Donegan and his Skiffle Group** (Pye Nixa N 15093), #1 (nineteen weeks on the chart. Donegan's second consecutive number one, a double-A side release and last to be released solely as a 78.)

14 June 1957: **All Shook Up**/That's When Your Heartaches Begin, **Elvis Presley** (HMV POP 359, #24 (one week on the chart, re-enters on 28 June, climbs to #1 and this time remains on the chart for a total of twenty weeks. Despite nine previous hits over here this was Elvis's first UK number one.)

27 September 1957: **That'll Be the Day**/I'm Lookin' for Someone to Love, **The Crickets** (Coral 45-Q 72279), #1 (Re-enters the chart at #29 on 10 January 1958 for one week only.)

6 December1957: **Peggy Sue**/Everyday, **Buddy Holly** (Coral Q 72293), #6 (Holly's first UK chart single issued under his own name; spent a total of seventeen weeks on the chart.)

27 December 1957: **Oh, Boy**/Not Fade Away, **The Crickets** (Coral 45-Q 72298), #3 (The follow up to 'That'll Be the Day', 'Oh Boy' charted for fifteen weeks.)

20 December 1957: Great Balls of Fire/**Mean Woman Blues**, **Jerry Lee Lewis** (London HLS 8529) #1 (twelve weeks on the chart.)

10 January 1958: **Raunchy**/The Midnite Man, **Bill Justis And His Orchestra** (Lead guitar played by Sid Manker), (London HLS 8517) #24 (Initially it was on the charts for just two weeks but on 31 January it re-entered the chart, climbing to #11 and spending some six weeks on the chart.)

7 February 1958: **Raunchy**/Mojo, **Ken Mackintosh And His Orchestra** (HMV POP 713), #19 (six weeks on the chart.)

20 November 1995: **The Beatles Anthology 1**: Disc 1, Track 3: **That'll Be The Day**, Track 4: **In Spite of All the Danger** – both sides of The Quarry Men 78rpm single recorded by Percy F. Phillips, July 1958. #1 (Billboard 200) USA, #2 (The Official Charts Company) UK.

1997 **Get Back – Together, John Lennon's Original Quarrymen** (Scorpion SCO 1007), fifteen track cd recorded by Eric Griffiths, Colin Hanton, Rod Davis, Pete Shotton and Len Garry at Music House Studios, Liverpool. Did not chart.

FILMOGRAPHY (SELECTIVE)

All films have their US release date unless otherwise stated.

30 December 1953: **The Wild One** (Columbia), starring Marlon Brando, Mary Murphy, Robert Keith, Lee Marvin. Directed by Laszlo Benedek.

10 February 1954: **The Glenn Miller Story** (Universal), starring James Stewart, June Allyson (featuring cameos by Louis Armstrong and Gene Krupa). Directed by Anthony Mann.

19 March 1955: **Blackboard Jungle** (MGM), starring Glenn Ford, Sidney Poitier, Vic Morrow, Anne Francis, Louis Calhern. Directed by Richard Brooks.

27 October 1955: **Rebel Without a Cause** (Warner Brothers), starring James Dean, Natalie Wood, Sal Mineo. Directed by Nicholas Ray.

2 February 1956: **The Benny Goodman Story** (Universal), starring Steve Allen, Donna Reed (featuring appearances from Lionel Hampton and Gene Krupa among many others). Directed by Valentine Davies.

21 March 1956: **Rock Around the Clock** (Columbia), starring Bill Haley and his Comets, Alan Freed, The Platters, Freddie Bell and the Bellboys. Directed by Fred F. Sears.

1 December 1956: **The Girl Can't Help It** (20th Century Fox), starring Tom Ewell, Jayne Mansfield, Edmond O'Brien, Henry Jones, Julie London (featuring musical performances

by Little Richard, Eddie Cochran, The Platters, Gene Vincent). Directed by Frank Tashlin.

8 November 1957: **Jailhouse Rock** (MGM), starring Elvis Presley, Judy Tyler. Directed by Richard Thorpe.

1958 (UK release): **Violent Playground** (Rank), starring Stanley Baker, Anne Heywood, David McCallum, Peter Cushing. Directed by Basil Dearden.

1 December 1959 (UK release): **Expresso Bongo** (Britist Lion), starring Laurence Harvey, Sylvia Syms, Cliff Richard, Yolande Donlan. Screenplat: Wolf Mankowitz. Directer by Val Guest.

PHOTO CREDITS

Front cover photograph courtesy of Charlie Roberts.

Photograph of The Quarry Men on p.167 courtesy of Geoff Rhind.

Back cover image of Colin Hanton with his original Quarry Men drum kit (1997 at Music House Studios, Liverpool) courtesy of Rod Davis.

Photographs pp. 2, 4, 5,10, 12, 18, 20, 28, 39, 66, 71, 324, 326, 368, 369, 370, 371 (Colin and siblings), 372 and 373 courtesy of Colin Hanton.

Photographs pp. 230 and 287, courtesy of The Quarry Men archive.

Photograph p.161 by James L. Davis and pp. 371 (The Quarry Men in Chicago) and 374 (The Quarry Men post-2005) courtesy of Rod Davis.

Photograph p.121 of Nigel Walley with John Lennon courtesy Nigel Walley.

Images pp. 134 and 135 of Nicky Cuff and the Connaughts and Phil Robinson and the Crossrocks courtesy of Colin Robinson.

Photograph p.15 Gonville Road, bomb damage 1940. Courtesy of Sefton Library Service.

Photographs pages 143, 145 and 148 of Charlie Roberts, Quarry Men Poster and Quarry Men in performance on Rosebery Street courtesy of Charlie Roberts.

Photograph p.161 of Ivan Vaughan courtesy of Jan Vaughan.

Photograph p.223 of Mr. Charlie McBain courtesy of Christine Westcott.

Photograph p.233 of John Lennon and Eric Griffiths courtesy of Relda Griffiths.

Photograph p.242 of Len Garry courtesy of Len Garry.

Photographs pp. 316, 317 and 320 of Percy Phillips, 38 Kensington Road and pages from Percy Phillips personal logbook courtesy of Peter Phillips.

Photograph p.63 of British teens courtesy of FOTO/FORTEPAN/Lipovits Karoly.

Photograph on pp. 417 courtesy of Liverpool Record Office, Liverpool Libraries

Record labels, album covers and other memorabilia sourced by Colin Hall.

'Postwar prefabs on Lineside Road, Liverpool, 1953'

MADE IN ENGLAND
vogue
78 R.P.M.
CORAL
102022
Q.72279
THAT'LL BE THE DAY
(Allison, Holly; Petty)
THE CRICKETS
with Orchestral Accompaniment
SOUTHERN MUSIC

Recorded by P. F. PHILLIPS
KENSINGTON
IN SPITE OF ALL THE DANGER.
Play with a light-weight pick-up
(McCartney, Harrison.)